THE GREAT DIVIDE

Counting his coups.

THE

GREAT DIVIDE:

*TRAVELS IN THE UPPER YELLOWSTONE IN THE
SUMMER OF 1874*

BY THE

EARL OF DUNRAVEN

Introduction by Marshall Sprague

WITH ILLUSTRATIONS BY VALENTINE W. BROMLEY

UNIVERSITY OF NEBRASKA PRESS · LINCOLN

First Bison Book edition October, 1967

*The Bison Book edition is reproduced from the 1876 edition
published by Chatto & Windus, London.*

INTRODUCTION

Windham Thomas Wyndham-Quin, who produced this enchanting book about his adventures in the American West, was a great deal more than an aristocrat called the fourth Earl of Dunraven and Mountearl in the Peerage of Ireland, second Baron Kenry of the United Kingdom, Knight of the Order of St. Patrick and Companion of the Order of St. Michael and St. George. Among other things, Dunraven was one of those talented writers from abroad who visited the United States and helped Americans to appraise their country at a time when they were too busy building a new world to think about it.

The Great Divide, which the earl wrote at the age of thirty-four, was the most popular of his half-dozen books about his travels. After its initial appearance in 1876, it ran through several English editions and an abridged American edition titled "Hunting in the Yellowstone." Of its reception, Dunraven said later, "Some clergy bought *The Great Divide* supposing it to be a theological work expounding the separation of the sheep and the goats; but if I remember right, the book did not rely much on that, and had a pretty good sale."

INTRODUCTION

The book delights us today as it delighted readers almost a century ago partly because of the joyous vigor, humor, and sensitivity of the writing. Dunraven could not compose a dull line, even if merely mentioning the pleasures of Denver's Corkscrew Club and Charpiot's Restaurant, or his guide's way of having a "tot of whiskey" before breakfast, or the look of sunrise from Fort Hall in Idaho, or meeting a man named Mahogany Bogstick. No better or more economical description of Montana's most sinful gold camp was ever penned than his "Virginia City! Good Lord! What a name for the place!" He could get off the subject and still hold his audience as when he explained in one of his books for no reason at all that the English name Fetherstonhaugh was shortened there to Fetherstone, became Firestone crossing the Atlantic, Pierre Fusil in Quebec and wound up Peter Gun in the United States.

But the writing is superb because the author is superb —one of the most attractive and entertaining of men, wise, witty, perceptive and vastly amused by everybody's pretensions including his own. In his mellow autobiography, *Past Times and Pastimes*, Dunraven explained that he was born in 1841 at Adare in the County of Limerick. He was smothered with affection by five sisters, having no brothers, and his parents decided to get him out from under so much sistering. However, they could not agree on the form of his early education so he had a bit of High Church instruction in Rome at first and then some other kind in Paris where he learned fluent and vernacular French around the Sorbonne and acquired all sorts of agreeable bad habits and an appreciation of fine wines and pretty girls. "It is most annoying," he said later, "that everything that is pleasant is all wrong."

He enjoyed his three years at Oxford as Lord Adair, son of the third Earl of Dunraven, though the cause of his enjoyment appears to have been that study was not an important part of the university curriculum. He had plenty of time to race his horses and play cricket and defend the honor of the Light Blues (Oxford) against "the insignificant Dark Blue" (Cambridge) in many a battle of flying whiskey bottles in the local pubs. Then he was a soldier briefly, seeing brisk action particularly during the campaign at Hyde Park in London when the Reform Leaguers threatened insurrection while attacking the anti-Reform Leaguers. In 1867, he became a practicing spiritualist under the renowned medium Daniel Dunglas Home but found that he could not approach the master's skill in making tables to tip and guitars to be played by invisible hands. Besides he felt that the men and women in this world were more stimulating than those Home had introduced him to in the next.

Soon after this spiritualist period, the *London Daily Telegraph* assigned young Dunraven to cover the British expedition against Emperor Theodore of Abyssinia who was alleged to have treated a couple of Englishmen discourteously. One of Dunraven's colleagues on this operetta assignment was Henry M. Stanley of the *New York Herald*, moving toward fame in deepest Africa and his historic greeting, "Dr. Livingston, I presume?"

Dunraven married Florence Elizabeth Kerr, of the high-born Lothian tribe, about this time, and the problem of where to go for the honeymoon gave him an excellent excuse to visit the United States. One could say that his preparation for writing *The Great Divide* began with the tales he had heard as a child about the American West. An uncle of his had known that mightiest of hunters, the incredible Sir St. George Gore, of Sligo, Ireland. The uncle had told him how Gore had shot down buffalo by the thousands all over Wyoming and Montana during the 1850's with an outfit of forty employees, one hundred and twelve horses, three milk cows, fifty staghounds and greyhounds, and enough champagne to drown in.

Dunraven's boyhood hero was the great Captain John Palliser of Tipperary who had stopped often at the Adair estate of the Dunravens and was not above playing trappers and Indians with the future fourth earl. Palliser had roamed the Upper Missouri country in 1847–1848 just for the fun of it. In the late 1850's he had conceived, organized and led the Palliser Expedition, which was the first official British exploration of the Canadian Rockies. Palliser tapered off his American adventures by spending a year as a Civil War blockade runner, smuggling contraband from Nassau to ports in the Confederate states.

With the deeds of men like Gore and Palliser to inspire him, Dunraven was in a thrilled state as he sailed with his bride to New York in the summer of 1869. "I was young," he recalled later, "not twenty-eight years of age; and my boyish brain-cells were stored to bursting with tales of Red Indians and grizzly b'ars; caballeros and haciendas, prairies and buffaloes, Texans and Mexicans, cowboys and voyageurs, and had not yet discharged or jettisoned their cargo. I was in search of such sport and adventure as, under the circumstances, were to be found."

Dunraven did not reveal what Florence Elizabeth, the bride, thought of such yearnings during their honeymoon when his boyish brain-cells were supposed to be concentrated on her. In any case, after landing in New York, the dutiful groom did the honeymoon rounds with his bride—the Brevoort House, Delmonico's, Newport, Lake George, Washington. Then, just as he thought of heading westward, he had a sunstroke in Virginia and so he returned to Ireland with Florence Elizabeth. He did not get back to the United States until the fall of 1871, after having covered the Franco-Prussian War for the *London Daily Telegraph*. His father had died recently and he was no longer Lord Adair but the Fourth Earl of Dunraven, master of thirty thousand ancestral acres in Ireland and in Wales. On this second attempt to go west, he followed the custom of British aristocrats by taking along his own doctor, George Henry Kingsley. Kingsley was a brother of Canon Kingsley, the *Water Babies* author, and an uncle of Rose and Maurice Kingsley who were in Colorado that same year helping to found the resort of Colorado Springs at Pikes Peak and giving it the English tone that caused it to be nicknamed "Little London."

INTRODUCTION

After landing in New York, Dunraven hurried with Dr. Kingsley straight to Chicago, having a letter of introduction to General Philip H. Sheridan, the Civil War hero who headed the western department of the U. S. Army. The earl found the general to be "a great soldier and a delightful man, with the one peculiarity of using the most astonishing swear words quite calmly and dispassionately in ordinary conversation." Sheridan had an antlered trophy hanging in his Army headquarters office. Dunraven called it a wapiti, a word Sheridan objected to as being affected and overly ornate. It was, the general said, a plain elk. His Lordship retorted that properly an "elk" was a "moose," explaining further that Americans called an elk an "elk" for the same reason, or lack of reason, that they call thrushes "robins" and grouse "partridges."

Next day, Sheridan wired Fort McPherson for hunting guides and sent Dunraven and Kingsley along by train from Chicago to North Platte, Nebraska. Two guides met them at the North Platte station—Buffalo Bill Cody and Texas Jack Omohundro, extraordinarily charming and able frontiersmen whom Dunraven took to at once. He described them in his autobiography as "tall, well-built, active-looking men, with singularly handsome features. Bill was dressed in a pair of corduroys tucked into his high boots, and a blue flannel shirt. He wore a broad-brimmed hat, or sombrero, and had a white handkerchief folded like a little shawl loosely fastened around his neck to keep off the fierce rays of the afternoon sun. Jack's costume was similar, with the exception that he wore moccasins, and had his lower limbs encased in a pair of comfortable greasy deerskin trousers, ornamented with a fringe along the seams. Round his waist was a belt supporting a revolver, two butcher knives, and, in his hand he carried his trusty rifle, the 'Widow'—now in my possession. Jack, tall and lithe, with light brown close-cropped hair, clear laughing honest blue eyes, and a soft and winning smile, might have sat as a model for a typical, modern Anglo-Saxon—if ethnologists will excuse the term. Bill was dark, with quick searching eyes, aquiline nose, and delicately cut features, and he wore his hair falling in long ringlets over his shoulders, in true Western style. As he cantered up, with his flowing locks and broad-brimmed hat, he looked like a picture of a cavalier of olden times."

Buffalo Bill and Texas Jack were well known in 1871 among big-game hunters but their greater renown came later as members of Buffalo Bill's Wild West Show. The earl was lucky to have such experts to introduce him to the West. Texas Jack was his guide once again three years later when he sat out from Denver's Corkscrew Club for Yellowstone Park to have the marvelous adventures that one reads about in *The Great Divide*.

It should not be imagined that this Yellowstone trek was the most exciting event of Dunraven's life. He was forever doing something exciting—trailing caribou in Labrador or fishing on the north shore of Lake Superior or admiring the northern lights in the Canadian Rockies or opposing sweatshop labor in the English House of Lords or working for Irish land reform. Although he was not the discoverer of Estes Park below Longs Peak in Colorado, he was the first to recognize its potential as a magnificently scenic summer resort. The English Hotel which he built in Estes in 1877 was the finest hostelry of that region until it burned down in 1911, four years after he sold the last of his Colorado holdings to F. O. Stanley, inventor of the Stanley Steamer.

The Estes Park project brought Dunraven much pain. In acquiring land for him there, his Colorado agents arranged homestead filings which were challenged in the courts during the late 1870's, and people squatted at will on some of the earl's best tracts. Stories in Denver papers accused him of being the shadiest of land-grabbers, and reported the doings of a man supposed to be Dunraven but actually an imposter who ran up bills in his name and behaved scandalously in Denver bawdy houses. A tale circulated that Dunraven and a young lady not his wife had been refused a room for the night in his own English Hotel because he and the young lady were making so much noise. His notoriety as a bad actor followed him back to New York, causing similar stories to appear in papers there. He complained of one of these in a letter to the Editor which was published in the *New York World*. His letter read:

> Sir: By your issue of Saturday last I perceive that I spent the previous evening at Booth's Theatre, but unless I am grievously mistaken as to my

own identity and the position of my body in space, I was listening to the excellent performance of the San Francisco Minstrels during the hours supposed to have been devoted to Julius Caesar. According to the pages of certain of your contemporaries, I have also since my arrival in New York eloped with a young lady, danced at a charity ball, dined out, been present at an evening reception, and have been concealed somewhere mysteriously, for no good purpose, in this city, while at the same time I was, to the best of my own belief, lying ill in bed at the Brevoort House. An Irish member of the British House of Commons is said to have once remarked that a man could not be in two places at once, barring he was a bird. At present it appears to be only necessary to reside under the shadow of the wings of the American Eagle to acquire from the magnanimous bird the faculty of being not in two but many places at once and the same time. This gift of ubiquity may be desirable, but it is inconvenient till one gets accustomed to it. Matters are getting rather mixed with me and, if things go on this way, I shall be compelled to hire a man to tell me who I am, where I am, and what particular commandment I am any given moment breaking. It would not be easy to find the right person to fill such a responsible place, for he would have to be intelligent, well-informed, religious and "reliable," but no doubt I might eventually procure such an one from the ranks of the new purveyors to the public press of this city. In the meantime, I should be glad to avail myself of your columns to assure my friends and acquaintances, who may have been startled by these reports, that I have left undone all those things I have done, and have done all those things

I have not done; and also to inform them that I am never to be found where I am, but may be successfully sought for where I am not.

Your obedient Servant,

DUNRAVEN

The American West saw no more of the Earl after the mid-1880s, but he lived on and on honorably, usefully, fully and joyously. He served Queen Victoria as her Undersecretary for the Colonies from 1885 to 1887. At the turn of the century he joined the cavalry in the Boer War. Sailing was his greatest pleasure next to roaming the wilderness. He raced his yachts *Valkyrie II* and *Valkyrie III* for the America's Cup off New York in 1893 and 1895, losing both races. He protested the second race on the grounds that commercial spectator boats were permitted to run on the course, and he was struck off the membership of the New York Yacht Club. His protest nearly caused a break of diplomatic relations between Britain and the United States.

To the end he was a gay blade, tall, lean, handsome, trim and debonair. He loved horses, the sea, pipe smoking, smart clothes, euchre, whiskey and good food—especially canvasback duck, soft-shelled crab and corn on the cob. He loved his London clubs and restaurants, intelligent conversation, and lovely women to look at. His friends included celebrities on both sides of the Atlantic—Oscar Wilde and Texas Jack Omohundro, Lord Kitchener and Jay Gould, General William T. Sherman and James McNeill Whistler. The novelist Elinor Glyn, creator of those shockingly erotic stories

INTRODUCTION

Three Weeks, *His Hour* and *Six Days*, was a favorite of the Earl's—"gifted in many respects," he wrote of her, "and in literature a genius."

He died at eighty-five in London on June 14, 1926. His finest memorial is this book, *The Great Divide*, bringing to us not only the pleasure of his company for a few hours but his own strong sense of what a privilege it is to be alive.

MARSHALL SPRAGUE

To my Wife

WHO BY HER COMPANIONSHIP WHEN PRESENT

AND FOND SYMPATHY WHEN ABSENT

HAS COMFORTED ME MUCH ON MANY EXPEDITIONS

THIS BOOK IS

WITH ALL AFFECTION

DEDICATED

PREFACE.

THERE are certain classes or families of reptiles and animals that are invariably associated in our minds with feelings of disgust, either on account of some real or fancied quality of danger inherent in them, as in the case of snakes, lizards, and scorpions, or by reason of something repulsive in the appearance of the creature, as, for instance, in the brown and spotty toad.

Such feelings may perhaps be traced to their peculiar causes, but there seems to be no earthly reason for associating with certain conditions of men the attributes that are universally supposed to be inseparable from them. Why is a sandboy jolly, or a hatter mad? What is there in the avocation of a tailor that should reduce the disciple of St. Christopher so far below the ordinary unit of humanity? And what has the tourist done that in the eyes of his fellow-creatures he should be an object of loathing and scorn? Is there anything radically wrong in his pursuits? Does the taint of original sin exhale a ranker odour among persons belonging to a class which would not exist but for the crime of curiosity? The individual tourist is no worse than his fellows, as far as personal excellence is concerned; it is the pursuit that brands him with infamy, that covers him with a halo of shame. At some time or other of our lives we are sure to have the tourist mania. It is as certain as the measles. Concealment is in vain, and the victim may as well wave aloft his Murray and with brazen front defy the sarcasms of the world, consoling himself with the reflection that the man who laughs at tourists, becoming one himself (as he is sure to do at some period of his life), will in his turn be exposed to the ridicule of others. In the Emerald Isle they call them 'Dingoes,' and use them as butts at which to aim the shafts of their Irish wit. The irrepressible North Briton on his native heath considers them poor 'fushionless' fools, and eyes them with a contempt he does not entertain for their purses. The females of the tribe are of course, if good-looking, exempt from the condemnation incurred by their companions (I use the word companions advisedly as implying a difference of sex). But the males are a race hated and despised. This is a fact full of instruction, and one that offers a sound argument against the believers in purgatory or any other transition state. If the adoption of a certain suit of clothes, coupled with a desire to visit strange or remarkable places, be sufficient to turn a good fellow into an ass, why should one hesitate to believe that perfect excellence or the reverse might follow as the immediate consequence of kicking off one's body?

Not only is the tourist scorned, but he is pillaged.

Early in summer, armies of open-mouthed expectant human sharks, dog-fish, and skate (I know many men bearing a strong resemblance to the latter fish) lie waiting for the shoals of tourists to approach their coasts. What a rush there is at them! How the victims vainly dash from side to side, protesting that they don't want a guide here, and don't care about going there; swearing that there is no enjoyment to be found in seeing a half-naked Arab skip down one pyramid and bound up another with inconceivable rapidity; objecting violently to rowing up the Middle Lake in a rain-storm; expostulating that they have no desire to ascend Snowdon in a fog! But it is of no use. The desire to squeeze is a law of nature among innkeepers and lovers, and must be obeyed; and in the autumn the shoals retire bedraggled, bewildered, bedevilled, robbed, pillaged, and sent empty away. Many a poor man, balancing his accounts after his hard-earned annual holiday, must truthfully say, ' I was a tourist and ye took me in.'

I may be excused for feeling strongly on this subject, for I have suffered much in the cause. Long-suffering and patient, I have trodden all the paths well-worn by pilgrim tourists' feet; have yawned through the interminable corridors of show places; have accompanied with an occasional ' Dear me !' ' Ah!' ' Really!' the monotone of the guide explaining the names of peaks, mountains or waterfalls, and telling me absurd stories of lovers' leaps and devil's punchbowls, and all the rest of it; have undergone through uncomplaining weeks the established routine of cathedral and museum and picture gallery of continental towns; have sought repose amid the dreamy languor of Oriental life, and been nearly *backsheeshed* to death; have worshipped at the shrine of Nature in many a lovely spot, desecrated by the sandwich-papers, orange-peel, and broken bottles of former devotees; have ascended many a breezy hill to commune with my own heart and refresh my weary soul with a draught from the cool deep-flowing spiritual fountains of Hippocrene, and instead have refreshed it with ginger-beer, and had my photograph taken for a shilling; and I have fought many a fierce battle with my landlord over the bill, and always come off second best. I have pretended not to see that the waiter expected half-a-crown, and have tried to dodge the housemaid and defraud guards, but I have invariably been worsted in the attempt. I therefore consider myself an authority on this subject, and unhesitatingly assert that the most nefarious act that can be perpetrated upon the tourist is the extortion of money for merely looking at the beauties of Nature. I do not mind so much the inordinate demands of the landlord, the pestering and pestilent guides, the awful charges or the preposterous bills which meet you at every turn; but it is utterly unbearable to be asked to pay for the privilege of walking about and looking. 'It is all yours, do what you like with it,' says Nature in a wild country. 'You may look but you must not touch,' civilised man may be suffered to say. But, not content with that restriction, he forbids you even to gaze. He will not withdraw the veil from the goddess save for a dollar or a shilling, as the case may be. Nothing is so abominable as the system of buying up scenery on speculation. The fencing-off of particular points of view, the dollar here and fifty cents there, the quarter in this place, the toll-bar at that, has it not disgusted every one who has visited that stupendous cataract Niagara? I remember going to see a waterfall in the Catskill Mountains in New York State. It was said to be a pretty sight—in fact, 'real elegant' I was in a beautiful frame of mind, ready to expand to any extent, full of expectant gush and controlled enthusiasm. But how ruthlessly was I disenchanted by finding that the water was dammed back, and could be turned on only by the application of a golden, or rather silver, key. Nothing is more revolting to our instincts, more disgraceful to our civilisation, than the system of trafficking in the charms with which Nature is so bountifully endowed. All honour then to the United States for having bequeathed as a free gift to man the beauties and curiosities of 'Wonderland.' It was an act worthy of a great nation, and she will have her reward in the praise of the present army of tourists, no less than in the thanks of the generations of them yet to come.

In January, 1872, a Bill passed through both Houses of Congress and received the President's sanction, to set apart and consecrate in perpetuity as a National Park this wonderful region. Under the provisions of this Bill the land cannot be bought or settled ; no fees therefore can be charged by private speculators to future visitors for the privilege of viewing the marvels of Nature, which it is enacted shall for ever be free to all nations and all people.

Being in the United States during the summer of 1874, and having two or three months of spare time, I determined to pay a visit in the autumn to the far-famed region of the Upper Yellowstone, and to judge for myself whether the thermal springs and geysers there situated were deserving of the superiority claimed for them over similar phenomena in New Zealand and Iceland. For two or three years—in fact, ever since the first vague accounts of the marvels to be seen upon its shores had filtered out into the world — I had longed to visit the Yellowstone. Its lakes had for me a magnetic attraction which drew me towards them with an irresistible impulse; and there was an atmosphere of mystery enveloping its upper waters like a mist, which I eagerly sought to dispel.

I did not undertake the expedition in the cause of Science. I do not pretend to anything but a very slight acquaintance with natural history, geology, and mineralogy. I had no instruments for taking measurements, nor the time, knowledge, and skill necessary to make an advantageous use of them. I have, therefore, whenever practicable, referred for distances and measurements to the different accounts contained in the reports of the Government expeditions of 1871-72 organised by Professor Hayden; and to that skilful and learned gentleman I owe a lasting debt of gratitude for his kindness in supplying me with details of routes and distances, for advising me as to guides and means of transportation, and for giving me many other items of information which turned out most useful to me in my trip. I am also anxious to acknowledge many favours I have received from the hands of General Sherman and General Sheridan, not only on the occasion of my visit to the Yellowstone, but on many other occasions. Without their valuable assistance and the benefit of their introductions, my explorations might frequently have failed altogether, or at any rate would have been conducted with great difficulty. To General Sweitzer also, and the other officers at Fort Ellis, my thanks are due for their unfailing kindness to me; and I take this opportunity of thanking my fellow-country-man, Mr. William Blackmore, for his goodness in allowing me to use in illustration some specimens selected from his beautiful collection of photographs of the Yellowstone district and Geyserland.

I had, moreover, heard the district spoken of as an excellent game-producing country; and the pursuit of large game is to me a great delight : but it was less for any special design of hunting than for the satisfaction of my curiosity and the gratification of my sight-seeing instincts that I really decided to attempt the trip.

I had intended making a somewhat prolonged tour, and proposed starting for the Yellowstone Lake from Rawlings Springs or some other convenient point on the Union Pacific Railway, not far west of Cheyenne. Had I done so I might have had something of greater interest to narrate. But I was prevented from carrying out my original intentions by the fact that hostilities broke out between certain of the Indian tribes and the Government, and I was therefore compelled to abandon all idea of penetrating to Geyserland from the east through mountain passes hitherto untrodden by the white man's foot, and to take a more ordinary and prosaic route. I must apologise for the fact that nothing happened to me or to any of my party. But, so far as I am personally concerned, it is useless to pretend that anything ever does happen to me. I never have an adventure worth a cent; nobody ever scalps me; I don't get 'jumped' by highwaymen. It never occurs to a bear to hug me, and my very appearance inspires feelings of dismay or disgust in the breast of the puma or mountain lion. I am not drowned or overwhelmed by sudden floods. I don't slide down precipices and catch by the seat of my breeches on a spike just as I am falling over a cliff 40,000 feet high. I don't ride for my life, the whirling· lasso of a wild Comanche just grazing my shoulder; so I have no opportunity of describing my mettlesome steed, ' swift son of the desert and the simoom.' My dog has never caught me by the coat collar just as I was sinking for the last time; so I have no excuse for making poetry if I could, and shedding a few tears over the faithful companion of my wanderings, lately deceased. Savages never throw tomahawks at me or stick my best hat full of arrows. It is true that I have often been horribly frightened, but generally without any adequate cause; and I have suffered fearfully from a too liberal admixture of saleratus in my bread, and terrible things happened to me in consequence, but only in my dreams. I don't get lost for weeks, and half starved; neither buffaloes gore me, nor wapiti spike me with their antlers. If I drew upon my imagination, the draft would probably be returned with 'no effects' written across the face of it : or, if there was any value to be found, some officious person would surely disclose that the notes were forgeries or the coin counterfeit. So the reader must reconcile him or herself to find in the following pages nothing more than a simple, but truthful, description of an ordinary humdrum trip.

If I have been guilty of technical errors in nomenclature, I pray to be excused ; my meaning will, I think, in any case be clear. I have not attempted to force into my narrative the typical Western Man, or to introduce much of his peculiar phraseology. I have also refrained from venturing upon second-hand imitations of American humorists, and from attempting to pourtray characters already drawn by skilful delineators of frontier life. Neither have I filled the mouths of my transatlantic characters with expressions which are erroneously supposed to thickly interlard the conversation of all Americans.

Of the illustrations in which Mr. Valentine Bromley has so graphically carried out my ideas, I will say nothing. The reader will agree with me that they speak for themselves.

If I am taken to task for using the term 'Geyser' as I do, I reply that, though it strictly is the proper name of a certain spring in Iceland, it has gradually come to be considered the generic term applicable to all springs of a similar character ; and therefore I am justified in using in that sense the expressions 'Geyser' and 'Geyserite.' So wonderful are the hot springs in the country referred to in the ensuing pages, that no language at my command can adequately describe their marvels. They must be seen to be believed; and I hope that any travellers or students of Nature who contemplate a visit thither will find in the pages of the ' Great Divide' some information that may prove serviceable on the trip.

DUNRAVEN.

CONTENTS.

LIST

OF

FULL-PAGE ILLUSTRATIONS.

THE GREAT DIVIDE.

CHAPTER I.

'WONDERLAND.'

NORTH AMERICA has frequently been compared disad-
vantageously, as regards scenery, with Europe and the
other quarters of the globe; and not without reason. Of
the western continent, the better known and more civilised
portions are very uninteresting. If I except the Hudson,
which is lovely, the soft beauty of Lake George, the
mountainous districts of New England, of Virginia, and
other spurs and offshoots of the Alleghanies, the general
character of the country, more especially between the
Alleghanies and the Rockies, is flat, dreary, and uninviting.
Exceedingly graceful is the maize plant when its silken
tassels droop in the hot sunshine amid the dark green
curving leaves, yet the eye wearies of interminable corn-
fields bounded by untidy and tortuous snake fences.
Nothing is more vulgar-looking and unkempt than recently
cleared land. The face of Nature, shorn of the beauty
of its natural covering, looks mean and dirty; and, as
compared with its appearance when clothed with forest,
resembles the contrast between a man's countenance when

disfigured by a coarse stubbly growth of a week old
and the same when adorned with the soft flowings of a
patriarchal beard. Blackened stumps stand thickly in the
foreground amid rocks and weeds, and the forest seems
to huddle itself back out of reach of the fatal axe. The
beauty of nature is destroyed, and is not succeeded by the
artificial beauty of civilisation.

The great plains, though fascinating from their vastness, and blessed with most glorious sunsets and clothed
with an exquisitely delicate colouring—so delicate that it
is not appreciated until a long apprenticeship to the prairie
has been served,—are, nevertheless, inexpressibly sad and
mournful. The mountains, grand as they are, cannot for
a moment compare in shape, form, and general beauty
with the Alps. No glaciers fill the upper portions of the
valleys; the thunder of the avalanche is seldom heard.
No peaks like the Matterhorn astonish with their rugged-
ness the traveller's eye. But the one attribute peculiar
to the continent is that of vastness. Everything is huge
and stupendous. Nature is formed in a larger mould
than in other lands. She is robust and strong, all her
actions full of vigour and young life. Storms are fearful
and violent, floods rise and sweep the country like seas.
Mighty rivers, with fierce ungovernable tide, in a night
scoop out fresh beds for themselves and laugh at man's
shackles and restraints, or, in their struggles to break the
chains that winter has bound around them, burst free
and carry off, like cobwebs, the toilsome results of engineering skill. Lakes are seas. There are great deserts
almost unknown and unmarked on any map. Through
thousands and thousands of square miles of primeval
forest, dark, impenetrable to the sun's rays, the north
wind wails and whispers; while for days you may
travel on the plains without seeing a tree, the horizon

forming an unbroken circle around you. The so-called Rocky Mountains extend the entire length of the continent, and in places are five or six hundred miles in width, comprising many ranges which contain important valleys, and divide great and fertile plains. Through these mountain-walls the rivers have burst or sawn their way, forming chasms (cañons as they are called) for which no parallel can elsewhere be found.

While this attribute of vastness marks the whole North American Continent, nowhere can you so well come in contact with and appreciate it as in the western wilds or far away territories; where Nature is very strong and man is very weak, and where the powers of science have not yet been called into play, to supplement and make up for his feebleness. And to no part of the 'Great West' should I sooner advise the traveller to go than to that marvellous country which I am about in memory to revisit.

Comprised in the territories of Montana and Wyoming there is a region which contains all the peculiarities of the continent in a remarkable degree, and which, moreover, is exceedingly interesting on account of its scenery, its geography, its mineralogy, and its sport. Although the altitudes are not so high as in other parts of the continent, it may be truthfully called the summit or apex of North America. Thence the waters flow in all directions—north, south, east, and west. There it is that great rivers rise, running through every clime, from perpetual snow to tropical heat. On the one side glance the currents destined to mingle with the tepid waves of the Gulf of Mexico; on the other up the rapids leap the salmon ascending from the distant waters of the Pacific Ocean. It is the geographical centre of North America. It is essentially 'The Great Divide.' Roaming at will through the trackless wastes that compose and surround this region, are to be found the best representatives of the fast vanishing aboriginal race. By the great bend of the Yellowstone are grouped the tall lodges of the gigantic Crows, men of six feet four or five inches in height, with long hair reaching in heavy plaits to their knees. From Idaho come parties of Bannacks, great raisers of stock and traders in horses. Peu d'Oreilles, Gros Ventres, Flatheads, Bloods, and Piegans, warlike Blackfeet, Assiniboins, and Sioux wander through the hunting grounds seeking their meat from God ; stealing horses, hunting, and warring upon one another in something like their natural freedom. Some of these are very hostile to the pale-faces, and much to be dreaded, like the well-armed and numerous Sioux, or as they style themselves ' Dakotahs ;' others are friendly to the whites, like the Crows, Snakes, Bannacks, and their kindred tribes. A few, such as Nez Percés and Bannacks, are semi-civilised, cultivating a little land, and raising horses and cattle, possessing farming implements, and using in war or for the chase the newest fashion in repeating rifles and the latest thing out in revolving pistols ; others, such as Blackfeet and Assiniboins, are primitive and unsophisticated, depending in a great measure upon their ancient weapons, the bow, the lance, and the club ; and subsisting entirely by the chase,—wanderers who have their homes far to the north in British territory. Sorely am I tempted to ' switch off' here, and dilate upon the manners, customs, rights and wrongs of the much-abused, long-suffering, and little-understood Red Indian race. Their very appellation is a misnomer ; their history is one long story of mismanagement, of rights withheld, treaties broken, and promises unfulfilled. With the bright exception of the Amalgamated Hudson Bay and North-West Fur Companies, their rulers have taken no pains to comprehend and provide for the necessities of their savage natures. But, as I know that I shall not be able to resist the temptation of alluding to this to me most fascinating subject later on when I come to speak of the Crow nation, I stay my pen here.

In this same region are still to be found great herds of wapiti—noblest representatives of the deer tribe, and soon to be numbered among things of the past. In the swampy flats among old beaver dams, where willows and alders grow, or among the thickest groves of young firs, still lingers the largest of existing elks, the moose. Poor Cervus Alces! your ungainly form has an old-time look about it ; your very appearance seems out of keeping with the present day. The smoke of the chimney, the sound of the axe, are surely though slowly encroaching on your wild domains. The atmosphere of civilisation is death to you, and in spite of your exquisitely keen senses of smell and hearing you too will soon have to be placed in the category of things that have been. In the valleys are both white-tail and black-tail deer. On the little prairies, open glades, and sparsely wooded slopes, grazes the small mountain bison or buffalo, whose race has also nearly vanished from the scene; and not very far distant are to be found herds of his congener, the great bison of the plains, for down in the Judith basin lie the hunting grounds where the Crows go every summer and winter in search of the prairie buffalo. In summer they kill them for their flesh ; in winter they utilise their skins to trade with the whites, and to make robes and houses for themselves. Prong-horn antelopes, the only specimen of the species on the continent, and the only known variety in the world that carries a branching horn, are very numerous on the plains and foot hills. Clear against the sky line, standing on some jutting crag, may not unfrequently be seen the massive stately outline of a bighorn or mountain sheep, a near relation to the moufflon or argali ; and far up in the wildest fastnesses of the range, among untrodden peaks, wild goats distantly allied to the eastern ibex have their inaccessible abode. If this list be not sufficient, and if it be considered that an element of danger is necessary, the sportsman will be glad to hear that nowhere, save perhaps in Southern California, will he be more likely to encounter Ursus horribilis, the grizzly bear. If he has ever pursued, or been pursued by that unpleasant beast, he will be gratified to learn that, as a rule, pine-trees are numerous and not difficult to climb.

It is a fortunate dispensation that the only dangerous variety of the genus in America cannot climb. The black bear, it is true, will ascend any tree that he can clasp with his muscular arms ; but he is a thoroughly reasonable animal, and is fully alive to the cogent logic of a bullet ; whereas the grizzly is an intractable brute. Happily, however, he is no gymnast ; and from the security of a tree-top a man can laugh his adversary to scorn.

Though game is abundant in many States and territories at certain times of the year, yet, taken as a whole, North America cannot for a moment compare with India or Africa as a hunting country. I have enjoyed pretty good sport occasionally myself, it is true : but it is difficult to get ; besides, it requires patience and perseverance, and entails hard work, and even then success is very uncertain ; and as there is nothing I so much dislike as being misled by accounts of the capabilities of a country in a hunting point of view, it is better, in order to avoid the possibility of myself offending in this respect, to say at once that in my opinion a man going to the States or to

British-American territory for big game shooting, and for nothing else, is almost sure to be disappointed. I cannot speak from personal experience; but, if the enthusiastic accounts one hears from the forests are not exaggerated, there can be no doubt that, if he can afford it, a sportsman can get far better deer-stalking in Scotland than anywhere else.

On the plains buffalo are still tolerably numerous and can always be met with if a man knows the right places to go to; but running buffalo ought scarcely to be considered a branch of the noble pastime. It is exciting; it calls into activity the savage instinct to shed blood that is inherent, though it may be dormant, in every man: but it is scarcely sport. Good sport cannot very well be attained without the expenditure of considerable time and trouble. It takes one a year or two to get acquainted with the country, and to learn something of the habits, manners, and customs of the wild beasts inhabiting it. And without this knowledge success is impossible. I have scarcely ever done much good on my first visit to any section, but I have managed to find out sufficient to ensure my being amply rewarded for my pains on a second attempt. Information generally comes from such unreliable sources, one hears such contradictory, absurd, and exaggerated statements, that it is wiser not to depend on local authorities, or indeed upon any authority at all, unless one is very well satisfied as to its trustworthiness. It is better to make up one's mind to spend one season at any rate in investigation, and then, if the prospects of sport are good enough to warrant the expenditure of much necessary trouble and a considerable sum of money, to organise a hunting expedition to that district. Take a limited, a very limited, portion of the United States, some natural section in the mountains, plains, or valleys, cut off by streams or ranges over or across which game are not likely to travel; even that area will be so enormous, the country will be so big, that unless it is literally swarming with deer it may be difficult to find them.

The herds of game move so much, also, according to the seasons. In Estes Park, for instance, near Denver, you might go out in winter or in early spring, when the snow is deep upon the Range, and shoot black-tail deer till you were sick of slaughter. I daresay you might—if you knew where to go to—sit down, and, without moving, get ten, fifteen, or even as many as twenty shots in the day. At other seasons you might walk the flesh off your bones without seeing a beast of any kind. Yet the deer are somewhere there all the time; and, if you can only find out to what deep recesses of the forest, or to what high mountain pastures they have betaken themselves in their search for cool shelter, or in their retreat from mosquitoes and other insect pests, you would be amply rewarded for your trouble.

It is the same with the wapiti. Sometimes the park will be full of them; you may find herds feeding right down upon the plain among the cattle; and in a fortnight there will not be one left. All will have disappeared; and, what is more, it is almost impossible to follow them up and find them, for they are much shyer than the deer. Where do they go to? Not across the snowy range, certainly. Where, then? Up to the bare fells, just under the perpetual snow, where they crop the short sweet grass that springs amid the débris fallen from the highest peaks; to the deep, black recesses of primeval forest; to valleys, basins, little parks and plains, hidden among the folds of the mountains, where the foot even of the wandering miner has never disturbed the solitudes.

Flying from the sound of the axe and the saw-mill, trying to escape from the sand-flies and mosquitoes during the summer months, they plunge into fastnesses known only to themselves, where it is well nigh impossible to find them, and from which they descend only when driven to lower pastures by stress of weather. At that season of the year the hunters of the country do not look for them, for they could not pack the meat down to market from those remote feeding-grounds; and they know that in the winter season there will be plenty of game in the foot hills close to the cities and the railway. The abundance of game is testified by the fact that in Denver deer-meat is in winter worth from three to three and a half cents a pound.

It is the same nearly everywhere, I believe. In Newfoundland the Cariboo migrate twice a year in vast numbers; crossing in the spring to their summer feeding-grounds on one side of the Island, and in the fall returning to their winter pastures on the opposite coast. Two years ago I was near Henry's Fork of Green River, in the spurs of the Uintah mountains. For about a month or six weeks in the fall, deer and wapiti come through the country in large numbers. Unfortunately I was too early on the ground, and had scarcely any success: but a party that arrived shortly after my departure, chancing to hit upon the right moment, enjoyed excellent sport. Their movements being regulated by the seasons, it is impossible to predict the arrival of the herds. In an open fall, a long delay is to be looked for; if winter, however, sets in early, their appearance is accelerated. Altogether it is a chance to find them, for they do not remain long; the bands quickly pass through and are gone. The same state of things exists in the Upper Yellowstone country, and indeed in nearly every district with which I am personally acquainted. A locality where game remains all the year round is hard to find.

Then the face of the country changes very rapidly, and the herds are in consequence continually and permanently shifting their ground. Valleys are ' settled up ' —' planted,' as would have been said in old Colonial days—in a single summer, and wheat-fields take the place of pasture-lands of short curly buffalo-grass. Tall maize plants shake their beautifully pendant dark-green glossy leaves where only a few weeks before thickets of coarse reeds and herbage grew. The whirr of the thrashing-machine is now heard where last year the silence was broken only by the coughing of deer, the barking of foxes, and the dismal howls of coyotes. I expect I should starve to-day in a place where four years ago I saw, I am sure, more than a thousand wapiti in one week. Even in a country which is not settled, if it is tolerably safe, and if small parties of white men can travel through it without much risk, the game will very soon be driven off or exterminated. And what wonder, when they kill millions of buffalo for their hides, and thousands of deer and wapiti for their skins alone, leaving the bodies to rot and fester in the sun?

Nothing irritates the aborigines so much as this wholesale destruction and waste of food. The red men are the game preservers of the country. Where Red Indians are numerous, you will be sure to find herds of wapiti, bands of white-tail and black-tail deer, antelope, sheep, buffalo, and everything else. There are certain tracts and districts, the marches between the hunting grounds of mutually hostile tribes, where nobody dares to go to hunt or trap, but across which strips of debatable land stealing parties and small war parties are frequently passing. That is the sort of place to go to if you want to see game ;

but there you may possibly see more than you bargained for; you may be a hunted, as well as a hunting, animal, and with the pleasures of the chase mingle the emotions of the chased.

As a rule, it may be truthfully said of America, ' No Indians, not much game; heap of Sioux, plenty of buffalo, elk, and deer.' There are exceptions to this rule, but not many.

Another difficulty in the way of the English sportsman is, that very few Americans care about what *they* call hunting, and *we* call shooting, as an amusement. There are, of course, exceptions; men who love the wilds, and take delight in running buffalo or wapiti, or stalking a deer; and year by year these exceptions are becoming more numerous : but, as a rule, the inhabitants of the United States take their holidays in quite a different style, or, if they do indulge in shooting at all, go in for prairie chickens and small game. Therefore it is not very easy for a stranger to procure reliable and disinterested information.

Having, I trust, by these few remarks, guarded against the possibility of misleading my brother sportsmen, I will return to Montana.

It is true that Montana has not fulfilled expectations as a gold-producing country, but this is attributable not so much to the absence of the precious metals as to the fact that communication is difficult and transportation laborious. Freights consequently are so high that working any but the very richest ores cannot possibly be remunerative. When it is considered that freights have to be hauled over almost impassable roads, from Corinne on the Union Pacific Railway, or have to ascend the Missouri in boats to the mouth of the Mussel Shell, whence they must be transported by mule or ox-trains, it is not to be wondered at that quartz mining does not pay.

In the early years of the settlement of the territory, prices ranged almost as high as they did in California during the period of great excitement there. Two dollars in dust per meal, and a dollar for a feed for your horse, were not uncommon prices. Flour reached as high as 75 cents per pound; hay was worth 80 dollars a ton, and all the necessaries of life for man and beast were charged for in like proportion. Such articles as picks sold at from 15 to 20 dollars apiece. Luxuries were ruinous; for lucifer matches, as an instance, you had to pay 75 cents or a dollar per small box. A friend of mine who put up a crushing mill at Stirling told me that he sold for $200 a saddle for which he had given $15 in St. Louis. Miners were paid $5 per day, with their board and lodging.

Against such exorbitant prices it was impossible for mine or mill owner to stand up. California, on the contrary, is practically self-supporting: its soil and climate will produce nearly every fruit, vegetable, and cereal that is of benefit to man; and it contains the finest pasture land in the world for sheep and cattle. Besides, it is accessible by sea, and consequently in that case 'supply' was not long in becoming equal to 'demand.' But Montana is remote from the sea, navigable rivers, and railways. As far as facilities of communication go, it is scarcely better off now than it was ten years ago, and the result is that prices, although they have declined, are still excessively high. Washing or gulch mining, therefore, is the only branch of the business which can be successfully carried on, and nearly all the gold exported from Montana is obtained by this process.

But there undoubtedly are in the country numerous

and fairly rich lodes of gold-bearing quartz, needing only the presence of a railway to become most valuable property. 'When the railway is made' is, in Montana, a sort of equivalent for our phrase 'when my ship comes home.' The Northern Pacific Railway was surveyed through the best parts of the territory, and under the benign influence of that great civiliser Montana would rapidly have developed into a prosperous State. But it is a case of 'If *hads* were *shads* there would have been fish for supper.' The Northern Pacific came to an untimely end. No one but Providence and financial agents can possibly say whether it is ever likely to be 'put through,' and in the meantime the northern territories are steadily 'advancing backwards.'

In spite of Montana's failure to rank among the principal gold and silver producing districts of the world, however, the mineralogist or geologist will find plenty to occupy and interest him. Nor need the lover of scenery or the Alpine climber be dissatisfied, for very beautiful are the mountains, prairies, streams, water-falls, and woods ; and, though the summits are higher in other portions of the great irregular elevation commonly known as the Rocky Mountains, yet nowhere, save in the great upheaval of the Sierra Nevada, are the outlines finer and more broken. The rugged, serrated range con-taining the three Tétons is, so far as I know, as picturesque as any on the continent. Although the highest mountains of North America are exceedingly easy of ascent, yet there are exceptions, for many a mountain is said to be inaccessible, and multitudes of peaks have never yet been trodden by the foot of man.

But the great centre of attraction to all, whatever their tastes and proclivities may be, is, of course, that extraordinary section of country not inaptly termed by the inhabitants 'Wonderland'—more accurately but not so euphoniously designated 'the Upper and Lower Fire-hole basin' or 'Geyser basin,' while the whole district is, for want of a better name, usually described as the 'Upper Yellowstone Country.' It is of this Geyser basin, the country immediately surrounding it, and the various routes leading thereto, that I propose to speak. It is accessible to all who have leisure, money, and inclination to travel, nor can it be pretended that a visit is attended by any alarming risk. To the territories of Montana, Wyoming, and Idaho in general I shall not allude. They are great hunting grounds, and there is much to be said about them ; but large portions of these territories—and those portions, for many reasons, the most prolific in game—are not very well known to me, and can be visited only at considerable risk owing to the restless hostility of the Indians.

The area contained in the reservation measures 3,578 square miles. It is, speaking roughly, within the meridians of 110° and 111° west longitude, and 44° and 45° north latitude. The general elevation is about 6,000 feet above sea level, while the mountain ranges that hem in the narrow valleys on every side attain to a height of from 10,000 to 12,000 feet. The winters are too severe for stock-raising, and, as frosts occur at night during nearly every month of the year, agriculture is out of the question. The rocks are generally volcanic, and there is but little chance of any mineral deposits being concealed in them. It is therefore for ordinary purposes a value-less region, capable of supporting only wild beasts and the wilder men who prey upon them. But, though useless for farming, mining, or manufacturing purposes, many circumstances have combined to render the National Park the most interesting and valuable district in the continent. It may be that the Yosemite Valley surpasses it in picturesque beauty. But the National Park does not rely upon its scenery alone. It is endowed with many and various attractions. It contains the most wonderful remains of volcanic activity at present known to exist. The Mammoth Hot Springs of Gardiner's River, and both the Geyser Basins, are situated in it. Entombed in its forests, at a height above the sea of 7,788 feet, lies a large and most lovely lake, which is, with four exceptions,* the highest body of water of any considerable size in the world; and in the snow that falls upon its summits are born four of the largest rivers of the continent. On the north are the sources of the Yellowstone; on the west, those of the three forks of the Missouri; to the south-west and south rise the springs of the Snake and Green Rivers, the former gaining the North Pacific, the latter finding its way to the Gulf of California; and lastly, on the south, head the numerous branches of Wind River. Thus it is, as auctioneers would say, a most desirable park-like property; and, if Government had not promptly stepped in, it would have been pounced upon by speculators, and the beauties of Nature, disposed of to the highest bidder, would have been retailed at so much a look to generations of future travellers.

There are five routes by which 'Wonderland' may be reached. First, and most obvious, is the regular stage line running from Corinne, a town situated on Great Salt Lake, thirty-two miles west of Ogden, to Virginia City and Helena. Ogden is the junction of the Union Pacific and Central Pacific Railways, and that fact is about the

---

* These four exceptions are lakes Titticaca in Peru, and Uros in Bolivia; which respectively are 12,874 and 12,359 feet above sea-level; and lakes Manasasarowak and Rakas Tal in Thibet, both of which lie at the enormous elevation of 15,000 feet.

only feature of any interest in the place. Corinne is about 2,508 miles from New York; up to that point the journey can be performed most comfortably in one of Pullman's cars; but at Corinne the traveller will find himself in the position of the young bear, with all his sorrows to come. A glance at the map will show that the most convenient course to pursue is to go direct from Corinne to Virginia City by stage, passing up Malade Valley. There the traveller should fit out, secure a guide, purchase or hire pack animals, and proceed to the Geyser Basins. Having examined these, he will pass by the Yellowstone Lake, the Mud Springs, and the Hot Springs of Gardiner's River; and crossing Mount Washburn—the summit of the ' Great Divide '—he will again emerge from the wilderness into civilisation at Bozeman. There he can take the stage, and return to Corinne, thereby making a round trip of it. The approximate distances are—Corinne to Virginia City, 330 miles; Virginia City to Lower Geyser Basin, 100 miles; Lower to Upper Basin and return, 20 miles; Lower Geyser Basin to Mud Springs, 25 miles; Mud Springs to Hot Springs on Gardiner's River, 50 miles; or Lower Geyser Basin to Yellowstone Lake, 30 miles; Lake to Mud Springs, 6 miles; Hot Springs of Gardiner's River to Boteler's Ranch, 40 miles; Boteler's to Bozeman, 35 miles; and Bozeman to Corinne, 400 miles. This is the simplest, easiest, and cheapest road that can be chosen, but it is the least interesting.

Secondly. Purchasing an outfit at Corinne or Salt Lake City, send it on to Fort Hall, Snake River Bridge, or some other convenient starting-point; take the before-mentioned stage line up Malade Valley till you join the outfit, and then launch out into the wilderness, taking a direction slightly to the east of north. After two or three days' travel through a dreary country of sage brush you will enter the Téton Basin, a fertile tract of 800 square miles in extent. Mr. Langford says of it : ' We entered the Téton Basin, which lay spread out before us like the land which Lot saw when he parted from Abraham. This basin is more than 800 square miles in extent, is covered with perennial grasses, well watered by large streams, fringed with an abundant growth of cotton-wood, furnishing sufficient timber for all the practical purposes of life, while the adjacent mountains are covered with tall pines, furnishing the best timber in the world.' From there you should visit the great Téton Mountains, of which the same authority states : ' The most northerly, or Grand Téton, which has received the name of and will hereafter be known as Mount Hayden, presents to the eye an outline very similar to that of the Matterhorn in the Alps. Its very appearance, unlike that of most of our mountains, seems to forbid all attempts to scale it, and for most of the distance the ascent can only be accomplished by climbing with both feet and hands. The face of the mountain presents an angle of 45°, and frequently 60°, much more abrupt than the steepest stairs. Glaciers of greater or lesser dimensions are met with every few hundred feet, and in several instances they prove almost insurmountable. The irregular stratifications of the rocks were often such as to leave us with no support other than our hands, at points and turnings where a failure in our hold would have precipitated us hundreds of feet down the face of the mountain. At one or two points when nearing the summit, we would have been obliged to have abandoned the task but for the aid we received by casting the rope over prominent projections, and pulling ourselves over them to places where we could obtain a secure foothold. In one of these efforts Mr. Stephenson came near losing his hold, and falling down a precipice nearly a thousand feet. Another of our company, while ascending along the edge of a glacier, losing his hold, slid down a smooth ridge of ice a distance of forty feet with fearful rapidity. His own presence of mind, in hastily throwing himself astride the edge of the glacier, and descending it in that position, caused him to fall into a snow-bed at the bottom, and on the extreme edge of the precipice. This saved him from falling at least 800 feet. Of nine of the company who commenced the ascent, Mr. Stephenson and myself alone were successful. We found on one of the buttresses, a little lower than the extreme top of the mountain, evidence that at some former period it had been visited by human beings. There was a circular in-closure about seven feet in diameter, formed by vertical slabs of rough granite, and about three feet in height, the interior of which was half filled with the detritus that long exposure to the elements had worn from these walls. It could not have been constructed less than half a century ago, when Indians only inhabited these regions.

'The summit of the Téton is very small, not more than 30 by 40 feet in diameter, with a precipitous descent on all sides. Its height by triangular measurement is 13,858 feet. The view from it embraces the valley of the Snake River, and territory contiguous, for a diameter of at least 160 miles. For grandeur, vastness, and variety, it is nowhere excelled in the region of the Rocky Mountains. Should the railroad to the Upper Yellowstone pass through this valley, the Téton range would form one of the attractive features of a visit to that wonderful country.

'On our descent of the mountain, while yet at a height

of 10,300 feet, we crossed a lake 600 yards long by 200 wide, of perpetual ice, which in thickness was about 3 feet, not unlike in character the description given of the most elevated glaciers of the Alps.'

You should then take a straight course for the northern branch of Snake River, which is called Henry's Fork, and, after ascending it up to Henry's Lake, cross the mountains by the Tyghee Pass, and enter the Valley of the Madison. Thence an easterly course will enable you to strike the trail from Virginia City to the Lower Geyser Basin, which passes within eight miles of the entrance to the cañon of Gibbon's Fork. Or the Snake River might be crossed in the proximity, but eastward, of the great bend it makes about Market Lake; and after fording the Pierré the course would lie through Falls-River Valley up to Beulah Lake. From that point the tourist would pass to Lewis Fork of Snake River, and wind his away along that stream till Lewis Lake at the foot of Mount Sheridan was reached. There the trail separates into two branches, the first taking a north-westerly course to the Shoshone Geyser Basin, and, thence crossing the main Rocky Mountains, divide at an elevation of 8,117 feet above sea-level, conducting you by the valley of the Fire Hole River, or east fork of the Madison; while the other, pursuing a north-easterly course, will conduct you, after crossing the main divide at a very easy gradient, to the Hot Springs of the Yellowstone Lake. As to distances—from Corinne to the neighbourhood of Fort Hall is about 125 miles, and from there to the north fork of Snake River about 60 miles. The following tables are from Mr. Hering's report to Professor Hayden :—

	Distance from Henry's Fork. in miles.	Distance from Corinne, in miles.	Elevation, in feet.
Henry's Fork Valley . .	0	145	5,130
Falls River	13	158	5,670
Entrance to Pass . . .	33	178	6,950
Beulah Lakes	39	184	7,525
Union Fork	45	190	7,800
Lewis Lake	56	201	7,828
Hot Springs, Yellowstone Lake	64	209	7,788
Yellowstone Falls . . .	94	239	7,700
Shoshone Geyser Basin . .	66	211	7,880
Divide	70	215	8,717
Upper Geyser Basin . .	80	225	7,390
Lower Geyser Basin . .	88	233	7,260

	Distance from Henry's Lake, in miles.	Distance from Corinne, in miles.	Elevation, in feet.
Henry's Lake	0	235	6,443
Tyghee Pass	10	245	7,063
Gibbon's Fork	33	268	6,808
Lower Geyser Basin . .	40	275	7,260
Upper Geyser Basin . .	48	283	7,390
Divide	58	293	8,717
Shoshone Geyser Basin . .	62	297	7,881
Lewis Lake	72	307	7,835
Hot Springs, Yellowstone Lake	80	315	7,788
Yellowstone Falls . . .	110	345	7,700

There can be no question that, if time be not an object, the latter route is very much to be preferred to the former, as it would exclude the long tiresome stage journey, and include a visit to the three Tétons.

Thirdly. If the map be consulted, a military post, by

name Camp Brown, will be noticed, situated about 120 miles north of Rawling Springs Station, on the Union Pacific Railway, with which place it is connected by a good stage road. From Camp Brown to the Geyser Basin cannot be more than 130 or 140 miles. The trail is said to be easy, the scenery beautiful, and game plentiful; wood, water and grass, in fact, all the necessaries of life, are found in abundance. In 1873 Captain Jones surveyed a trail from Camp Brown to Fort Ellis, with a view to connecting the National Park and the mining districts and towns of Northern Wyoming and Montana with the railway, by a waggon road more direct than the existing one from Corinne. It had always been reported that the Yellowstone Lake was unapproachable from the south. Impassable mountain ranges, which an old trapper described as being so 'high and rugged that a crow couldn't fly over them,' were said to bar the way. But these obstacles turned out to be purely mythical. The expedition, after a most interesting journey, arrived safely at the Yellowstone Lake without having experienced any great difficulty, having met with no serious obstacles to overcome in the way of steep gradients.

The result of this investigation proves that the distances from the Union Pacific Railway to the National Park have been much over-estimated. It seems clear that from Point of Rocks Station a stage line could be made to the Yellowstone Lake *viâ* Camp Brown, which would not exceed 250 miles in length. The only drawback to this route is that it is sometimes very unsafe on account of Indians. It is actually in the Snake country, and the Snakes, or Shoshones, are friendly; but, once clear of Camp Brown, there is no harbour of refuge to make for, nothing to keep in check and overawe the natives. Under these circumstances friendly Indians are just as likely to steal your horses as anybody else; and I should not at all fancy being caught alone by half a dozen young braves eager to gain the distinction of having taken a scalp. Never trust an Indian, even though the tribe be at peace, unless you have very good reason to know that you can do so. It may seem surprising, but the women are at the bottom of all the mischief. The chiefs, steady old fellows, long ago settled and done for, have arrived at the same conclusion as Solomon—that all things are vanity—and have transferred their affections from the fickle sex to the constant pipe, adopting as their motto 'anything for a quiet life;' so that these old dignitaries are most anxious to be at peace and receive their annuity goods regularly; and they do their best to keep the young men quiet. But courage and craftiness are virtues highly prized in savage communities. The brightest smiles, the sweetest glances await the youth fortunate enough to have struck an enemy. He becomes a man; his words are listened to with respect; his friendship is courted; his love not often refused. The old women tell the girls long stories of what men their forefathers were, and descant upon the doughty deeds they performed before daring to aspire to the hand of their mistresses. The vanity of the 'dusky maiden' is aroused; she determines to be not too cheaply bought or too easily won; and she taunts and goads her lover into committing some act that frequently brings a terrible retribution, not upon him alone unfortunately, but upon whole families and tribes of innocent persons.

Can we not imagine the scene? The lovers pacing the moonlit sward chequered with the drooping shadows of the pines, the rustle of the trailing robe, the twinkle of the little naked feet among the flowers, the glance of the tender eyes, the throbbing pulse and beating heart, the half-concealed outline of the little swelling bosom heaving in responsive agitation, the gentle pressure of the hand, the warm soft rounded form yielding to the persuasive arm, the whispered ' Darling, wilt thou be mine ? Fly, oh fly with me to yonder grove, there on soft carpeting of moss to plight our troth and swear eternal constancy.' And the prudent reply, ' Yes, dearest, I am sure it would be very charming, but what would papa say? How many scalps a year have you got ? How many horses can you steal? Have you taken any ponies lately, nice piebald ones? ' Fancy his conscious blush of shame, and her indignant ' What! have you killed nobody yet? Unhand me, villain ! Is it thus you dare to address the daughter of the " Skunk that creeps in the grass "? '

No! I don't think the young brave is to blame. What can he do? ' Needs must when the devil drives ; ' and, if the old song of St. Anthony's temptation is to be credited, there lurks in the sweet smile and shyly inviting glance of woman the most dangerous and irresistible imp of the whole satanic crew.

For these reasons, when he is in pursuit of a particularly lovely or hard-hearted damsel, I should prefer keeping out of the way of the enamoured swain. So it is not wise to trust too much even to the Snakes. But the country is liable also to incursions of the Sioux, those scourges of the plains, who are so much dreaded by the Snakes that it would never do to trust to the latter for escort or protection. They would most likely abandon you upon the first sign of danger. These remarks apply only to small parties ; but ten or twelve men might, except under very extraordinary circumstances, travel with perfect safety.

Fourthly. There is what may be called the Missouri

route. Until late in summer the river is navigable to
Fort Benton, which is distant from Helena about 80 or 90
miles by stage road; and by taking this road the traveller would have an opportunity of visiting, if he so
desired, the great Falls of the Missouri. From Helena
either Bozeman or Virginia City may be readily reached
by stage. The transit from Bismarck, a town situated on
the Missouri and the present terminus of the Northern
Pacific Railway, to Benton would occupy ten to fifteen
days. Much interesting country would be traversed,
especially the *mauvaises terres*, or 'bad lands' of
Dakotah; but it would be a tedious journey, and devoid
of comfort. A better plan would be to disembark at
Carrol, near the mouth of the Mussel Shell, and, having
ordered horses to be in readiness for you, to take the
waggon trail from there to the Crow Agency at the great
bend of the Yellowstone River, and thence to Fort Ellis
and Bozeman. The total length of the land journey
would be about 150 miles, through a prairie country
abounding in antelope and buffalo. The river is navigable to Benton only at high water, but communication
is kept up pretty regularly with Carrol. It is only at
extreme low water that the steamers fail to reach the
mouth of the Mussel Shell; and then the traffic is carried
on in Mackinaw boats.

A very good plan for a party starting, say early in
June from England, would be to sail for Quebec, the
prettiest and pleasantest town in the Dominion, and
thence to go by steamer to Montreal, up the noble river
St. Lawrence, and through the lovely scenery of the
Thousand Islands to Toronto. From there by rail to
Collingwood, a journey of only four hours, and then
again by steamer across the great lakes Huron and

Superior, through the Sault St. Mary ; skirting the wildly picturesque north shore of Lake Superior, and touching at various places, Bruce Mines, Michipicotton, Neepigon —famous for trout—Silver Islet, Prince Arthur's Landing, Fort William, Pigeon River, &c. &c., to Fond du lac, now called Duluth. The course would then lie over the embryonic Northern Pacific Railway to Bismarck, and up the Missouri to Carrol. From Collingwood to Duluth would take about a week ; Bismarck is about 440 miles from Duluth, and the ascent of the river would occupy about 10 to 15 days.

The mention of the north shore and of Prince Arthur's Landing, which is one of the gateways to the ' North-West Territory,' leads me to the fifth direction from which the National Park may be reached—namely, from the British possessions.

Among all the modes of progression hitherto invented by restless man, there is not one that can compare in respect of comfort and luxury with travelling in a birch-bark canoe. It is the poetry of progression. Along the bottom of the boat are laid blankets and bedding ; a sort of wicker-work screen is sloped against the middle thwart, affording a delicious support to the back ; and indolently, in your shirt sleeves if the day be warm, or well covered with a blanket if it is chilly, you sit or lie on this most luxurious of couches, and are propelled at a rapid rate over the smooth surface of a lake or down the swift current of some stream. If you want exercise, you can take a paddle yourself. If you prefer to be inactive, you can lie still and placidly survey the scenery, rising occasionally to have a shot at a wild duck ; at intervals reading, smoking, and sleeping. Sleep indeed you will enjoy most luxuriously, for the rapid bounding motion of the canoe as she leaps forward at every impulse of the crew, the sharp quick beat of the paddles on the water, and the roll of their shafts against the gunwale, with the continuous hiss and ripple of the stream cleft by the curving prow, combine to make a more soothing soporific than all the fabrications of poppy and mandragora that can be found in the pharmacopœia of civilisation.

Dreamily you lie side by side—you and your friend —lazily gazing at the pine-covered shores and wooded islands of some unknown lake, the open book unheeded on your knee; the half-smoked pipe drops into your lap; your head sinks gently back; and you wander into dreamland, to awake presently and find yourself sweeping round the curve of some majestic river, whose shores are blazing with the rich crimson, brown, and gold of the maple and other hard-wood trees in their autumn dress.

Presently the current quickens. The best man shifts his place from the stern to the bow, and stands ready with his long-handled paddle to twist the frail boat out of reach of hidden rocks. The men's faces glow with excitement. Quicker and quicker flows the stream, breaking into little rapids, foaming round rocks, and rising in tumbling waves over the shallows. At a word from the bowman the crew redouble their efforts, the paddle shafts crash against the gunwale, the spray flies beneath the bending blades. The canoe shakes and quivers through all its fibres, leaping bodily at every stroke.

Before you is a seething mass of foam, its whiteness broken by horrid black rocks, one touch against whose jagged sides would rip the canoe into tatters and hurl you into eternity. Your ears are full of the roar of waters; waves leap up in all directions, as the river, maddened at

Canoe shooting a Rapid.

obstruction, hurls itself through some narrow gorge. The bowman stands erect to take one look in silence, noting in that critical instant the line of deepest water; then bending to his work, with sharp, short words of command to the steersman, he directs the boat. The canoe seems to pitch headlong into space. Whack! comes a great wave over the bow; crash! comes another over the side. The bowman, his figure stooped, and his knees planted firmly against the side, stands, with paddle poised in both hands, screaming to the crew to paddle hard; and the crew cheer and shout with excitement in return. You, too, get wild, and feel inclined to yell defiance to the roaring hissing flood that madly dashes you from side to side. After the first plunge you are in a bewildering whirl of waters. The shore seems to fly past you. Crash! You are right on that rock, and (I don't care who you are) you will feel your heart jump into your mouth, and you will catch the side with a grip that leaves a mark on your fingers afterwards. No! With a shriek of command to the steersman, and a plunge of his paddle, the bowman wrenches the canoe out of its course. Another stroke or two, another plunge forward, and with a loud exulting yell from the bowman, who flourishes his paddle round his head, you pitch headlong down the final leap, and with a grunt of relief from the straining crew glide rapidly into still water.

Through the calm gloaming, through the lovely hours of moonlit night you glide, if the stream is favourable and the current safe; the crew of *Metis*, or French half-breeds, asleep, wrapped in their white capotes, all but the steersman, who nods over his paddle and croons to himself some old Normandy or Breton song. Or, landing in the evening, you struggle back from the romance of leaf tints and sunset glows to the delicious savouriness of a stew, composed of fat pork, partridges, potatoes, onions, fish, and lumps of dough ; and having ballasted yourself with this compound, and smoked the digestive pipe, sleep on sweet pine-tops till you're *levézd* by the steersman in the morning, when you pursue your way, not miserable and cross, as you would be at home after such a mess of pottage, but bright, happy, and cheerful ; capable of enjoying to the full the glories of the daybreak, watching the watery diamonds from the paddle-blades flashing in the sun, and listening to the echoing notes of *À la claire fontaine*, or some other French-Canadian song.

Dear me! What a lot might be written about Fort William, the Kamanistiquoia River, and the lovely chest-nut-tinted falls upon it, of the hospitality of Mr. M'Intyre, and of the great old days gone by of the North-West Fur Company, when the traders were little kings in Montreal ; when the old hall at Fort William echoed the voices of over a hundred retainers of the Company at a time ; when fleets of large north-west canoes, manned by twelve men each, would come up the still reaches from the lakes, and flotillas of lighter vessels, laden with costly furs from far-distant northern wilds, would sweep down its rapid current, their half-savage crews imitating the cry of the beast representing the department from which they came.

But I have already rambled out of the way too much. All I meant to say was, that canoe travelling is very pleasant ; but it is somewhat expensive. If therefore a party of friends, not *very* particular about expense, would like a canoe journey, and not object to a long ride or drive, I should advise them to take the last given directions as far as Prince Arthur's Landing or Fort

William, and go up by canoe to Fort Garry, visiting Kakabeka Falls, passing through the soft beauties of the Lake of the Woods and Rainy Lake and River, stopping a day or two at Fort Francis, if many lodges of Chippeways or Saulteaux happen to be congregated there, and traversing the wild grandeur of the Winipeg River. From Fort Garry they could either ride or drive in about three weeks to Fort Benton, following the Assiniboin River, and shaping their course gradually south by Q'appelle Lakes; or else, riding up the valley of the Saskatchewan to Carlton, they could thence strike due south to the South Saskatchewan, and onwards by the Cypress Hills to Milk River, and so to Benton. Good men, understanding the natives and well acquainted with the country, are to be found at Fort Garry; and there ought to be no danger from Indians, except perhaps a little just in crossing the boundary. But the risk would be so slight that it is scarcely worth considering. Indians who are hostile in the States are friendly in the British possessions; and, though going from Benton north might be uncomfortable, I should have little apprehension in crossing to Benton from the Canada side in the company of a single half-breed upon whom I could rely.

Finally, you may approach the Park from Walla Walla on the west; but, as I personally know nothing about that country, I think the less I say about it the better. I believe there is a road following the Hell-Gate and Bitter-Root Rivers; the Indian tribes are friendly, and the traveller would have the advantage of journeying through a country little known to civilised man, and reported to be full of game. Further than this deponent sayeth not.

Having thus attempted to 'locate' the Geyser region, and describe the paths leading thereto, I shall proceed to take up my parable and follow my trail in memory from Salt Lake City to Wonderland and back.

Pi-ta-ne-sha-a-du, PRINCIPAL CHIEF OF THE PAWNEES.

CHAPTER II.

OFF TO THE GEYSERS.

MY first act after making up my mind to undertake the trip to Geyserland was to write to my old friend, hunting companion and guide, Mr. John Omohondro, better known as Texas Jack, and endeavour to secure his services for the expedition. Jack and I in company had run wapiti and buffalo many times upon the plains. He started for me my first bison, a solitary savage old bull, down on one of the tributaries of the Republican; under his auspices I slew my first elk also, and, though it was not a very large one, I thought it the most magnificent animal the world had ever produced; together we once made the most successful run at elk that I have ever heard of, and enjoyed a day's sport such as I shall never see again, but to which I hope to allude later on in this volume, if space will permit me. Many a long day had we hunted together, and been in at the deaths of numerous antelopes and white-tail and black-tail deer; and many a waggon-load of meat, the produce of our chase, have he and I sent into the Fort. I cannot tell you exactly what fort it was, O sporting reader, because if there be any game left in that locality, which I very much doubt, I want selfishly to reserve it for my own especial benefit, for I hope to shoot there once again before I die.

I had had plenty of experience therefore of Jack, and knew him to be just the man I wanted; but since those merry days among the sandhills and on the plains, he had settled down in life and married; and whether he could be induced to leave his wife and comfortable home, and to brave the hardships and dangers of a hunting or exploring trip to the far West, I was very much in doubt. I was therefore much pleased one fine day, as I was lying dozing during the heat of noon in my tent, pitched close to the never-melting snows on Long's Peak, to receive a letter from Jack, forwarded from the post-office of the rising little town of Longmont, saying that he was ready for anything, that he would be delighted to come, and was prepared to accompany me anywhere. He added that I should find him at Charpiot's Restaurant, Denver, in a couple of days.

Jack was a great acquisition to our party, which consisted, besides myself, of Dr. G. Kingsley; my cousin and good friend, Captain C. Wynne; Maxwell, a gentleman of colour, who fulfilled the important functions of barber and cook; Campbell, my henchman or servant, a limber-limbed lengthy Highlandman, whose legs were about as long as his drawl; and last, but not least, in his own estimation at any rate, if not in mine, the faithful companion of many wanderings, my much-beloved colley dog 'Tweed.'

Maxwell had been with me before in the sunny South, sailing down the broad reaches of the Indian river, camped among the oak and palmetto scrub fringing the sands of Merrit's Island, or on some hummock under the shade of the pines and palms of fragrant Florida; and I knew him to be a good cook, and took him with me gladly, but with some misgivings as to whether he could stand the cold. Campbell was fresh from his native hills. Wynne and I were old friends, who knew by experience that we should get on well together. On this occasion, however, he caused me a fearful amount of anxiety, for which I hope he has repented long ago in sackcloth and ashes; for he was delayed a month in England, and after waiting as long as possible, I was forced to start without him. On three separate occasions we halted a week for him, and it was more by good luck than by good management that he succeeded eventually in joining us in Montana: but I must admit that by his cheerful and genial companionship he subsequently atoned fully for all previous misdeeds. Dr. Kingsley and I were not strangers, for we had travelled together in America before; had hunted in company, eaten out of the same battered iron pot, and drunk out of the same pannikin. Altogether, our party contained within itself the elements necessary to ensure, if not a successful, at any rate an enjoyable trip.

It was late in the month of July when I got Jack's letter, and, acting upon it, I on the following day bade adieu to the happy hunting-grounds of Estes Park and drove down to Denver, the capital of Colorado, a distance of 60 miles. While still at some distance from the town I became aware of a great coruscation, which I took to proceed from a comet or some other meteorological eccentricity, but which on approaching nearer resolved itself into the diamond shirt-studs and breast-pin shining in the snowy 'bosom' of my friend Texas Jack, who had already arrived from the classic east winds of Boston to share the fortunes of the trip. Pork and beans and pickled cucumbers had failed to sour his genial smile; æsthetic dissipation had not dulled the lustre of his eye. Jack at Denver in broadcloth and white linen was the same Jack that I had last seen upon the North Platte, grimy in an old buckskin suit redolent of slaughtered animals and bodily deliquescence. How we did 'haver' and talk over old times that night, occasionally making enquiries as to the tenor of the historical telegram sent by the Governor of North Carolina to the Governor of South Carolina, which I may as well mention is said to have been to the effect that it 'was a long time between drinks.' Far into the night we discussed our future plans, and finally decided that as General Sheridan, who had kindly given me the benefit of his advice in Chicago, would by no means recommend the route *viâ* Camp Brown, which he considered dangerous for a small party that year, owing to hostilities having broken out with the Sioux, our best plan would be to take the ordinary road from Corinne by stage.

Corinne is, as I have already mentioned in the preceding chapter, picturesquely situated on the shores of Great Salt Lake about 32 miles west of Ogden, the terminus, or rather junction of the Union Pacific and Central Pacific Railways. Deseret, or, as it is now universally called, Salt Lake City, is two or three hours distant by train south of Ogden. It was therefore a little out of our way; but as the office of the Montana stage line was there, and as it offered by far the most convenient market for us to fit out at, we made up our minds to betake ourselves first of all to Salt Lake City. Our movements after that were to be guided a good deal by circumstances. Our general intention was to stage it from Corinne to Virginia City in Montana, and from there to get on as best we could to Fort Ellis or Bozeman in the same territory. There we proposed to purchase horses, mules, and whatever was necessary for the expedition. If Wynne joined by the time we were ready to take the field, we meant to have gone straight on from Fort Ellis to the Geyser district, and, having seen the wonders of that country, to have devoted some time to hunting in the mountains about the sources of Clark's Fork of the Yellowstone. We were obliged, however, to modify our plans a little, and do our hunting first, in order to give Wynne an opportunity of overtaking us.

Having a great antipathy to stage travelling in promiscuous company, I determined, throwing prudence to the winds, to make myself as comfortable as circumstances would allow, regardless of expense; and accordingly I sent Jack on ahead to Salt Lake City to negotiate terms and charter the entire vehicle for our own sole and particular use, while we took our ease in our inn at Denver. On receiving a telegram from him to say 'all right,' we joined him at Deseret, and spent a couple of days in that city of saintly sinners, making a few necessary purchases, such as saddles, buffalo robes, and bridles.

Deseret is a very pretty town, beautifully situated on a plain almost surrounded by spurs of the Wahsatch Range. It looks clean from a distance, and on inspection it justifies its appearance. Perhaps the houses are whiter than the characters of some of its inhabitants. Formerly it enjoyed a very evil reputation; but, allowing for the discordant elements that mingle there, it may be said to be a tolerably respectable, though very peculiar place. It is like a jar of mixed human pickles, the population being composed of a conglomeration of saints and gentiles, elders and sinners, Mormons and Christians, and very much 'mixed' indeed. But there is no occasion now to give any description of Mormonism and the Mormons. Everybody knows all about that.

I enjoyed myself very well, and was introduced by

Jack to many estimable acquaintances, and to many
curious scenes. But I am not sure that on the whole I
benefited much, pecuniarily, from his assistance. True, I
acquired a considerable amount of second-hand renown,
and, like the moon, shone with borrowed splendour. Jack
was dressed in beaded buckskins and moccasins, fringed
leggings and broad felt hat. Jack is a tall, straight, and
handsome man, and in walking through the well-watered
streets of Deseret in his company I felt the same proud
conscious glow that pervades the white waistcoat of the
male débutant when for the first time he walks down St.
James's Street, arm in arm with the best dressed and most
fashionable man about town. It was obvious to all that
I was on terms of equality with a great personage, and
on that account cigars were frequent and drinks free.
But I don't know that there was any great reduction in
buffalo robes and saddles.

All our preparations being at length completed, we,
on a lovely afternoon in the first week in August, took
the train from Salt Lake City, and, after changing cars
at Ogden, arrived at Corinne, where we slept at a very
comfortable little inn. We knew it would be our last
night in bed for some time, so we made the most of the
luxury. The following morning, at 6.30 A.M., we piled
ourselves and traps into a lumbering, heavy, old-fashioned
stage-coach, and, under the guidance of a whisky bottle
and an exceedingly comical driver, started for Virginia
City. Jehu was a very odd man and wore a very odd
head-dress, consisting of a chimney-pot hat elongated by
some strange process into a cone, having the brim turned
down and ventilated by large gashes cut in the sides. He
was very garrulous, and, I grieve to add, profane. I
might now give you, O reader, the 'Comical Coachman,'
and introduce the story of Mr. Greeley ; but, as I am not

inclined to cause needless suffering, I refrain. The coach was a strange vehicle, mostly composed of leather. It was decorated with decayed leather; the sides were leather curtains; the top was leather; it was hung upon leather straps, and thongs of the same material dangled from the roof.

The arrangements along the road are not good. The accommodation for travellers at the stations, and the food supplied, are, with one or two exceptions, infamously bad. The horses are grass-fed all through the summer, and the poor brutes are quite unfit for the work they are called upon to perform. As they are generally out grazing on the prairie or hill-side when a coach arrives at a changing place, and have to be driven in and caught, a great deal of time is lost and delays are frequent. In fact nobody dreams of being in time; and, unless you arrive at the station for changing teams six or eight hours or half a day late, you will probably find no one at the ranch. The boys will have gone out visiting or shooting, not expecting to see you so soon. The consequence is that meals get very 'mixed;' you find yourself having dinner at 7 A.M., supping at noon, and breakfasting somewhere about sundown, or in the middle of the night. As all the repasts are much the same, consisting of beefsteaks, pork, potatoes, hot biscuit (a hot roll is in America termed a biscuit, and what we call biscuit is there denominated a cracker) and coffee, this dislocation of meals does not so very much signify.

The interior of the coach was occupied by three seats, the spaces between which we filled in with baggage, and over the comparatively level surface thus formed we were shot about like shuttles in a loom for four days and nights. The vehicle laboured a great deal in the heavy roads, producing at first in most of us a feeling of sea-sickness, which gradually wore off. Friday, our first day out, was not pleasantly spent. The sun was intensely powerful The road, many inches deep in alkaline dust, traversed a level plain, following the course of Bear River ; and there was nothing to break the dull monotony of the scene, except a few stunted artemisia and sage bushes, and very distant views of mountains. Clouds of the salt dust, agitated by the sultry breeze, covered our clothes, and filled our eyes, ears, noses and mouths ; dinner-time and tea-time were hailed with delight, and a little private eating and drinking was also indulged in to while away the tedious hours. There was no difficulty about eating, but to take a drink amidst the heavings and kickings of the carriage, without swallowing bottle and all, required considerable skill.

At length the long-wished-for shades of evening began to fall. The shadows of the mountains crept over the plain. The wind died away ; the clouds of white powder settled down ; the delicious crisp coolness of a summer night at those high altitudes succeeded to the enervating suffocating heat of day, and refreshed our irritated nerves. Rolling ourselves in blankets, we stretched out as well as we could upon the baggage and passed a very tolerable night. It was bright moonlight, and I lay awake for a long time watching the big jack-rabbits scudding over the plain, and admiring the jovial grinning countenance of the full moon ; till, finally, in spite of the jolting, I fell into a sound sleep, broken, however, occasionally by Tweed—who with almost human malignity would lie down on my stomach instead of in the place allotted to him—and by the piercing Indian yells which the driver emitted to announce his approach to each station for changing horses.

Towards evening the plain narrowed into a valley,

and the road became fearfully rough, littered with blocks
of stone, and pitted with holes full of water. The depth
of these pools not being properly laid down upon any
chart, our driver was obliged to get off and sound them
with his whip-handle, thereby delaying us very much.
During the night we crossed the mountains, and a little
before sun-rise awoke to find ourselves at a small change
station close to the summit, and near to where the road
branches off to Fort Hall.

Many people prefer sun-sets to sun-rises. I must
confess that, notwithstanding the superior gorgeousness of
colour of the evening hour, to me there is something
infinitely sad about the decline of day ; all things, vegetable as well as animal, sink so wearily to rest ; whereas
with the morn come hopes renewed and energies restored.
The grass is green and cool, and the flowers, fresh after
their bath of dew, look saucily up at the sun. The birds
sing ; all animals, save those that prey by night, re-
joice ; and new life seems to thrill through the frame of
man.

On this particular Saturday morning the breaking of
the day was very beautiful. There had been a slight
frost. Not a single shred of vapour obscured the perfectly
cloudless sky, not a breath of wind disturbed the marvellous transparency of the atmosphere. We stood on a
very elevated plateau close to a solitary shanty. In the
background were some half-dozen native lodges, from
each of which rose in a straight line a thin blue thread
of smoke. Crouched on the ground, his blanket drawn
up over his mouth and nose, sat one Indian, and the
gaunt figure of another was discernible stalking towards
us in the rapidly decreasing gloom. The western con-
stellations were still brightly shining, but the splendour
of the morning star was waning before an intenser light.

The dawn approaches, flinging over all the eastern sky a veil of the most delicate primrose, that warms into the rich lustre of the topaz, hiding the sad eyes of the fading stars. The yellow light sweeping across the sky is followed by a lovely rosy tint, which, slowly creeping over the arch of heaven, dyes the earth and firmament with its soft colouring, and throws back the mountains and valleys into deepest gloom. Stronger and stronger grows the lusty morn. Higher and warmer spreads the now crimson flood; timid Nature, with hot conscious blush, drops from her burning brow the veil of night, and shrinking, yet eager, steps forth in naked loveliness to meet the sun. The mountains all flush up; then blaze into sudden life. A great ball of fire clears the horizon, and strikes broad avenues of white light across the plain. The sun is up! and it is day. What is more, the horses are hitched; and, with a cry of 'all aboard,' away we roll to undergo another twelve hours' dust and heat.

Not very far from Fort Hall the road crosses Snake River at a point where the waters have cut through a basaltic outflow, and exposed a remarkably fine section to view. The basalt is columnar and regular, full of 'pot-holes' of various sizes, some being two or three feet deep, though only five or six inches in diameter; others, broad and shallow, occasionally containing the stones that, whirled constantly round by the action - of water, have worn out the cavities. We passed a good deal of volcanic matter, which appears to have been originally poured out into water, and covered with a deposit of fine volcanic sand and ashes. The evidences of water action are numerous. The whole great plain and valley of the Snake River is, I presume, formed by erosion, the 'Three Buttes' and other detached fragments remaining as monuments to show the former level of the land.

More recent signs, too, are abundantly to be seen. Several clearly defined old beaches, indicating the various levels at which the waters of the lakes have at different periods stood, are noticeable on the sides of low spurs and bluffs. Large districts look as if the waters had but quite lately retired from them, and even now great tracts are submerged after heavy rains. I should say that a very low dam across the rivers draining it would suffice to flood the whole country, and turn it into another great Salt Lake or inland sea.

Sunday was by no means a day of rest to us. We were all getting stiff and tired with incessant jolting, and longed to be at our journey's end. Tweed became so disgusted that he yielded to the seductions of a most undesirable acquaintance picked up at dinner-time, and could not or would not be found when the coach started. He came on by the next stage, and arrived in Virginia City 'sober and sorry for it.' We were all becoming dilapidated, and Maxwell especially so, for in addition to the ordinary fatigues of the journey he had also undergone the perils of starvation and assassination. Having a very proper antipathy to sit at the same table as his master, and there being but one table prepared, he ate nothing at all at first. When I discovered the cause, I recommended him sooner than starve to sit down with us, which he accordingly did at breakfast on Sunday; upon which up jumps an irascible Texan who was going to drive us, and, smashing his fist down on the table, swears that he is not going to eat with any wretched nigger. And, under ordinary circumstances, he would have been right. White and black should not associate ; both are excellent, but mutually disagreeable to each other. The perfume of the rose is sweet, the savour of the onion delicious ; but each possesses in respect to the other a most incompatible aroma.

We passed in the afternoon through a strange wild gap in the mountains, and emerged into another interminable plain bounded by nothing anywhere, except on the west, where rose the savage rocky crest of the ' Big Hole' Mountains, a continuation of the 'Flat Head' range ; in the hidden recesses of whose valleys the lordly moose still linger in considerable numbers, and among whose inaccessible crags the wild mountain goat finds a congenial home.   On the east the general level is broken only by the jagged tooth-like outlines of the distant Tétons.

Nothing is more extraordinary and wearisome than the levelness of the road.   From Corinne to Virginia City you drive along a series of apparently perfectly flat plains, connected with each other by short cañons and valleys.   Occasionally the road ascends, but by a very easy gradient.   There are no precipices, no torrents, no avalanches, no glaciers ; nothing grand, terrible, or dangerous.   The idea that you are surmounting a portion of a great and important watershed, that you are crossing the backbone of the continent, and scaling a vast mountain range, appears preposterous.   A field-day in the Long Valley, Aldershot, towards the end of July, with its concomitants of heat, dust, flatness, and general disagreeability (if there be such a word), resembles the passage of the Alps by Napoleon I. just about as much as does the ideal crossing of the great Rocky Mountains resemble the tame reality.

As I do not consider it a wise thing to cook stories or varnish facts when one is sure to be found out, I must beg the reader to excuse my unfolding any hairbreadth escapes, and to suffer me to introduce him or her thus prosaically to Virginia City, where we arrived on Monday morning, in fair condition, but by no means according to sample, if one had been taken of us on leaving Deseret.

Virginia City. Good Lord! What a name for the place! We had looked forward to it during the journey as to a sort of haven of rest, a lap of luxury; a Capua in which to forget our woes and weariness; an Elysium where we might be washed, clean-shirted, rubbed, shampooed, barbered, curled, cooled, and cock-tailed. Not a bit of it! Not a sign of Capua about the place! There might have been laps, but there was no luxury. A street of straggling shanties, a bank, a blacksmith's shop, a few dry goods stores, and bar-rooms, constitute the main attractions of the 'city.' A gentleman had informed me that Virginia *city* contained brown stone-front houses and paved streets, equal, he guessed, to any Eastern *town*. How that man did lie in his Wellingtons! The whole place was a delusion and a snare. One of the party was especially mortified, for he had been provided with a letter of introduction to some ladies from whose society he anticipated great pleasure; but when he came to inquire he found, to his intense disgust, that they were in Virginia City, *Nevada*, 'ten thousand miles away!' However, we soon became reconciled to our fate. We found the little inn very clean and comfortable; we dined on deer, antelope, and bear meat, a fact which raised hopes of hunting in our bosoms; and the people were exceedingly civil, kind, obliging, and anxious to assist strangers in any possible way, as, so far as my experience goes of America, and indeed of all countries, they invariably are as soon as you get off the regular lines of travel.

Virginia City is situated on Alder Gulch. It is surrounded by a dreary country, resembling the more desolate parts of Cumberland, and consisting of interminable waves of steep low hills covered with short, withered grass. I went out for a walk on the afternoon of our arrival, and was most disagreeably impressed. I could not get to the top of anything, and consequently could obtain no extended view. I kept continually climbing to the summit of grassy hills, only to find other hills, grassier and higher, surrounding me on all sides. The wind swept howling down the combes, and whistled shrilly in the short, wiry herbage ; large masses of ragged-edged black clouds were piled up against a leaden sky ; not a sign of man or beast was to be seen. It began to snow heavily, and I was glad to turn my back to the storm and scud for home.

Alder Gulch produced at one time some of the richest placer workings of the continent. It was discovered in 1863, and about 30 millions of dollars' worth of gold have been won from it. Of late years very little has been done, and at present the industrious Chinaman alone pursues the business of re-washing the old dirt heaps, and making money where any one else would starve. In truth, he is a great washerwoman, is your Chinaman, equally successful with rotten quartz and dirty shirts. Alder Gulch is about twelve miles in length and half a mile broad. It is closed at the head by a remarkable limestone ridge, the highest point of which is known as ' Old Baldy Mountain,' and it leads into the Jefferson Fork of the Missouri. Along the sides of the valley may be seen many patches of black basalt, and the bottom is covered entirely by drift, composed of material weather and water worn out of metamorphic rocks, the fragments varying in size from large boulders to fine sand and gravel. In this drift the float gold is found. In Montana the deposits of the precious metal generally occur in metamorphic rocks, belonging probably to the Huronian or Laurentian series. These are clearly stratified, not unfrequently intercalated with bands of clay or sand, and underlie the whole country, forming beds of great thickness, very massive and close-grained in their lower layers, but growing softer and looser in texture towards the surface. The superimposed formations, carboniferous limestones, and others, appear to have been almost wholly removed by erosion. In this part of Montana, indeed, the forces of erosion must have acted with great vigour for a long period of time. The general character of the country where placer mines exist may be said to be a series of deep gulches, frequently dry in the height of summer, but carrying foaming torrents after heavy rains and in snow-melting time, leading at right angles into a principal valley, and combining to form a little river, or, as it would be locally called, a creek. This principal stream courses in a broad valley through the mountains for perhaps 60, 80, or 100 miles, and at every two or three miles of its progress receives the waters of a little tributary torrent, tearing through the strata in deep cañons for ten or twelve miles, and searching the very vitals of the hills. Down these gulches, cañons, and valleys are carried the yellow specks torn from their quartz and felspar cradles, hurried downward by the melting snow, and battered into powder by falling boulders and grinding rocks, till they sink in beds of worthless sand and mud, there to lie in peace for ages amid the solitudes of primeval forest and eternal snow. Some fine day there comes along a dirty, dishevelled, tobacco-chewing fellow— 'fossicker,' as they would say in Australia, 'prospector,' as he would be called in the States. Impelled by a love of adventure, a passion for excitement, a hatred of 'the town and its narrow ways,' and of all and any of the steady wage-getting occupations of life, he braves summer's heat and winter's cold, thirst and starvation, hostile Indians and jealous whites; perhaps paddling a tiny birch-bark canoe over unmapped, unheard-of lakes, away to the far and misty North, or driving before him over the plains and prairies of a more genial clime his donkey or Indian pony, laden with the few necessaries that supply all the wants of his precarious life—a little flour, some tea and sugar tied up in a rag, a battered frying-pan and tin cup, a shovel, axe, and rusty gun.   Through untrodden wastes he wanders, self-dependent and alone, thinking of the great spree he had the last time he was in ' settlements,' and dreaming of what a good time he will enjoy when he gets back rich with the value of some lucky find, till chance directs him to the Gulch.   After a rapid but keen survey, he thinks it is a likely-looking place, capsizes the pack off his pony, leans lazily upon his shovel, spits, and finally concludes to take a sample of the dirt.   Listlessly, but with what delicacy of manipulation he handles the shovel, spilling over its edges the water and lighter mud ! See the look of interest that wakens up his emotionless face as the residue of sediment becomes less and less ! Still more tenderly he moves the circling pan, stooping anxiously to scan the few remaining grains of fine sand. A minute speck of yellow glitters in the sun ; with another dexterous turn of the wrist, two or three more golden grains are exposed to view.   He catches his breath ; his eyes glisten ; his heart beats.   Hurrah ! He has found the colour ! and ' a d—d good colour too.'   It is all over with your primeval forest now ; not all the Indians this side of Halifax or the other place could keep men out of that gulch.   In a short time claims are staked, tents erected, shanties built, and ' Roaring Camp ' is in full blast with all its rowdyism, its shooting, gambling, drinking, and blaspheming, and its under-current of charity, which never will be credited by those who value substance less than shadows, and think more of words than deeds.

Although the float gold undoubtedly had its origin in

the metamorphic rocks through which the streams have cut their way, yet, strange as it may appear, the exceptions where paying lodes have been found at the head of rich placer mines are extremely rare. No discoveries of any value have been made in the rocks towards the head of Alder Gulch, from which the tons of gold-dust, panned out from the bed of the stream, must have come. It would appear as though the upper portions of the strata contained all the metal, and the inferior layers were either very lean, or entirely destitute, of ore. The lodes throughout all this section have a general north-east and south-west strike, and dip nearly west at an angle of fifty or sixty degrees. The matrix is felspar and quartz, exhibiting various degrees of hardness in texture, and occurring generally in gneiss. The trend of the whole metamorphic series is about north-west and south-east.

There was nothing to interest us in Virginia City, or in the neighbourhood. The chances of good sport appeared on inquiry to be very doubtful, and so, as soon as we had rested ourselves, we decided, after a council of war, to go to Fort Ellis, and have a week's hunting in that locality, while we were waiting for Wynne, who *ought* to have joined us long ago.

The road to Fort Ellis and Bozeman passes, in a nearly due north direction, down the valley of the Madison river, deflecting towards the little village of Stirling and the mining (or would-be mining) settlement of Midasburg. It then crosses the Madison, and, surmounting a low watershed to the east, projects across the Gallatin or eastern fork of the Missouri. I had some inquiries to make at Stirling; and accordingly, on Wednesday, Jack and I drove over there while the rest agreed to follow us the next day. The morning was cold and stormy, and the first snow of the year lay several inches deep on the slopes and summits of the two low divides over which the road passes. The country was dreary and mountainous, the only sight of interest being the house of the late lamented Mr. Slade, the 'boss murderer' of the West. If any one wants to know about him, of the deeds that he did, and the men that he murdered, and the cunning tricks with which he deluded his victims to take them unawares, ; of the ears and noses he cut off, and how he turned the unfortunate Jules into a target and shot him to death by degrees, taking a whole day and a great many drinks about it ; and what a good and faithful stage-agent he was, and what a gentleman-like quiet man when sober and in good-humour; and, finally, of how he cried and kicked and screamed, and begged and prayed, when they were going to hang him in Virginia City ; and how devoted his wife was to him, and how she was just in time to be too late to see the hanging—are they not written in the books of the Chronicles of Bret Harte, or can they not be heard from the lips of a gentleman of the Irish persuasion who rode behind me to Stirling, and scared me consumedly with his tales of highway robbery and the like ? Slade was a remarkable man in his life and death. Few have equalled him in the cruel courage and calm daring he exhibited so frequently during his career ; but it is very seldom that border desperadoes have shown the white feather at the last as he did, most of them taking their departure in a similar frame of mind to that of the individual who, being told, when the rope was round his neck, that he had five minutes law to say his prayers, replied, 'Go on with the hanging, gentlemen ; *my* prayers would not reach a yard high.' The coolness exhibited by some of these desperadoes is marvellous. A worthy, rejoicing I think in the name of ' Big Ed,' was hanged in company with two others at Laramie during the railway-making days. The ropes were fastened to a beam projecting from the top of a log-built corral or inclosure, and the ' hangees ' had to walk up a ladder, stand on the top of the fence, and jump off. When ' Big Ed ' got half-way up the ladder he turned and asked the assembled gentlemen whether they had any objection to his taking off his boots. The gentlemen ' hangers ' replied that they had not the slightest objection, upon which 'Ed,' after divesting himself of his Wellingtons, mounted to the top of the inclosure, and, just when about to plunge into eternity, called out to a man in the crowd, ' Say! Bill, you just tell Hank (these names are imaginary, for I do not remember the true ones) that he has lost his bet after all, for I have not died in my boots ; you get the twenty dollars, and pay it over to my girl Sal.' To die in one's boots is, in the West, a periphrase for dying a violent death.

Stirling *was* to have been ' quite a place,' a mighty city—in fact, the metropolis of Montana. At present it consists of a post-office, a store, and one or two houses, and seems destined to revert at no distant date to the wild sheep and goats that from the rocky crags surrounding it surveyed the labours of the Midas Mining Company, and others, when, in 1864, they commenced their building operations at Midasburg. The Company erected a very spacious and solidly-built mill of cut stone, the engines, machinery, and crushers for which were brought at enormous cost from California. The mill contains fifteen stamps, worked by engines of eighty-horse power ; and it is capable of crushing from one and a quarter to a ton and a half of hard rock per day per stamp, using five screens ; but not a single ounce has yet passed under the stampers, and of course the building material, plant, and even engines are utterly valueless, the expense of removal being so prodigiously high.

The original cost of the building and plant must have been considerable, and to that must be added a large item for the transport of the ponderous machinery for 1,200 miles through Arizona and Utah, the most dangerous and desolate regions in the United States. It is a sad thing to see such a waste of energy and money. Better days may come; but, if Mr. Jackson (the manager of the Company, to whom I gladly take this opportunity of tendering my best thanks for all his kindness) thinks so, he must be a sanguine man. At present he has nothing to do but buy and melt gold-dust and look after the property of the Company.

At Stirling we found a most extraordinary little Irishman. He was very diminutive, could drink six or eight quarts of milk at a sitting, called himself Mr. Mahogany Bogstick, never touched beer, spirits or tobacco, was partial to petticoats, and held that if only England would legislate justly for the Sister Isle, all the Irishmen in the world could reside comfortably and happily at home with plenty to eat and drink, lots of land to live upon, and not a hand's turn of work to do. I think he invented his extraordinary name on the spur of the moment, from a mistaken notion that Jack was chaffing him, when in reply to his inquiries he informed him that Omonhondro was his *nom de famille*. He was a very funny character, and amused us greatly during the evening.

We bought a pony at Stirling, and, having now been joined by Dr. Kingsley, on Friday we left this *fiasco* of a city and drove to Fort Ellis, a distance of 45 miles. Our recent purchase was the occasion of some little anxiety to us at starting. He was a native pony, of mixed Spanish and American blood. Like all half-bred mustangs, he was not destitute of the diabolical accomplishment of ' buck-jumping,' and he exhibited a slight disposition to indulge in the pastime; but, as he evidently was not a thorough proficient at it, Jack found no difficulty in subduing his early efforts; after which his behaviour was most exemplary. The doctor and I drove in the buggy, and Jack (whom I beg to introduce pictorially to the reader, on p. 58) on the newly-acquired Broncho, galloped gaily alongside in great form, full of spirits—I mean animal spirits, not whisky—singing, whooping, and yelling. It was a lovely morning; the snow had all disappeared, and the sun shone out bright and warm. The horses were fresh, and we rattled gaily along a good and level road, following the direction of a little creek and passing many evidences of the short period of prosperity that succeeded the discovery of gold in 1864, in the shape of old placer workings, dams for heading-up water to work crushing-mills, tumble-down houses, and deserted shanties. The only inhabitant now left was fishing for trout, and catching them too in an abandoned mill-dam.

The road, after pursuing a north-easterly direction for a few miles, crosses the Madison by a toll-bridge, and bends to the north along the margin of the stream. The Missouri, as I suppose all geography-taught folks are aware, heads in three principal streams, the Jefferson on the west, the Madison in the middle, and the Gallatin to the east. The Madison is, at the point of crossing, a fine, broad, rushing river, flowing with a current discoloured by the washings of many placer mines, through a rich alluvial plain. In its shallow stream, warmed by the tributary waters of the Fire Hole River, the usual fluviatile vegetation flourishes with more than ordinary luxuriance, and fills the air with a clean, sea-weedy smell. Leaving the river-bed and turning again in an easterly direction, we crossed the low divide separating the Madison and Gallatin Valleys. This divide is a broad ridge, furrowed and water-worn into a series of rounded grass-covered hills. Although I should not estimate the highest point at more than 300 feet above the level of the plains, yet the ridge affords a fine view of both valley systems. The two basins are very similar in character, and of the same geological formation ; having been lake basins originally, and at no very distant period of time. The old beaches can be very distinctly traced in the former valley. Turning from it and looking east, the Gallatin Valley is spread out before you, the course of the river marked by a heavy growth of dark-green cotton-wood trees ; and beyond it, in the distance, rise the mountains dividing the waters that flow into the Yellowstone from those seeking the Missouri. Dimly visible in the hazy north are the ' Crazy Woman ' Mountains and the peaks about Shields River ; on the southern horizon the Great Tétons hang like a blue cloud ; and to the west are the soft outlines of the water-shed between the Madison and Jefferson. Dotted among the cotton-woods may be seen the white houses of prosperous settlers, and at the northern or lower end of the valley, where the divide on which you stand melts into the plain, two or three white objects denote the position of Gallatin City, which is situated at the junction of the Three Forks. The outlines of the neighbouring mountains are fine, especially some great masses of trap and porphyry protruding through the limestone. Many of the mountains show old crater forms, and the courses of the lava streams that have flowed from them can in some cases be distinctly traced.

We reached the clear swift-flowing waters of the Gallatin about two in the afternoon, and, picking out a nice shady place, went into camp for a couple of hours.

While some of us unhitched and unharnessed the horses, picketed them and gave them their corn, others proceeded to the river and speedily returned with a dozen or so of beautiful trout. A fire was soon lighted, and with fresh-broiled trout and some farinaceous food, taken in a concentrated and liquid form out of a black bottle, we made a luncheon not to be despised, and then lay down in the cool shade to rest and wait till the cattle had finished their feed.

Oh! the comfort of lying flat on your back on the grass, gazing up at the blue sky and the flickering green leaves of the trees ; flat on your back in your shirt-sleeves without any collar—by no manner of means must you have a collar ; it is sure to get tight and half choke you when you lie down—to take your rest in the shade on a hot day, the breeze playing round your head and stealing down your back and chest. That is luxury indeed! No apprehension of catching cold disturbs your mind, while you are soothed by the distant chirruping of grasshoppers in the sunshine, the murmur of bees in the tree-tops, and the *carillon* of the rushing stream. You are not trespassing and nobody can warn you off. There is plenty of fish in the river, some whisky left in the bottle, lots of bread in the buggy ; and you run no risk of being disturbed, for there is not another human being within miles. You can go when you like, or stay as long as you choose. You can stretch your arms and kick out your legs without any danger of treading on a sensitive corn, or of poking out somebody's eye ; and you can throw back your shoulders, expand your chest, and inhale a full draught of fresh pure air; with a sense of glorious independence only to be enjoyed in a large country. I believe a man under such circumstances positively is nearly as happy as a cow in a clover field. Think of it, ye fashionables, ye toilers of the season, who pass laborious days panting in the dusty jam of a London summer, and spend perspiring nights struggling on a staircase, inhaling your fellow-creatures, absorbing fat dowagers, breathing men and women! Think of it, and give an affirmative answer to the lines in Bret Harte, 'Is our civilisation a failure, or is the Caucasian played out?'

It is sweet to do nothing; but we could not linger very long, for our destination, Fort Ellis, was at a distance unknown to us; so, hitching up the horses, we tucked ourselves into the buggy, crossed the Gallatin River, and pursued our way.

The valley of this river affords about the finest agricultural and pasture land in the territory. It is about forty miles in length from south to north, and varies in breadth from five to fifteen miles. It is watered by the Gallatin, the banks of which are very heavily bordered with poplars and bitter cotton-woods, and by several little tributaries, some rising on the eastern flanks of the Gallatin Range, and others towards the north, in a series of broken, detached, and unnamed mountains. Small fruits, vegetables, and all cereals (with the exception of Indian corn, which would never be a valuable crop) flourish luxuriantly. The great drawback to all this region, however, is the interval of cold that invariably comes in about the time of the autumnal equinox. At the latter end of September there is a fortnight of very cold stormy weather, which completely destroys unharvested crops and ungathered fruit.

This is true of a very large tract of country, including Montana, Idaho, Wyoming, and all Northern·Colorado, in which latter section it not unfrequently happens that more snow falls during September than in any other month of the year. This cold snap is succeeded by fine bright warm weather, answering to the Indian summer of Virginia, which lasts usually till Christmas, and not unfrequently till the stormy months of February and March. Were it not for these so-called equinoctial snows, the warm September and October sun which is so much needed in these north-western territories, where the springs are very late and the summers short, would ripen to perfection apples, pears, peaches, and Indian corn. As long as these peculiar climatic effects obtain within their borders, these territories cannot compete in the production of fruit, vegetables, and maize with other countries situated as far, or even farther. to the north, but which are not subject to such sudden atmospheric changes.

At the upper or south end of the valley stands the clean, all-alive, and wide-awake town of Bozeman ; and three miles further on, almost in the jaws of Bozeman Pass, is Fort Ellis, the most important military post in the north-west. The term ' Fort ' is in this, as in most other cases, a mere figure of speech. All trading establishments of the Hudson Bay and other fur Companies, and all military establishments, are designated forts, though there may be nothing whatever fortified about them. Fort Ellis consists of a large square, two sides of which are occupied by the soldiers' quarters, while the remaining side is devoted to the officers' houses. All along the inside of the square runs a wooden sidewalk, beside which a few unhappy trees are striving to grow ; and the interior space, the centre of which is adorned with a tall flag-staff, is gravelled, forming a commodious parade-ground; while the angles are flanked and protected by quaint old-fashioned-looking block houses, octagonal in shape, loop-holed, and begirt with a broad balcony, upon which sentries pace everlastingly up and down. Beyond the buildings forming the square are other soldiers' quarters, washerwomen's houses, stables, stores, billiard-room, blacksmiths' and saddlers' shops, and the like, the whole being surrounded by a sort of stockade fence; and furthest removed, on a breezy elevation, are the hospital buildings, and some large stores and magazines.

Strategically, the situation of Fort Ellis is well chosen, for it commands the valleys of the Yellowstone and of the three forks of the Missouri, in which is contained all the richest and best land in the territory—in fact, all that is really available for cultivation; and, in connection with Fort Shaw and Fort Benton, it commands the navigation on the Missouri, and the three principal passes which break through the mountains from one river system to the other. These gaps are very important as being natural thoroughfares, for through Flat Head, Bridger, and Bozeman Passes the Bannacks and Flat Heads make their way to hunt buffalo on the Mussel Shell, Upper Missouri, and Lower Yellowstone; and through them also the hostile Indians of the plains make their raids into the Gallatin Valley, killing and plundering the settlers, and lifting their stock. These predatory expeditions had latterly become rare, and it was hoped that they had been renounced altogether; but only last year the Sioux made a dash, ran some stock off from under the very walls of Fort Ellis, and killed two white men near the Crow Mission. The Crow Indians are the best guards.

Their young men are always roaming through the country in the hope of picking up something; and they smell out a war-party long before it occurs to the soldiers that there is a hostile red-skin within a hundred miles. 'When the Crows are away the Sioux will play,' but, when the tribes of the Absaraka return to their Agency, those thieving worthies discover that important business necessitates their presence at home.

It was late in the afternoon when we arrived at Fort Ellis. With some difficulty we found our way to General Sweitzer's quarters, where, upon presenting our letters of introduction, we were most kindly received. By the time we had completed our ablutions, after which we stepped out on the 'stoop,' or verandah, to enjoy the cool breeze, the sun was nearly down. It was a most lovely evening. The atmosphere was 'smoky,' as it is termed in the West, and imparted a dim grandeur to the distant mountains, while the glowing valley lay basking in the sunlight; and far to the west the dark masses of the Madison Mountains bounded the horizon. Close by, the summits of Bridger's Peaks reared themselves distinct and clear, catching the full blaze of the setting sun; and to the north and east the blue cloudy heights of 'Crazy Woman' Range swam and trembled in the haze. The air was perfectly still; the 'star-spangled banner' hung motionless. Two or three cloud-islands, or rather reefs of clouds, lay in the clear blue sky, dazzling under the slant rays of the sun. The clouds grew crimson, their edges flashing like red burnished gold, and the horizon was tinted with lovely greens, purples, and yellows, splendent but fading imperceptibly into each other. Lower and lower sank the sun, while the evening star shone bright through a great gap in the eastern range. A puff of white smoke, a loud echoing report; down floated the Stars and

Stripes, and one more peaceful and monotonous day had passed over the heads of these exiles in a remote frontier post, these watchers on the confines of civilisation.

TEXAS JACK.

CHAPTER III.

THE CROW TRIBE.

A FEW pleasant days we lingered at Fort Ellis, much enjoying the kind hospitality of General and Mrs. Sweitzer and the officers of the garrison ; discussing hunting and shooting, trapping bears, stalking elk or trailing Redskins; listening to awful tales, which I trust were a little highly-coloured, of Indian devilry and cunning, how they creep upon you unawares, how they impale you on a young pine-tree, and leave you there to squirm your life out in writhing agonies, or lay you, stripped naked, flat on your back on the ground, your arms and legs extended, and, lighting a small fire on your stomach, dance round you in enjoyment of the spectacle.

Wild stories, too, we heard of weary marches ; of want of food and want of water; of hazardous scouting expeditions ; and of awful sufferings in winter snows, when men lost their toes and fingers, or fared like the carpenter in the voyage through the Straits of Magellan, who, 'thinking to blow his nose, did cast it into the fire.' Perhaps some fastidious fair one may think the carpenter in question must have been a vulgar person. Any one who has been to a cold climate will, however, allow that if you blow your nose at all, you must use the implements of nature, not of art.

So we chatted, spun yarns, played billiards, and drove about, while Jack, by no means idle, was purchasing stock at Bozeman ; and, finally, everything being nearly ready, I left orders for the outfit to proceed direct to Boteler's Ranch, and started off myself to have a look at the Crow Agency.

The distance from Fort Ellis to the Agency is about thirty miles. The road is easy and not very remarkable in any way. The cañon or gorge by which it breaks through the first range of mountains is rather fine, the pass being in some places hemmed in by very massive precipitous walls of rock. The road then winds along for some distance, a little above the creek level, over the usual hilly deposit of detritus that invariably borders the foot of the mountain ranges; and at length, when you begin to think the distance must have been miscalculated, you gain the summit of a rise and get your first view of the Yellowstone River and of its plain, fading in the dim unbroken distance to the east, and bounded to the south-east by the great range of the Yellowstone Mountains. I had heard so much of the Yellowstone—of the signs and wonders that attend its birth in the mountains, and of the lovely and mysterious lake at its source; of the region, fire-haunted and full of portents, which no Indian dare visit, and which until a year or two ago was unknown to civilised man; of the stupendous cliffs of its cañon, and of the wild tribes that roam along its banks—that when the sheen of its waters glittering on the evening sun struck my eye, I pulled up and gazed on the scene with something of the silent enthusiasm of a pilgrim who sees in the far distance St. Peter's dome or the minarets of Mecca, towards which for weary days he has dragged his feet.

The Mission is well situated on the south side of the river near the great bend, where, after bursting through the mountains, it suddenly turns its course from north to east. As the road runs on the north bank of the Yellowstone, we had to cross the river.

The current is deep, broad, and rapid, flowing over a bottom of loose rolling stones ; and though the waters were low at the time, it was by no means easy to ford. With the river bank-full it is impassable. A fine grassy prairie surrounds the Mission, extending on both sides of the river for some distance, and gradually expanding on the south side into the great plains that lie between the Yellowstone and Missouri. North of the river are the Crazy Woman and Sheep Mountains. Near at hand on the south is a high triangular peak, on the top of which the Crows occasionally light a great fire ; but whether it is done at stated seasons, and is connected in any way with some religious observance dimly shadowing the former prevalence of fire-worship, or whether it is used merely as a signal, I could not discover. Further to the south is the great snowy Yellowstone Range. The buildings of the Agency comprise a small barrack, which was garrisoned by a non-commissioned officer and ten men ; traders' stores, church, school-house, houses for the various employés, and comfortable quarters for the agent and his family and the missionary. I had some interesting conversation that evening with the Agent and Missionary on the subject of evangelising the red men. To most lay travellers the word missionary is as a red rag to a bull. I feel tempted to say something on the topic ; but it is an exciting one, and, if once I began to write thereon, I should unduly swell the proportions of this book. So I prefer to abstain from the question of the proselytisation of nations in general, omitting even to account for the fact that too frequently, among Indians in particular, the words heathen and honest man, thief and Christian, are convertible terms.

The Absaraka, as they call themselves—or Crows, as the whites designate them—are a fine race, tall, straight, clean-limbed, well-proportioned, and light in colour. Men of six feet two, three, and even four inches in height are not uncommon; and they look taller than they really are, partly on account of their wearing drapery which adds to their apparent stature, and partly because, like all other savages, they lack the robust proportions and strong muscular development of the white man, and in consequence their limbs look long, rounded, and woman-like. The beauty of long locks, with us a crown of glory to the fair sex, is, in the lodges of the Crows, appropriated entirely by the men; who take infinite pains with their hair, usually wearing it in long heavy plaits. I don't know how it is with the women, but probably they have not time or opportunity to cultivate it or keep it in order, for among Indians it is the men who spend hours in beautifying themselves and looking in the glass, who run up long bills for finery and make use of powder and paint. They reserve to themselves all the tricks and artificial aids of the toilet. For their glossy locks the greasy bear is shorn of his fat; for them are the reddest cloth, the brightest beads, the bravest plumes, the rarest shells. The young men monopolise the trinkets, necklaces, and earrings, dress themselves in shirts adorned with porcupine-quill embroidery, and throw over their shoulders blankets of vivid red or green. The women, poor drudges, have no time for these vanities. The wife has to unpack the horses, set up the lodge poles, stretch the skin-covering over them, cut the wood, light the fire, draw the water, spank the baby, cook the supper, and light the pipe for her lazy lord, who sits at ease, master of the situation, indolently beautifying his ugly person, smearing a stripe of yellow ochre across his Roman nose, painting his broad face in alternate stripes of black and red, or colouring his dusky skin a lively pea-green. A girl has a poor chance of retaining any little article of finery that may be given to her. Unless she is comely, well-formed, a recent acquisition, or a very great favourite, it soon finds its way into the wardrobe of her husband.

They are great dandies these young bucks, and take immense pains about their get-up, carrying with them, on friendly expeditions, their paint and finery, and always halting to dress before entering a strange village. They are exceedingly careful of their war-bonnets and feather head-dresses, folding them in neat little band-boxes of birch-bark or hide, and are very proud of their ornaments, earrings, bracelets, and garniture.

Nothing tickles the fancy of an Indian so much as to be stared at by a white man. His vanity is gratified; he sees that he has made an impression, and it never enters into his head that the impression could be anything but favourable.

The sole end and object of his existence, the point on which all his thoughts and energies are concentrated, is to appear formidable to his enemies and attractive to the women. If he can scare his foes by the hideousness of his war-paint and the ferocity of his appearance, he is delighted, because he may, perhaps, without risk to himself, shoot one of them in the back while running away; and having done so, he and his friends would scalp the body, and kick it, and dance round it, and stamp upon it, and abuse it, and stick it full of knives and arrows, and have a 'gay old time generally,' and then go home and be afraid of the dead man's ghost. At any rate, he would argue that, even if he killed no one, he would not be killed himself, which would be a highly satisfactory reflection to his selfish mind. And if he sees that the bright vermilion partings of his hair, and the carefully-designed and artfully-painted stripes and patches on his face and chest, are making an impression ; if shy glances of approval note the swing of his gay blanket and the style of his leggings, and if soft eyes brighten at the sight of his shell earrings and the silver plates in his back hair, he is also delighted, because—well, for the same reason anybody else would be.

In short, he is the greatest coxcomb on the face of the earth, not to be surpassed even in London for inordinate vanity, stupendous egotism, and love of self. His features may not be strictly classical, according to our standard of beauty. His cheek-bones might be considered somewhat too prominent, and his paint certainly is inadmissible with us : but, to do him justice, I must allow that he is not a bad-looking fellow in his way. Take, as an example, a young warrior of the Bannacks whom I saw riding through a street in Virginia City from their camp in the neighbourhood. Smooth and easy as a hawk's flight he sweeps along, sitting his foam-flecked mustang with the yielding gracefulness of a willow bending to the breeze; swaying his lithe body with every bound of the animal beneath him. Before him, across the pommel of his saddle, he bears his rifle in embroidered elk-skin cover adorned with long fringes, which, mingling with the horse's mane and the tags and tassels of his gay leggings, spread out behind him on either side. His long black hair, plaited and tied with knots of scarlet ribbon, streams out in the wind, and uniting with the horse's tail seems almost to touch the dust. Slung across his back are his lion-skin quiver and his bow ; by his side hangs a revolver, silver-mounted, and shining in the sun. With the toes of his beaded moccasins he touches the loops that serve him for stirrups ; his left hand lightly holds the bridle ; and from his right wrist hangs by a thong

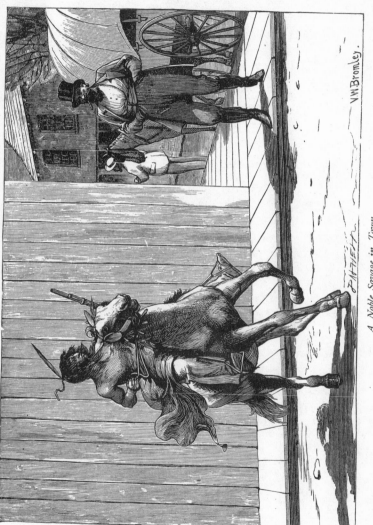

A Noble Savage in Town.

his buckhorn-handled quirt or whip. As he gallops down the street, all his gay trappings fly out in disorder behind him ; and, when with a pull at the cruel Spanish bit he steadies into a walk, the folds of his scarlet blanket settle down and hang gracefully from his shoulders, and he passes, an embodiment of savage life, full of wild beauty and bright colour, and no doubt attractive to the female eye ; glancing with supreme and undisguised contempt upon the plug-hat, black store coat and pants of some newly-arrived representative of civilisation.

It is only the young men who indulge their love of dress and finery. The tried and seasoned warriors wear with pride their feather head-dresses, every plume in which commemorates some notable incident in their lives ; but they care little for beautifying their weather-beaten countenances. Indeed, it is considered *de rigueur* that a great chief should assume a studied simplicity of garb and demeanour, be his age what it may. Though his government, such as it is, is a species of despotism, yet the Red Indian is a thorough Republican at heart, and a great stickler for the equal rights of all. He is the most independent man in the world, each head of a family being in his own lodge supreme. The chiefs hold their position by an exceedingly precarious tenure, inasmuch as their popularity, and consequently the numerical strength of their following, fluctuates as good or evil results attend their undertakings. Before starting on a war expedition or buffalo hunt, the chief 'makes medicine;' that is, he wraps himself in his blanket, and sits down without eating, speaking, or smoking for forty-eight hours or so. If no evil omens occur, if he is impressed with a feeling that the hour is propitious, the party will set out, full of confidence and ready to obey him in every respect. But if bad luck pursues them, if the enemy discovers their proximity before a blow has been struck, or if they fail to find game, or cannot approach the herds owing to a bad wind prevailing for two or three days, the chief in charge of the party never fails to abdicate voluntarily, and some one else is chosen to see if he can make better medicine.

War chiefs are selected for their skill, courage, and cunning, and they are most anxious to show that their whole energies are devoted to the advantage of the public, and not used for the benefit of themselves or their families. The great man therefore is generally no better housed or clothed than the average of his tribe He is among the first to feel the pangs of hunger, and it would be considered exceedingly wrong in him to take advantage of his position and to provide himself against the numerous vicissitudes of savage life.

But, to return to the Crows: This tribe is divided into two bands—the Mountain Crows, numbering about 3,200 souls, including half-breeds; and the River Crows, about 1,200. Each division is in their own language called by a distinctive name, which indicates significantly certain customs which the sub-tribes have adopted as suitable to the nature of the country in which they dwell; but which, being translated, would be very shocking to ears polite.

Their present reservation, secured to them by treaty with the United States in 1868, comprises about 6,272,000 acres of land, situated north of the Yellowstone. It contains every variety of land, mountain, plain, valley, forest and meadow; is well watered by several important confluents of the Yellowstone, and is in parts heavily timbered. In other words, it is well adapted to the purpose for which it was set aside, namely, the support of a wandering race of people living by the chase. But gold was found or heard of on Rosebud or Big Boulder; white men flocked in, the land was wanted, and the Crows were 'requested' to exchange their reserve for one of 3,625,000 acres, about half the size of their original territory in the Judith Basin, south of the Missouri; a land certainly not flowing with milk and honey, not even with milk and water, or water alone—a country small in size and sparsely timbered. It is true that it is a fine game country, and it abounds or abounded in buffalo; but it is a hunting-ground over which many tribes had a right of common-age. One of the inducements held out to the Crows was that they would thenceforth have it all to themselves;—truly a heavy undertaking to keep out all the Sioux, Bannacks, Nez Percés, Flat Heads, Black Feet, Assini-boins, Piegans, &c. &c., who have from the beginning of time been running buffalo on these plains. The whole lives of the new-comers will be spent in Chancery, de-fending their newly-acquired privileges against the right of immemorial usage claimed by the others. However, when Uncle Sam 'requests' a small tribe to exchange their reservation, it is much the same as when Policeman X 220 'requests' an obstructionist to move on. After a little remonstrance the tribe, like the individual, sees the force of the argument and accedes to the request. So the Crows, after much speechifying and remonstrating at a convention held at their Agency in 1873, expressed their willingness to go, entreating (poor fellows!) that Major Pease, who had for some time been their agent, and for whom they evidently entertained great respect and affec-tion, should continue to act in that capacity, and asking for assistance against their enemies, the Sioux, whom they declared to be better armed and supplied than they were, despite the fact that the Sioux are hostile to the whites. Indeed, they seemed to fancy that the Dakotah had been favoured on account of their hostility. It is a dangerous thing to allow Indians to suppose that by making themselves troublesome they can obtain privileges they would not otherwise enjoy.

The territory claimed by the Crows at the time of their meeting with the Commissioner in 1873 had been conveyed to them in the usual terms by the United States in 1868, and the Government had, moreover, undertaken certain obligations, such as yearly payments of money and supplies of goods. In 1869 their agent wrote to Washington complaining bitterly that the treaty obligations were not carried out by Government, and that, in consequence, he had much difficulty in restraining his Indians from making common cause with the neighbouring hostile tribes. In 1873 the United States proposed to take up their land and place them on the new reservation, and offered to make a new treaty decreeing that 'the following district of country, to wit, ... shall be, and the same is, set apart for the absolute and undisturbed use and occupation of the Indians herein named.' The text of the treaty went on to say that ' the United States now solemnly agree that no person except those herein designated . . . . shall *ever* be permitted to pass over, settle upon, or reside in the territory described in this article. . . . . And the United States agree to set apart the sum of one million of dollars, to hold the same in trust for the Crow tribe of Indians, the principal to be held in perpetuity and the interest thereof to be expended or invested.' All this doubtless was very satisfactory ; but, considering that only five years had elapsed since the former treaty at Laramie, it is not likely that the Crows would again attach much importance to the proviso that no person should *ever* disturb them in their new possession, which was nominally to be for their absolute use. Neither would they be inclined after their last experience to attach a very high value to the interest on their one million dollars.

The Crow tribe will not, in all probability, cumber the earth for many generations; and the one million dollars, held for their use in perpetuity, are likely to revert to Uncle Sam before very long; but in the meantime, the adhesiveness of the material used in paying Indian annuities being proverbial, it would be interesting to know how much of the interest will fall into the Crows' hands and how much will stick on the way.

In fact, the value of the whole new treaty does not amount to that of a row of pins, for the fulfilment of it depends entirely upon whether anything of value is discovered on the new reserve, in which case the Absaraka will be again 'requested' to take up their beds and walk. No one can appreciate this more fully than the Indians themselves, who have learned by hard experience the true value of such treaty obligations. No people can feel more keenly the pain of parting from their old hunting-grounds, from the burial-places of their fathers and the birthplaces of their sons. But what can they do but make the best case they can for themselves and bow to fate?

In the last instance, however, they did succeed in making better terms than usual, and managed to retain some of their old reserve. Whether the new treaty has up to the present been enforced I am not aware. At the time of my visit the Agency buildings had not been removed, and I am under the impression that the treaty has not yet been confirmed at Washington.

I should like to have inserted *in extenso* an account of the meeting of the Commissioners appointed to negotiate the new treaty with the head man of the Crow nation, for it would convey a good idea of the feelings of the natives on the subject. Want of space forbids me to do so, but I will quote a few extracts from the Reports of the Commissioners of Indian affairs in 1873.

Mr. Brunot represented the Government, and Black-foot, second chief of the Mountain Crows, was the principal speaker on their side. Many other Indians also spoke; complaining that the Government had not fulfilled the stipulations of the treaty made at Laramie in 1868, protesting that they were not assenting parties to that treaty, expatiating on the bad quality of the goods supplied to them, begging that the agent they liked might be left with them, praying for a large reservation, pleading hard to retain their own country, and asking for assistance, in the shape of weapons, against their enemies. Blackfoot first addressed the meeting. He commenced, as usual, with an invocation, pointing the peace-pipe at each appeal in the direction of the sky, the earth, and the four cardinal points; then handing it to the Commissioners, who passed it to the chiefs, he said :—

' You call the Great Spirit Jesus in your language; we call him, in the Crow language, E-so-we-wat-se. I am going to light the pipe, and talk to the Great Spirit.' Here he lighted the pipe, and, looking up reverently, added : ' The Great Spirit has made the red man and the white man, and sees all before Him to-day. Have pity upon us! May the white man and the Indian speak truth to each other to-day! The sun that looks down upon us to-day, and gives us light and heat, sees that our hearts are true, and that what we do is good for the poor red man. The moon that shines on us in the night-time will see us prosper and do well. O earth! on which we walk, from which we come, and which we love as our mother—which we love as our country—we ask thee to see that we do that which is good for us and our children. This tobacco comes from the whites; we mix it with bark from the Indian trees and burn it together before thee, O Great Spirit. So may our hearts and the hearts of the white men go out together to Thee and be made good and right. . . . .

'I am going to have a long talk with you. The Great Father sent our friends to see us. We see each other; that is good. You came here last summer; we were sent for to see you. We were at back of the mountains when we heard of you; but high waters and the mountains prevented our coming. You said you did not see us, and you were sorry for it. We could not come any faster. This summer we were on this side near the Yellowstone, where we were getting skins to make lodges. In the fall the traders will want our robes. We will then go over the Yellowstone to Judith Basin to hunt. Since I was a boy I recollect that is what the Crows always did. When the Crows meet a friend they always give him something; so we do with you. You say you have a book that tells about the Great Spirit. We always give the Great Spirit something; I think that is good. We see the sun, we give him something; and the moon and the earth, we give them something. We beg them to take pity on us. The sun and the moon look at us, and the ground gives us food. You come and see us, and that is why we give you something. We are men like each other; our religion is different from yours. . . . .

'The old folks are dying off, then who will own the land? I went to Fort Laramie; the old Indians signed the treaty. We came back to the camp and told the young men, and they said we had done wrong, and they did not want to have anything to do with it. They said:

" We love the Great Father, and hold on to the hands of our white friend. All the other Indian tribes fight the whites; we do not do so. We love the whites, and we want them to leave us a big country." . . . .

'All the other Indians go and talk to the Great Father; you take them to Washington. They are bad; they hide their hearts; but they talk good to the Great Father, and you do more for them than for us. This I want to tell you; yesterday you spoke to us, and we listened to you. If you wish to have peace with all the Indians, get them all together and make peace with them. Then I will make peace with them too. . . . .

'The Great Spirit made these mountains and rivers for us and all this land. We were told so, and when we go down the river hunting for food we come back here again. We cross over to the other river, and we think it is good. Many years ago the buffalo got sick and died, and Mr. Waldron gave us annuity goods, and since then they have given us something every year. The guns you gave us we do not point at the whites. We do not shoot our white friends. We are true when we look in your face. On our hands is no white man's blood. When you give us arms to go and fight the Sioux, we fight them to keep our lands from them. When we raise our camp and go for buffalo some white men go with us; they see what we are doing: they see that we jump over the places that are bloody. On the other side of the river below, there are plenty of buffalo; on the mountains are plenty of elk and black-tailed deer; and white-tailed deer are plenty at the foot of the mountain. All the streams are full of beaver. In the Yellowstone River the whites catch trout; there are plenty of them. The white men give us food; we know nothing about it. Do not be in a hurry; when we are poor we will tell you of it. At

Laramie we went to see the Commissioners. Now Commissioners come to see us, and we listen to what you say. The Commissioners told us at Laramie if we remained good friends of the whites we should be taken care of for forty years. Since we made that treaty it is only five years. You are in a hurry to quit giving us food. I am a young man yet, my teeth are all good. They told us at Laramie that we should get food till we were old and our children after us. . . . .

'When we set up our lodge poles, one reaches to the Yellowstone; the other is on White River, another one goes to Wind River; the other lodge is on the Bridger Mountains. This is our land, and so we told the Commissioners at Fort Laramie; but all kinds of white people come over it, and we tell you of it, though we say nothing to them. On this side of the Yellowstone there is a lake; about it are buffalo; it is a rich country, the whites are on it. They are stealing our quartz; it is ours, but we say nothing to them. The whites steal a great deal of our money. We do not want them to go into our country. We would like needle-guns to get game and fight the Sioux; this we tell you.'

And so on through a long speech, discussing the question of boundary, commenting on the quality of supplies, asking for help against their enemies, &c. &c.

Mr. Brunot, Chief Commissioner, thus replied:—

'Blackfoot says that the white people are digging in the mountains, taking away your gold. I know that myself. I saw them go there. I told them it was not right. The Great Father has heard about it, and he has said that the Crows had better let the people have the gold, and he will pay you for the land. The Crows have done well. You have not hurt the white people who are on the reservation and in the mines, and you tell us you are the white man's friend. The Great Father does not want any of these whites to hurt the Crows. He says, for us to tell the Crows, that if you let the white people have the land, he will give you things you need for many years. I have been looking about over your reservation. I see you do not go much where the mines are. I think it would be good for you to let the white people have the land, and the Great Father for many years will give you what you need for yourselves and your children. I do not want this on account of the people who are on your land, but I think it will be good for you and your children. It is your land, and you can do what you please with it. If you want to keep it, I have nothing to say; but I think it would be good for you to sell it.'

Iron Bull then observed, in reference to the quality of stores doled out to his tribe :—

' I went with Shane the interpreter. They gave me blankets : I could blow through them, and they went to pieces; they gave us nothing that was good. I asked them to do something for us. They said ' " Yes ; " but they have done nothing for us.' And, in speaking of Major Pease, he added : ' Here is our agency : we were looking for a white man to take charge of it. We know Pease's face. All the people, old men, young men, women, and children, know Pease. If you put anybody else here as agent, we will not feel like living here any more.'

Then Low Horn and Crazy Sister-in-Law, and many others, added :—

' We love him, and want to keep him. We all love him and want him to remain with the Crows. . . . . We do not want Pease to go away. My boy does not want him to go away. He gives you a horse to keep

Pease here.' (Here he gave the Commissioner a stick as a pledge to represent the horse.)

Even the children seem to have had real affection for the agent, as the Report says that Mountain Chief's daughter and Crazy Sister-in-Law's little daughter presented robes, saying, ' We want Pease to stay with the Crow tribe.' All the children gathered about Major Pease to hold on to him. To which appeals Mr. Brunot replied :—

' One thing I want you all to understand. You say you want Mr. Pease for agent. You know his face and like him ; so do I, and I think the Great Father likes him too. The Great Father when he has his men he puts them where he wants them to go ; he puts them where he pleases. General Baker was over at Fort Ellis ; the Great Father took him away and sent another man there. When I came here I knew Major Pease was here ; these gentlemen knew Pease was here, and that is all we know about it. If the Great Father wants to take him away, you must think it is all right.'

Mr. Brunot then made a long speech explaining the terms of the proposed arrangement, indicating the new boundary, and putting forward the various reasons that made it so desirable to negotiate a fresh treaty. Amongst others he mentioned the railway, and said :—' The Great Father is making the railroad. It is like the whirlwind. I cannot stop it. Nobody can. I might as well try to stop the Yellowstone with my hand. I cannot do it. The Sioux thought they had stopped the Great Father's soldiers last summer.'

Blackfoot, who must have a strong sense of humour combined with the Indian gravity of his temperament, and who, despite the solemnity of the occasion, evidently could not resist the temptation to vent his feelings a little in sarcasm, answered Mr. Brunot: 'What you have said we have listened to, and we think it is true. At Laramie the treaty was made. We did not feel right. We had made a long journey, and were tired and sick. They gave us some horses. They thought they were doing a big thing and making us a big present. But the horses were wild like the antelope. We caught them with the lasso. They jumped and kicked ; we held on tight to them, but they got away from us ; we were sick hunting them, and when we got home nearly all of them were gone. The Commissioners told me that we should have plenty of food given us for forty years. They were big men who talked with us ; they were not drunk when they told us. We were men and heard them, and so it ought to be written in the treaty. I told the Commissioners at Laramie that I had seen the Sioux commit a great massacre ; they killed many white men. But the Sioux are still there, and still kill white men. When you whip the Sioux come and tell us of it. You are afraid of the Sioux. Two years ago I went with the soldiers ; they were very brave ; they were going through the Sioux country to Powder River and Tongue River. We got to Prior Creek just below here in the Crow country. I wanted to go ahead into the Sioux country, but the soldiers got scared and turned back. I was there, and so were the others who are here ; they know what I say is true. The soldiers said they were going to Tongue River, but they got frightened at the Sioux and turned back. The soldiers were the whirlwind ; they went towards the Sioux country, but the whirlwind turned back. Last summer the soldiers went to Prior Creek again ; again they said they were going through the Sioux country, but they saw a few Sioux ; they were afraid of them ; they got scared and turned up to the

Mussel Shell and went back again. Again the whirlwind was going through the Sioux country, but again the whirlwind turned back. We are not the whirlwind, but we go to the Sioux; we go into their country, we meet them and fight, but we do not turn back; but we are not the whirlwind. You say the railroad is coming up the Yellowstone; that it is like the whirlwind, and cannot be turned back. I do not think it will come. The Sioux are on the way, and you are afraid of them; they will turn the whirlwind back. If you whip the Sioux and get them out of the way, the railroad may come, and I will say nothing.

'We were born on this side the Yellowstone and were raised here. It is good land. There is plenty of good land here. Timber and grass and water are plenty, and there is much game in the mountains. You talk about Judith Basin, and say you are going to give us plenty to eat. We do not want to exchange our land. You are my friend. If we were to go to the white man's country, and bloody it as they do our country, you would not like it. For many years I have known the whites. You have a big heart, but it is not so with the white men who come into my country. Some of them never sucked their mother's breasts. I think they were raised like the buffalo, and sucked a buffalo cow for their mother. They have no hearts. I was not raised in that way. I am a man. I was raised and sucked milk from my mother's breasts. There is no white man's blood on our hands, and I am not ashamed to shake hands with you. What I say is true. I am your friend. The sun sees me, and hears what I say. The Great Spirit hears me, and knows it is true. Did I ask these white men to come here and crowd me? Buffalo robes are my money; we have some buffalo left yet. If I go to the buffalo country and bring no robes back, the traders will not look at me. They won't be glad to see me, and shake hands with me and say " How, how," as they would if I had plenty. I think you had better leave Pease with us as he was before. If you put anybody else here, very soon they will kick me in the face with their foot. All the men who have Crow women we don't want them sent away. They are my friends, and I want them to live as I do.'

Speaking of the treaty of 1868, he said : ' It is all lies; we do not want to hear any more. Wrap it up and throw it all away. We will not have that treaty. . . . . . We wanted to know just what was in that treaty, and my friend has told us. I have said before that we are friends, and that we like each other, yet we have different thoughts in our hearts. The first time I went to Fort Laramie and met the Peace Commissioners, to what each said to the other we said, " Yes, yes." The second time we went, we signed the treaty ; but neither of us, my white friends nor the Indian chiefs, said " Yes, yes " to what is in that treaty. What we said to them, and what they said to us, was, " Goo l." We said " Yes, yes " to it, but it is not in the treaty. Shane was there the first time, and what he interpreted to us are not the words that are in the treaty. The first time we went we did not sign the treaty ; we only said " Yes, yes " to each other. The Indian way of making a treaty is to light a pipe, and the Indians and their white friends smoke it. When we were in council at Laramie, we asked whether we might eat the buffalo for a long time. They said " Yes." That is not in the treaty. We told them we wanted a big country. They said we should have it, and that is not in the treaty. They promised us plenty of goods and food for forty years—plenty for all the Crows to eat ; but that is not in the treaty. Listen to what I say. We asked, " Shall we and our children get food for forty years?" They said "Yes;" but it is not that way in the treaty. They told us when we got a good man for agent, he should stay with us; but it is not so in the treaty. We asked that the white man's road along Powder River be abandoned, and that the grass be permitted to grow in it. They said "Yes, yes;" but it is not in the treaty. The land that we used to own we do not think of taking pay for. We used to own the land in the Mud River Valley. These old Crows you see here were born there. We owned Horse Creek, Stinking Water, and Heart's Mountain. Many of these Indians were born there. So we owned the country about Powder River and Tongue River, and many of our young men were born there. So we owned the mouth of Mussel Shell, and Crazy Mountain, and Judith Basin. Many of our children were born there. So we told the Commissioners. They said "Yes, yes;" but there is nothing about it in the treaty. We told them there were many bad Indians, but that we would hold on to the hands of the white man, and would love each other. We told them the Piegans, the Sioux, and other tribes have killed white men. We told them the whites were afraid of them. I asked them to look at us; that we had no arms, and they should not be afraid of the Crows. They said "Yes, yes;" but it is not so written in the treaty. The treaty, you say, has bought all our land except on this side of the river. And what do we get for it? I am ashamed about it. We sell our land, and what do we get for it? We get a pair of stockings, and when we put them on they go to pieces. They get some old shirts and have them washed, and give them to us; we put them on and our elbows go right through them. They send us tin kettles; we go to get water to carry to our lodges. We dip the water up, but it all runs out again.   This is what we get for our land. . . . . . They said, " Will you sell the Powder River country, Judith Basin, and Wind River country ? "   I told them no ; but that is not in the treaty.   When Major Camp came here as agent, we gave him a present of a large number of robes to send to the Great Father.   We never heard that the Great Father got those robes ; we would like to hear about them.   The Crow tribe want Major Pease to remain with us as our agent.   Some of the young men want him to take them to see the Great Father at Washington. You ask us to tell you what we want.   We want Mexican blankets, elk teeth, beads, eagle feathers, panther and other skins.   We like fine horses and needle-guns.   These things are to us what money is to you.'

At the last three sittings of the council, the question of the new boundary was eagerly discussed.   Blackfoot, who would be invaluable as an against-time talker, and would have done good service in the late debates on the Peace Preservation Acts in Ireland, after making a very long speech to his own people, observed to Mr. Brunot— ' We have talked three days, and my tongue is not tired. . . . .

Mr. Brunot having explained the provisions of the new articles of agreement, Blackfoot proceeded to prove the vigour of his tongue : —

' On this side of the river and on the other side is our country.   If you do not know anything about it I will tell you about it, for I was raised here.   You mark all our country, the streams and mountains, and I would like to tell you about it ; and what I say I want you to take to your heart.   You make us think a great deal to-day.   I am a man and am talking to you.   All the Indian tribes have not strong arms and brave hearts like we have ; they are not so brave.   We love you and

Crow Chiefs.

1. Etchci-re-kash-cha-racha (Poor Elk).   2. Kam-de-wat-se (Black Foot).   3. A-pats-ke (Long Ears).
4. I-sa-sush (He shows his Face).   5. Mit-cho-ash (Onion).

shake hands with you (taking Mr. Brunot's hand). We have gone to Judith Basin a great deal, and you wish us to take it for a reservation. All kinds of men go there; trappers and hunters go there, poisoning game; the Sioux Indians, Crees, Santees, Mandans, Assiniboins, Gros Ventres, Piegans, Peu d'Oreilles, Flat Heads, the Mountain Crows, the River Crows, Bannacks, Snakes, and Nez Percé Indians, and white people, all go there. You wish us to take the Judith Basin for a reservation. All these Indians will come, and we will likely quarrel; that is what we think about it. Judith Basin is a small basin, a good many people go there; we all go there to eat buffalo. I have told you about the Sioux when they come to fight us. We go a long way from our camp. All Indians are not as strong as we are; they give up and run off. If you have two dogs, and they go to fight, and you catch them and pull them apart, when you let them go they fight again. So it is with the Sioux and the Crows. . . . . I will tell you what we will do; neither of us will live for ever; in time both of us will die. We will sell the part of our reservation containing the mountains from Clarke's Fork; below the mountains and the valleys we will not sell. The Crow young men will go to Washington and fix it up, and come back and tell us about it. We will sell the range of mountains to Heart's Mountain and Clarke's Fork. The young men will sell it at Washington, and they will say to the Great Father at Washington that the Crows have a strong heart and are willing to sell their land. When you buy this and give us plenty for it, we will talk about the rest if you wish to buy it. Those mountains are full of mines. The whites think we don't know about the mines, but we do. We will sell you a big country, all the mountains. Now tell us what you are going to give for our mountains. . . . . I want to know what you will give for the mountains; then we will talk about the rest of our land. . . . . In Gallatin Valley are plenty of cartridges, the Crows have none. If the Sioux come, I do not know what we shall fight them with. See all these old women; they have no clothing, the young men have no good blankets. We would like the Nez Percés, when they raise camp, to come here; they die with the Crows, they help to fight the Sioux. The last Commission told us we could eat buffalo a long time. While we are here the Flat Head Indians take our horses; I would like you to take our part and stop them.'

At last, however, Blackfoot, finding himself in a minority, gave in, and the treaty was agreed to and signed. Poor fellows! Driven about from pillar to post, it will not be for long that your unreasonableness in persevering to exist, and your impudence in supposing that you have any right to do so, will trouble statesmen. And what conflicting accounts will be given of you, varying from the poetical and exaggerated but most fascinating delineations of Fenimore Cooper, down to the equally untrue dictum of the prairie man, who thinks that ' all Injuns are pison' !

Blackfoot may fairly be regarded as a representative man. Superior to the mass of Red Indians, he is a good specimen of the ruling class among them. Endowed in no slight degree with the gift of eloquence, and, as the preceding quotations sufficiently testify, provided with a sharp tongue to give utterance to the suggestions of a keen and caustic wit, he is one of many of his race who, had they been properly directed, might have exerted their well-merited influence in the improvement of the condition of their tribe. To call such a man a mere savage and to assert that his race are irreclaimable barbarians who should no longer be allowed to cumber the ground, is as untruthful as it is absurd. I am glad to be able to submit the foregoing extracts to the reader. They will serve to show what manner of man the Indian really is.

There were a good many Crows at the Agency when I arrived, and I was formally introduced to several of the leading men. The accompanying illustration is an accurate presentment of five of them. They are invariably named from some peculiarity of appearance, or some striking incident in their lives; and the names in some instances are very expressive, such as—

Thin Belly—*Ella-causs-se*.
Shot in the Jaw—*Esa-woor*.
Boy that Grabs—*Seeateots*.
Rides behind a Man on Horseback—*Ma-me-ri-ke-ish*.
Charge through the Camp—*Ash-e-ri-i-was-sash*.

How other names were obtained it is not so easy to see, such for instance as—

Old Onion—*Mit-hu-a*.
Calf in the Mouth—*Nak-pak-a-e*;

which are rather puzzling. A few might be appropriately applied to our own friends, such as—

The One who Hunts his Debt—*Ash-e-te-si-Oish*.

During the evening a number of them came up from the camp and gave us a *coup* dance. Among those present at the dance were Blackfoot, Little Soldier, The Spaniard, Boy that Grabs, Two Bellies, Pretty Bird, and several other notabilities whose names have escaped my memory. Blackfoot and an old medicine-man were masters of the ceremonies and conducted the arrangements, but took no active part themselves.

A *coup* dance, as it is called by the whites, is not a dance at all. The Indians call it counting their *coups*, and it is a sort of history lesson in which the young braves and warriors narrate their deeds in war, an interlude of stamping and singing taking place between each speech. As each adventure is detailed, those among the crowd of listeners who can bear witness to the truth of the speaker's statement strike the ground with their whip-handles in token of approval; and it is customary for the speaker at the close of each description to produce the trophies which he won on that particular occasion—a gun, a club, a pistol, and perhaps a scalp. Thus the records of the tribe are kept green and fresh in the people's memories. Old feuds are fanned and kept alive, and the young men are urged to emulate the brave deeds of their fathers by hearing those deeds proclaimed and applauded.

At one end of a large room sat the agent, Dr. Wright, one or two white squawmen,[1] the interpreter, and all the rest of us; before us lay spread in tempting show a large sack of sugar, a great pile of gingerbread-nuts, a box of black tobacco, and a lot of cartridges; and along the other three sides were ranged the Indians. The sublime and the ridiculous, the comic and the tragic element, are so absurdly blended in these people that at one moment you are convulsed with laughter at their ludicrous appearance, and at the next are astonished at the dignity of their gestures, the ease of their carriage, and the grand simplicity of their movements. It is but fair to say that the ludicrous element is due to the adoption of articles of civilised dress which do not accord

---

[1] 'Squaw man' is a term commonly used to describe a white man married to, and living with, an Indian woman. He draws annuity goods, and is to all intents and purposes a Red Man.

well with their native attire. There were twenty or thirty Indians present. With the exception of Blackfoot, who wore only a shirt of grey flannel and a blanket, they were dressed in all their finery ; and their costumes were varied and peculiar, the only garments common to all being the waist-cloth and moccasins. Some used leggings of antelope or deer skin, fringed with human hair; others preferred them made of scarlet or blue cloth; while many dispensed with them altogether. Flannel and cotton shirts were rather fashionable, but the great swells sported shirts, or rather tunics, of buckskin embroidered, fringed, and adorned with skins of the ermine weasel. Every man carried a blanket—scarlet, green, or striped ; some had fabricated them into a rude resemblance to a Mackinaw coat or Hudson's Bay Company capote : but in most cases they were just thrown over the shoulders or belted round the waist. *The* correct thing—the latest novelty out—was a short braided cavalry jacket, or very skimpy diminutive tail-coat, such as one may see in old pictures of postilions. The varieties of head-dress were very numerous. The most approved style was a tall puritanical-looking hard felt hat, encircled by several bands of tri-coloured ribbon tied in bows, the loose ends being suffered to hang down on either side. A few of the braves wore ordinary felt hats. Some had beautiful feather-work head-gear, while others were content to pride themselves upon the natural luxuriance of their heavy plaits. Of course those who were apparelled in their native costume looked well, in our eyes at least, while there was something exceedingly mirth-provoking in the aspect of the warriors who sported the short-tailed coats and tall hats. They presented somewhat the appearance of French revolutionists, and looked as if they had bought up the properties of some strolling company. All the Indians had left their weapons outside with their ponies, but each man carried, suspended to his wrist, his whip, which consisted of a very thick heavy wooden or elk-horn handle about 18 inches long, with two or three elk-hide thongs as a lash. The whip is in reality a formidable club.

The Indian is by no means the taciturn melancholy individual he has been described to be. On the contrary, when he has enough to eat and is warm he is loquacious enough, and is a very jovial, joke-loving fellow. When we entered the room we found the chiefs and braves all seated round, leaning against the walls, smoking, laughing, talking, and carrying on great chaff with the interpreter, who was bantering them upon their love affairs, and displayed an intimate acquaintance with the domestic vicissitudes of some of the party, which was much relished by the others. The doorway was blocked by a mass of boys and youths who had come to hold the ponies and attend upon their elders and betters.

The ceremonies on this occasion were opened by Dr. Wright, who put me forward, blushing in a dirty flannel shirt, to be glared at by the assembled braves, while he made a speech introducing me. Every sentence had of course to be interpreted, and it took therefore some little time to explain, in flowery and poetic language, how I had travelled so many moons to see the Crows; how I had crossed great oceans in big canoes; traversed prairies, swum rivers, crossed mountains, and all to have the honour of seeing the Crows. In fact, according to the eloquent doctor, the supreme moment of my life had arrived; the aim of my existence was gained :—I had seen the Crows! All this time I stood in the middle of the room, feeling very uncomfortable, trying to look dignified in shirt and trousers,—which is an impossible feat,—and not knowing what the mischief to do with my hands; for, the room being very hot, I had taken off my coat and waistcoat, and my deer-skin continuations were not endowed with pockets. When he had made an end of speaking, I lifted up my voice, and, in shaky accents, told them that I was unaccustomed to public speaking, that I had come a long way to see them, that I was very glad to see them, and that I considered them to be, to quote from a well-known story, 'Crows, very fine Crows, d—d fine Crows, the finest Crows I ever saw in my life.' I then deposited myself on an empty candle-box, but had to get up again to shake hands with every individual in the room, each man approaching me singly, taking my hand with a grip that sometimes was unpleasantly warm, shaking it in a most affectionate manner, the while gazing solemnly into my eyes, and gutturally emitting 'How!'—to which salutation I with much dignity responded 'How!' After this Blackfoot got up and made an oration, dilating upon the extreme poverty of himself and his nation, expatiating upon the great virtues of wool, especially in the form of blankets, in counteracting the bad effects of cold, and extolling the hygienic properties of flannel shirts. It was a fine speech to have delivered before a Dorcas Society. I thought the allusions and hints were somewhat pointed, but gave them to understand that a few blankets might be forthcoming if they gave us some good dancing, an intimation that was received with a grunt of applause.

I cannot describe an Indian dance. The only way to convey an idea of it would be for me to put on a blanket and 'jump around loose,' and for some one else to take shorthand notes of my appearance and antics. I tried it the other day in my English home: but the shorthand writer had a fit; my elder children howled in terror; the baby went into convulsions, and had oil poured on its head; the wife of my bosom fled shrieking from the room, and my nearest male relative threatened to apply for a writ 'de lunatico;' so I abandoned the attempt.

When a chief wishes to organise a war-party, he goes out himself to recruit, and, having no military band to help him, is obliged to make great play with his own lungs. He paints and feathers himself, dances his war-dance, and sings the song of battle. Thus does he fire the inflammable hearts of the young men, who also feather and paint, mingle their yells with his, and join him in striking the war-post. It is the same all over the world. I wonder how many 'civilised' deaths are due to the screams of the maddening bag-pipe, the shrill notes of the fife, the exciting roll of the drum, or the pulse-quickening war-strains of a brass band!

At their religious ceremonies they sing and dance, even as David did before the Ark.

If death is imminent, and if he *wish* to die, the Indian will fold his blanket around him, lie down, and sing himself clean out of the flesh; for in common, as I believe, with all natural peoples he can help to loosen the fetters that bind his spirit, and assist himself to die.

His medicine-song is very sacred, and is most religiously reserved for his own and his guardian spirit's ears alone.

Indian singing, too, is very peculiar. They have their religious songs, their war-songs, their death-songs, their mysterious medicine-songs. About the time that a youth enters upon manhood, and before he embarks upon any serious undertaking, he goes away by himself and fasts for many days. In his dreams he then sees mapped out his course through life, and learns whether he is to strive to be a warrior, a peace-chief, or a medicine-man. Whatever animal—beast, bird, or fish—then appears to him, he takes as representing his guardian spirit. However pressed by hunger, he will not kill or injure that creature, and to it he addresses himself in his medicine-song, which, though to our ears a string of utter nonsense, is to him a serious and sacred composition. These are all songs with words, but, like Mendelssohn, they are very great at songs without words. All their ceremonies are accompanied by a rhythmical chant, to the tune of which the feet and hands keep accurate time. The music consists of guttural exclamations, or rather of a violent jerking out of all the breath in the body. They expel the sounds spasmodically from the caverns of their broad chests, with their mouths open, or hiss them out savagely through the closed teeth. They sit in a circle, their bodies bending, their heads nodding, feet going, all in most perfect time, gradually growing more and more excited, till every muscle and nerve jerks and twitches in unison with the stamp of the feet and the taps of the drum. There is such a rhythm and ' go,' such an amount of nervous energy and physical force is exhibited, that the excitement is contagious, and it is hard to restrain one's-self from joining in. I should like to go into the subject of the origin of Indian dances, whether religious or otherwise, but it is too large a question to embark upon now. Personally, I delight in witnessing them. But to return to our *coup* dance.

After a short silence an old medicine-man led off, chanting to a drum accompaniment a monotonous song. He was speedily joined by the rest, and away they all went at score, squatted on their haunches on the floor, hands, feet, and head all keeping time to the music, which consisted of sharp, energetic ejaculations—' Hey ah! hi hi ah! hiyah hi hiyah!' &c. &c., expelled convulsively from the chest. They kept this going till they had worked themselves up to the proper pitch of excitement, and then from the far end of the room a tall young man arose, and, gathering up the folds of his blanket, stood in the centre of the floor. He wore the universal waist-cloth; scarlet cloth leggings and beaded moccasins covered his legs and feet; and a sleeveless deer-skin shirt or tunic, fringed with ermine skins, half concealed his brawny chest. He wore no head-gear to adorn the long luxuriance of his coarse black hair. His arms were bare and circled with bracelets.

For a minute he stood, his left foot slightly advanced, a perfect picture of natural dignity and ease, looking proudly around him; then sweeping back his robe and making a circling gesture as though to signify that he addressed himself to the whole assembly, he advanced a step or two, stretched out his right arm with a grand gesture, and commenced to speak. I could not of course understand a word that he said, but you can gather a great deal of an Indian's meaning without knowing one syllable of his language, so appropriate and well chosen are his gestures and actions. In fact, two good sign-talkers can converse fluently together without the utterance of a word. It is a curious fact, and worthy the notice of ethnologists, that whereas some of the plain tribes talk by signs very well, others, to whom this method of imparting information and obtaining knowledge is equally important, have never been capable of acquiring the art. Well, this young brave postured so cleverly, and signified so plainly by his signs what he was doing, how long he was out, when he met his enemy, &c. &c.; so faithfully delineated all the circumstances of the fight and the result of it, that I could pretty well make out his meaning without the aid of the interpreter, who rendered into English his actual words.

His speech, being very liberally translated, was some-what in this style :—'Oh ka hé!' he said, 'oh ka hé; listen to me. It was last spring, soon after the snows had melted from the hills, about the time when those infernal east winds do blow, raising clouds of dust in the King's Road, Chelsea, that I and five others (Charley Smashington led the party) who had come up to town to see the Oxford and Cambridge boat race, drove up to Cremorne in two hansoms. We were in our war-paint, white ties encircled our necks, our feet were shod in patent leather ; our hearts were good, our backs strong, our bellies full of inferior dinner and bad wine. We were all partially disguised in liquor, and our hearts and faces were Light Blue. Elated with our late triumph, we danced the valse-dance far into the night, and loudly proclaimed the great deeds of our tribe and jeered at the insignificant Dark Blue. I was standing on a chair waving a champagne bottle round my head, when without a moment's warning the war-cry of the Dark Blues rang through the air. I received the contents of a tumbler of B. and S. full in the face, and, stunned and dripping with drink, was pulled out of the conflict by my friends and my heels.

'What a row there was !—bottles flying, glasses smash-ing, tables falling, fists smacking, yells, howls, screams, oaths, and every other kind of missile hurled through the air. I espied a timid youth in spectacles crawling terror-stricken beneath a table. Yelling " I'll have those gig-lamps," I sprang upon him ; with one blow I knocked his hat off ; another, and the crimson flood flowed out upon his vest ; I dashed the glasses from his face, I ground him in the dust, I tore the reeking necktie from his dis-honoured head, and with a howl of triumph fled from the scene, followed by my friends. They are here, and know that my tongue is not forked, and that I speak straight, and here is the tie.' After waiting for the witnesses of his deeds to corroborate his statement he proceeded to other topics.

And so every brave in turn graphically narrated to us his deeds; described his fights with Black Feet or Assiniboins, upon the Sun, the Marias, or the Milk Rivers; and told of his encounters with the Sioux in the Judith Basin, or on the Missouri, producing as trophies of his valour the scalps torn from the heads of enemies, and laying down as evidence of his truthfulness the guns and pistols captured from them. And after each speech we had a chorus of 'He hi hiyah hiyah! Hi hiyah hiyah!'

After this we all smoked, and Blackfoot delivered another oration, still harping upon the same string, and explaining the marvellous properties of woollen blankets and flannel shirts; and, being a practical man, he also took occasion to speak to the agent about some cattle-straying and horse-stealing grievances.

Then, when the performers were rested, they indulged in some more violent exercise in the shape of bull-dances and bear-dances, dances mimicking the chase and war. About a dozen of the braves got together in a corner and formed a small circle, sitting close together and facing inwards, and commenced to sing. On this occasion the tune was faster and more lively, and the inflexion of their voices much greater. They ran up and down the scale, from shrill falsetto to the lowest rumbling of a basso profundo with a cold in his head. They broke out occasionally into most awful war-whoops, yells, and whistlings. They rattled gourds and banged drums, and made altogether a most diabolical and highly exciting row. Their heads all bobbed in unison; their elbows began to work; faster and faster went the music, louder and louder grew the din;

and then, as they warmed up to the proper pitch, the outsiders would start up, bound into the centre of the floor, and form a large circle facing inwards and revolving round the room. Sometimes they would all spring round and face us, grimacing and contorting their bodies, their facial muscles and their limbs working and writhing with nervous excitement. Then they would jump round again, and present a back view to our gaze. High in the air they would leap, coming down with a spank of their flat moccasined feet upon the boards that made the rafters ring again. Now they would imitate the death of a buffalo, plunging headlong on the floor, rolling over and over in apparent agonies; now, mimicking attack, pursuit, or flight, they would yell their war-cries, and brandish their guns and pistols. Their bodies quivered with emotion, and perspiration poured from their faces; but the singers kept stimulating them to renewed exertion. They had no time to rest except when sometimes the music would slacken a little, and they would all join in a circle and sidle gently round the room. There was one old fellow whose appearance on these occasions, as viewed from behind, was very absurd. He was a middle-aged man and very stout; he wore a waist-cloth and leggings. Now an Indian's leggings reach only half way up the thigh; there is a spacious hiatus between them and the waist-cloth. In fact, when an Indian sits down he does not sit on his leggings, or on anything else except his own skin. A very short-tailed coat covered his shoulders, and his hair hung down behind in long plaits; he had cast aside his blanket, and a felt hat was on his head. When he capered facing inwards, brandishing a pistol in one hand, and a rifle in the other, his flesh shaking and quivering in a jelly-like manner, and his little coat-tails and long hair flapping up and down, it was almost too much; and it was with difficulty that we maintained a decorum suitable to the occasion.

It was midnight before they finished the bull-dance; yet they showed no signs of exhaustion, and would no doubt have gone on till morning : but the room, even when we entered it, was warm; a stove burnt fiercely at one end, the door was blocked with human beings; and after two or three hours of dancing and perspiring, what little oxygen the apartment had originally contained had been replaced by free Indian, and the atmosphere became stifling and oppressive. So after a few complimentary speeches, and an invitation given and accepted to visit the camp next day, we separated, the Indians riding back to their lodges and the whites retiring to bed.

The following morning Mr. Shane, the interpreter, and I rode down to the Crow village.

The lodges are tall, circular dwellings, composed of long fir-poles planted on a circle in the ground. These slope inwards and form a cone, meeting and leaning against each other at the apex; and upon them is stretched a covering of buffalo hides. They make very comfortable, clean and airy houses, and are far preferable to any tent, being much warmer in winter and cooler in summer. A tepee will hold from twelve to fifteen or even twenty individuals; several families, therefore, generally occupy one in common. The earth is beaten down hard, forming a smooth floor, and in the middle burns the fire, the smoke finding an exit through an aperture at the top. The portions of the tepee assigned to each family or couple are divided by a kind of wicker-work screen at the head and foot, separating a segment of a circle of about eight or ten feet in length and five or six in breadth, closed by the screen at either end, and at the outer side by the wall of the lodge, but being open towards the interior. The fire is common property, and has a certain amount of reverence paid to it. It is considered very bad manners, for instance, to step between the fire and the place where the head man sits. All round, on the lodge poles and on the screens, are suspended the arms, clothing, finery, and equipment of the men and their horses. Each lodge forms a little community in itself.

The tepees are pitched with all the regularity of an organised camp, in a large circle, inside which the stock is driven at night or on an alarm or occasion of danger. Outside the door is struck a spear or pole, on which is suspended the shield of the chief and a mysterious something tied up in a bundle, which is great medicine. If a hawk or eagle happens to be the totem of the chief, one of those birds will very commonly be seen perched on the shield. These totems are, in fact, their escutcheons or coats of arms, and they are exhibited without the lodge in the same manner as and for the same reason that knights used to display their shields and banners before their tents.

Let us suppose that we dismount and picket our horses at the lodge of the 'Bear that sits on his haunches,' or some other warrior of renown. A few grave, dignified braves saunter up and look at us with a mixture of curiosity and contempt; a lot of obese little boys and girls, stark naked, gaze with undisguised astonishment; and a crowd of laughing, chaffing youngsters, clothed in the inevitable blanket, gather round. Some are completely shrouded in the folds of their blankets, but others, the day being warm, have lifted their skirts rather high. An Indian youth of sixteen or seventeen is generally very tall, thin, and angular, and if, as is sometimes the case, he has for coolness gathered his blanket up about his shoulders, his aspect is very peculiar. The interpreter sticks his head through the opening, pulling aside the buffalo hide that serves for a door, and, stooping low, draws himself into the tent. I follow, and, stepping carefully round the far side of the fire, seat myself by the chief, shake hands, and say 'How!'

This tepee was shared by three families. In one compartment were seated, on soft buffalo robes, the chief and myself; in another were two women, young and rather comely, and several papooses; incumbrances of the chief, —though among savages wife and children can scarcely be called incumbrances. In a third lay a very old man and an extremely fat woman, with whom the interpreter struck up an animated conversation, which, to judge by her wrigglings and giggling, must have been highly complimentary. Nature had made a good deal of her, and she was accustomed to being made still more of by the men, for her proportions were vast, and fat is highly prized among all dwellers in cold climates; and for that matter, I believe, by nearly all savages, in whatever clime they live. A fourth division was occupied by a young couple, a nice clean-looking girl and a fine tall young man, who was evidently a great dandy, being feathered, painted, and dressed in his best clothes. A woman was bending over the fire looking after some cooking, and in a corner lay a man flat on his back and fast asleep. A lot of starved dogs were driven out when we entered, and the aperture through which we had come was speedily filled with peering curious faces of small boys and girls.

The young couple attracted my attention; they appeared so fond of each other that I judged they must be a newly-married pair. The wife had not got a new dressing-case and did not appear elated, neither did the man look conscious or uncomfortable; but there were other signs sufficient to enable one to form a correct diagnosis. When we came in they were engaged in the pleasant pastime of eating beans and grease together out of the same dish. The repast finished, she reclined gracefully against a lodge pole, and he, covering his lithe limbs in the folds of his blanket, stretched himself out—replete, happy, and full of beans—to repose his head upon her lap, and to his head she without more ado applied herself. I thought she was going to plait his hair; but no, it was on a far nobler errand that her nimble fingers so swiftly sped. Man does not monopolise the pleasures of the chase, though he alone pursues the plodding buffalo and jumping deer. For his helpmate is reserved a smaller but more vivacious species of game, in the pursuit and capture of which she must take great delight, to judge by the interest portrayed in this case on the countenance of the lady, as with unerring eye and unfaltering hand she, through the thick tangles of her husband's hair, hotly pressed the bounding fugitive, or, like the relentless bloodhound, surely tracked to his lair the slow-crawling and unmentionable one.

Of course the pipe was not long in making its appearance, since nothing can be done in an Indian's house without that implement. A young man cut up some black plug tobacco on a board, mixed it with willow bark, filled the calumet, stuck a hot ember in the bowl, and presented it to the chief. He first blew a whiff to each of the four quarters, to the earth, and the sky, then drew a volume of smoke into his own interior, expelled it (I don't mean his interior, but the smoke) slowly with a satisfied sigh, and handed the pipe to me. I took a pull or two and passed it on, and so it went to each man from left to right. The pipe must never be passed against the sun; but, when the last man to the right of the starting-point has smoked, it must be handed across and sent round again from left to right.

After the smoke we had some dried meat and coffee, and then the son of the chief, a little fellow about five or six years old, stark naked, with his little stomach sticking out like a drowned puppy, came and presented me with a handsome pair of embroidered moccasins. The gift was accompanied by a very pretty and hospitable speech from the father to the effect that he was very sorry he had nothing better to give me, but that he had done the best he could; that he was very glad to see me; that he was a great warrior and a great hunter; that he lived on hunting, and cared only for hunting. All was said in the simple, poetical, eloquent language that Indians invariably employ.

Then I noticed that his arm had once been broken, and questioned him about it; and it turned out that it had been done by a bear, and that led to the whole story, so graphically told, and with such an infinite variety of appropriate action, that I only wish I could attempt to repeat it. He observed that I wore a dog-whistle made out of an alligator's tooth, and of course he must needs know all about that; and I had to try and convey to his mind some idea of Florida, and what sort of beast an alligator was, all of which was, I daresay, retailed to the rest of the tribe with such embellishments that they probably put me down as the biggest liar who had ever come out of the East.

And so an hour or two went quickly by; and, having many visits of ceremony to pay, we shook hands, ' howed!' and departed to another lodge. In every tepee we met with the same sort of reception; drank some coffee, tasted a morsel of meat out of compliment, and smoked. The chief would then present me with something—a

Cache.

buffalo robe, a knife scabbard, or pair of embroidered leggings; apologising for the insignificance of the offering, and making a speech to welcome the stranger and to extol himself, something to the effect that he was glad to see you in his house; that his heart was open and felt good towards you; that he was a great man and had struck many enemies; that this scar was received in battle with the Sioux, that in a skirmish with the Black Feet; that he was and always would be friendly to the whites; that he was a hunter, and would always live by hunting; that to eat the flesh of buffalo was his great delight; that he was fond of elk, deer, and all small game, and that to chase them was what his heart loved best. As we were returning to our horses I was attracted by a great drumming and singing going on in a lodge; and looking in we found six men gambling for the cartridges they had received the preceding night. They were playing at a game of chance called 'Cache.' On the floor, in the centre of the lodge, was spread a large buffalo robe to form the gaming-table, and on either side of this knelt, or squatted, four young men facing each other.

The play of 'Cache' is a game which, like Ah Sing, 'I do not understand.' It is a pretty pastime, and somewhat resembles the noble, physiognomical, and instructive game of Coddam. In fact, the latter is but a civilised development of the former. In the one case half-a-crown is used—that is to say, in polite circles; lower in the social scale, the more cumbrous and odoriferous penny may be substituted; in the other case, the players have not got half-a-crown or even a penny, and so a piece of shell or bit of bone takes the place of the circulating medium.

As far as I could judge, Cache is played in the following manner. A buffalo robe or blanket usurps the uses of a table, and the performers gamble with an amount of liveliness and animation that would not be tolerated in the serene circles of polite society; betraying their happiness at winning, and their disgust and disappointment at losing, with a childlike simplicity and guilelessness that, while gratifying to one's moral sense, is occasionally inconvenient to one's personality.

In one way civilised performers surpass savage players. Careful study and lifelong attention paid to the art of unblushingly deceiving their friends, and incessant practice in telling taradiddles—varying in grade and texture from the delicately tinted and neatly fashioned white lie up to the crude, rough-hewn, stupendous crammer—have resulted in the acquirement by most educated beings of a power of controlling the countenance and concealing the emotions that is invaluable in such games as poker, brag, or coddam. In this respect poor Mr. Lo [1] cannot compete with us. His ingenuous countenance betrays all too readily—the allusion is not to blushing—the passing emotions of his soul; his 'untutored mind' leads him to express freely and forcibly the feelings of rage or exultation that agitate it, and so he is obliged to keep up a continual singing, drumming, and brandishing of his arms, to conceal by outward movements the varying passions that agitate him within.

The game of Cache may be played by any number of persons, half being on one side and half on the other. The performers sit or kneel upon the ground opposite each other in two lines, a couple of yards or so asunder. Each party has a drum, and on this instrument the man stationed at the further end of the room keeps up, while

---

[1] Throughout America, but principally in the Canadas, the Indian is called Mr. Lo, from Pope's lines in the 'Essay on Man,' beginning, 'Lo! the poor Indian.'

his side is in, an incessant banging and tamborining (if I may be allowed to coin the word), hoping thereby to encourage the holder of the cache in his efforts at dissimulation, and trying to bewilder his adversary and thwart him in his attempts at discovery. The stakes having been agreed upon, they are placed upon the robe; an equal number of small sticks are given to the two leaders wherewith to score, and play commences.

The man on the left of the line takes in his hand the cache, which consists of a certain number of bits of bone or shell, or buttons—in fact, any small objects will do. He sits opposite the player who has to guess, and his great object is of course to deceive him and prevent him from indicating correctly which of his hands contains the bones or shells. With great rapidity and much violence of gesticulation he brandishes his arms, flourishing them in the face of his adversary, slipping his hands behind his own back, shaking them above his head, and continually passing and shifting the cache from one to the other. The drummer whacks upon his drum, and pumps out a spasmodic song; his companions slap their hands, jerk their bodies, and grunt in unison; and the player, stimulated by the contagion of their rhythmical excitement, becomes more and more wild, and at last, when he thinks that his opponent is quite confused, dashes out both clenched fists and leaves him to guess in which hand and in what position lies the cache. If he indicates the wrong hand, his party lose one point. The holder of the cache goes on again, and his side set up one stick.

Each player has a certain number of chances, and, when he has expended them all, he goes out till his turn comes round again, and the next man has the guess. Every time some one guesses correctly. the cache is transferred to his side, and the others have in their turn to try and discover who has possession of it. Occasionally a man is found out directly; sometimes a player is so lucky and can so skilfully deceive his adversaries that he scores ever so many points before he is put out. Thus they go on winning and losing, putting up sticks and having them taken down again, until one side or the other have got possession of all the markers, when the game is over, and the stakes are paid to the fortunate party and divided among them.

When we looked in the game was at a most critical stage. One side had acquired very nearly all the sticks; they held the cache, and the others were pointing and pointing very unsuccessfully. The winning side looked triumphant. The fellow with the cache shook and brandished his fists, and dashed them out confidently, as much as to say, ' You know you can't; you will never guess it right.' The opposite players were frantic; their drummer beat with all his might; they spirted out their song through their set teeth in sharp spasmodic jets; they violently struck their ribs with both elbows in unison with the time, expelling their breath in guttural grunts; their bodies shook, their muscles quivered and twitched with intense excitement; the veins in their temples stood out in knots, and beads of sweat trickled from their brows. Their eyes were starting from their heads with eagerness, as they noticed the rapidly diminishing pile of sticks, and watched the actions of their guesser. He literally danced upon the ground as he sat—if a man in such a position can be said to dance. He seemed an incarnation of nervous energy, and his anxiety as he threw out his hand and guessed was painful to see. The better to get at his naked body he held the tail of his shirt in his teeth, and at each unsuccessful venture he would smite his open palm with a resounding smack upon his brawny ribs, throw his body back on to his heels and swing it about, dashing his hands together above his head, as if suppli cating for better luck next time.

We did not stop to see the end of the game, but altogether it appeared to be a fine pastime, and would be useful I am sure at home, to burn up superfluous carbon on wet days when the soul-destroying croquet or most excellent game of lawn-tennis cannot be indulged in. There might be some difficulty about the adaptation, however; our clothes certainly would be somewhat in the way; and without the power of smacking one's-self, or, at any rate, one's neighbour, if one were losing, the game would lack half its charm.

After seeing all that was worthy of notice in the camp we rode back to the Mission, and that evening met all the chiefs again. I distributed a few blankets among them; and Dr. Wright made a speech recommending them to come to Sunday School, at which they all grunted. One of them then got up and invited me formally to accompany them and the Bannacks on their annual fall hunt in the Judith Basin; and, when I reluctantly refused, they wished me all sorts of good luck in hunting, and begged me to make good medicine for them. I promised to do so, and in turn wished them ' heaps of buffalo and plenty of good wind to hunt them, an open winter, and not much snow ;' which sentiment they very much applauded, striking the floor with their whip-handles, and ejaculating an unspellable exclamation which Fenimore Cooper writes *hugh*, but which sounds to me more like *ahé*.

They were very pressing in their invitation to join in their buffalo hunt; and I regretted not being able to do so. I should have been treated with great consideration. For an honoured guest the best lodging and food are prepared, and all that the wild man thinks best in the world would have been freely given. Many little delicate attentions, flattering but awkward, would have been paid to me. I should have had a tepee to myself with heaps of buffalo robes, and replete with all the comforts of camp, and all the luxuries in and out of season. Plenty of food for myself, lots of grass for my horses, a damsel strong and vigorous to cut grass and wood, draw water, and attend to the external economy of the establishment; and a more interesting young person to do the cooking, spread the robes, sew on my buttons, minister to all my personal wants, and look after the interior household arrangements, would doubtless have been provided. I should have had all I wanted and more besides. Our route to the buffalo range would have passed through a country reputed to be full of wapiti, deer, and bears. I longed to accept the invitation, but lack of time would not allow of it; and so after another 'howing' and handshaking we parted the best friends.

Nor will I stop to calculate how much tea and sugar, pork and tobacco, suffice to convert a tribe or individual; or to notice how, in consequence of this peculiarity among the natives, Christianity rules high in years of scarcity, and has a downward tendency when buffalo are plenty. However degraded their religion may be, I doubt if a change ever is morally beneficial to a savage race.

Roman Catholicism suits the Red men best, with its spiritualism in some respects so like their own, its festivals and fasts at stated times resembling their green-corn dances and vigils; with its prayers and intercessions for the dead, its ceremonial, its good and evil spirits, its symbolism, its oblations, its little saints and medals. The Red Indian does not see such a great difference between the priest and the medicine-man. It is a difference of degree, not of kind; and, if backed by a little pork and flour, he is apt to look upon the cross and medal as greater talismans than claws of beast and bits of rag and skin, and to think that the missionary makes stronger medicine than his priest.

The dry, cold philosophy of the Methodist finds little favour with an imaginative race, worshipping the Great Spirit in the elements and in all the forms and forces of Nature; thanking the Principle of Good for success in hunting and in war; propitiating the Evil Principle that brings the deep snows and stamps the lakes and rivers into solid ice, and carries in its train fever and starvation —that broods over them at night with the black shadows of its wings—that rides upon the wind, and hurls the arrows of its anger at them in the thunderstorm; asking advice of the shades of their ancestors; and peopling the air with ghosts and shadows, and the woods and mountains with phantasms good and evil.

To the Indian's mind there is nothing intrinsically good or desirable in the doctrines of the various Christian sects; nor is there anything whatever in our mode of living or in our boasted civilisation to prepossess him in favour of the religion of the white race. These red-skinned savages have no respect whatever for the pale-faces—men whose thoughts, feelings, occupations, and pastimes are entirely at variance with their own. Aliens they are to us in almost all things. Their thoughts run in a different channel; they are guided so much more by instinct than by reasoning. They have a code of morals and of honour differing most materially from ours. They attach importance to matters so trifling in our eyes, are gratified or offended by such insignificant details, are guided through life by rules so much at variance with our established methods, that it is impossible for us to foresee what, under particular circumstances, their conduct will be. They are influenced by feelings and passions which we do not in the least understand, and cannot therefore appreciate. They show reverence to superstitions and religious ceremonies, which we, knowing nothing whatever about them, declare at once to be utterly foolish and absurd; and they attach much importance to observances which seem to us almost as utterly meaningless and ridiculous as many of the doctrines preached by our missionaries must appear to them. White men who have dwelt all their lives with the Indians have to confess that they know very little about their inner lives, and understand nothing of the hidden springs of action, and of the secret motives that impel them to conduct themselves in the strange and inexplicable manner they sometimes do. A man may live for years and years with a tribe, have grown-up children among them, be in all things as one of themselves, and even be looked up to, liked and appreciated by them ; yet occasionally a shadow will seem to get between him and his adopted brothers ; their hearts feel bad towards him ; his wife will tell him that he had better leave the town for a few days ; and if he is wise he goes away out of sight, and lies quiet for a time. His wife brings him food, till after three or four days the cloud has blown over, and he can return to his lodge. Nobody would think of looking for him ; but if he persisted in remaining in the village, and the men happened to meet him during such a period of excitement, he would probably fall a victim to his obstinacy. It is impossible to account for the strange, unreasonable moods which occasionally possess these people.

Judged by our standard, the Indians are as a rule cowards, and we suppose therefore that they must be convinced of our superiority in courage. Not a bit of it. They look upon our bravery as the height of folly, and find us lacking entirely in those great qualities they so much admire. We cannot endure the tortures of physical pain or starve as they can. Their mode of carrying on war is quite dissimilar to ours, and they do not appreciate that desperate, bull-dog courage that leads a soldier to struggle to the bitter end against overpowering odds ; nor do they highly esteem a man who is ready at all times to sacrifice his life for the cause. On the contrary ; they would regard such an one as a fool who had parted with a valuable commodity, namely his life, without obtaining an adequate return for it.

Those chiefs are disgraced who bring back the war party with diminished ranks. Occasionally they make up their minds to a great effort, and expend a number of lives to compass the destruction of the enemy, as in the case of the Fort Phil Kearney massacre, when the Indians lost severely, but killed, if I remember aright, over eighty officers and men. Why it should be called a massacre, by the way, I don't know. If the Indians had all been killed instead of the soldiers it would have been a battle. They are not, I think, very prone to fight, and their great object in war is to do as much damage as possible without the loss of a single man.

By hunting they live; and to keep their hunting-grounds intact, to drive off intruders, they must have many young men, the more the better, for there is no danger of an excess of population in an Indian tribe. It would not do to lose warriors in battle with the troops, and then fall an easy prey to the other divisions of their own race, always waiting for a chance to seize their tribal hunting-grounds and to drive them from the best portions of their territory. A life is very valuable to them. Hence it is that they admire the man who can creep, and watch, and lay out for days and nights in bitter cold and snow without food or warmth, and who, by infinite patience, cool courage, and a nice calculation of chances, secures a scalp or a lot of horses without risk to himself, but who, if he found circumstances unfavourable and the odds against him, would return without striking a blow. That is the man they look up to. So we do not impress them a bit by our superior bravery; they view with indifference the reckless courage and devotion upon which we set such store, and value very highly those qualities which we are inclined to despise.

They know and acknowledge that we are numerically much more powerful than they are. They see that we make better weapons, clothes, and ornaments than they can; but dollars or hides will buy our rifles, pistols, shirts, beads, and blankets, and they are quite contented that we should make and that they should use them. They consider us very convenient as traders and producers, but attach no importance to our superiority over them in these respects. They would as soon think of estimating a squaw at a higher figure than a man, because she beads and makes his moccasins, and tans the robes.

The whites they come in contact with are not, as a rule, the best specimens of the race, and the Indian sees that we are lacking in many virtues that rule his actions and guide his life. A few of the leading men in various tribes are taken to Washington and New York, with a view of awing them with the evidences of our overwhelming numbers and of our skill and power. They are astonished at the numbers of men they see. The agent who accompanied a party, I think it was of Arapahoes, told me that one chief took a stick with him to count the warriors of the pale faces, cutting a notch in it for every man he saw. Poor fellow! he soon got to the end of his stick, and finally went partially crazy, so bewildered was he with the vast multitudes of human beings in the Eastern towns.

But in these great cities they see just enough to degrade the inhabitants in their eyes. They can learn nothing of the blessings and advantages attendant on civilisation. How can they appreciate our hospitals, schools, and charitable establishments, or our artistic, literary, and scientific associations? What can they know of the thousand-and-one emanations of our artificial mode of life, which make existence pleasant to certain classes among us? They see the worst only—the squalor, the wretchedness, the dirt, the crowding together of the population, and they are startled at the discordant life of a great town. As to taking any wider or deeper view of our civilisation, and looking forward to future benefits which, growing out of present miseries, may, when the machine is in better working order and runs smoother, gladden the days of generations yet to come—that they are incapable of doing: the present is sufficient for them.

Besides, on the whole question as to what civilisation is, the two races are hopelessly at variance. While we think we are advancing, they assert that we are going back. We hope and trust that we are on the right path; they say that we are hopelessly off the trail. They consider our lives altogether wrong, and look upon us with contempt, perhaps with a little pity. While fully acknowledging the fact of our preponderating strength, while seeing plainly before them the extermination of their race, and bowing their heads to sad necessity, they yet will not admit that we are in any respect their equals, man to man. They are the most strong-hearted, hard-headed people in this matter, submitting to the inevitable, but sturdily maintaining their self-respect.

As to our railways, our waggons and carriages, our bridges, roads, houses, villages, towns, and cities, they are all utterly abhorrent to the Indian. He cannot understand what satisfaction we can find in the pursuit of business or in the pleasures that form the sum and substance of our lives. He cannot realise the state of society in which we exist, our thoughts and actions, our eating and drinking, our sleeping and waking, our occupations and our pastimes; in fact, our whole scheme of life is so repulsive to him that he looks with surprise and contempt upon a race that finds existence bearable under such circumstances.

Even when poor, cold, half-starved, he would not change places with any white man. With enough to eat, tobacco to smoke, horses, guns, and hides to trade for beads and finery, he is the happiest man on earth, for he is thoroughly contented with his lot. He is free, and he knows it. We are slaves, bound by chains of our own forging, and he sees that it is so. Could he but fathom the depths of a great city, and gauge the pettiness, the paltry selfishness of the inhabitants, and see the deceit, the humbug, the lying, the outward swagger, and the inward cringing, the toadyism, and the simulated independence; could he but see Mrs. Grundy enthroned in all her weighty majesty, paralysing with her conventionalities all originality in the brains of her subjects; could he but view the lives that might have been honourably passed, spent instead in struggling for and clutching after gold, and see the steps by which many a respected man has climbed to fortune, wet with the tears of ruined men and women; could he appreciate the meanness of those who consider no sacrifice of self-respect too great, provided it helps them to the end and object of their lives, and pushes them a little higher, as they are pleased to call it, in society; could he but glance at the millions of existences spent in almost chronic wretchedness, lives that it makes one shudder to think of, years spent in close alleys and back slums, up dismal rotting courts, without a ray of sun to cheer them, without a mouthful of sweet fresh air to breathe, without a flower or even a blade of grass, or any token, however humble, to show that there is somewhere a beautiful Nature—without one vestige of anything to make life graceful, but closed in for ever with surroundings sordid, dismal, and debasing;—if he could take a broader view of the land, and note how we have blackened and disfigured the face of Nature, and how we have polluted our streams and fountains, so that we drink sewage instead of water;—could he but see that our rivers are turned to drains, and flow reeking with filth, and guess how by our manufactures we have poisoned our rivers, destroyed our fish, and so impregnated the very air we breathe that grass will not grow exposed to the unhealthy atmosphere;—could he but take all this in, and be told that such is the outcome of our civilisation, he would strike his open palm upon his naked chest, and thank God that he was a savage, uneducated and untutored, but with air to breathe, and water to drink; ignorant but independent, a wild but a free man.

Nor is this feeling of contempt for white men confined to the pure-blooded Indian. I have never seen a half-breed that did not cleave to the savage and despise the civilised race. Many children of mixed marriages cannot speak a word of English; and the half-breed, whether Scotch, American, or French, invariably prefers the society of his relations on the mother's side. Many of them, too, have had ample opportunities of understanding all the benefits of our system. But the one sentiment is almost universal. They will admit that the benefits which our advanced state of society has poured upon the human race are numerous and great. They will allow that there is much to be admired in the order of our lives; but, all the same, give them the forest and the prairie, the mountain and the vale. Let the rushing of great rivers, the wailing of the wind be their music; let their homes be the birch wigwam or skin tent; let trees, and stones, and flowers, and birds, and the forests and the wild beasts therein, be the books for them to read. The two lives are different utterly; both are good they will say, but the wild life is the best.

So it is difficult for missionaries to make much head against the pride and prejudice, the instincts and feelings, of a race they scarcely understand.

However, Dr. Wright was very sanguine, and I sincerely hope that good success may crown his efforts. Christianity may do something towards granting an euthanasia to a fast-vanishing, much-enduring, and hardly-entreated people. Let us hope that it will.

I should much have liked to stay a few days at the Mission, and to have devoted a little time to a more careful study of the Crow tribe of Indians. I have always felt a keen interest in the Red men; for though there is much to disgust us in their practices, pursuits, and manners, and though their ideas and customs are in most cases repugnant to us, yet a great deal that is instructive is also to be found among them, and valuable lessons may be learned from a people who, though far beneath us in many respects, are in some things our superiors. Many qualities, almost lacking in us, they have cultivated and brought to great perfection.

I am by no means an enthusiast on the Red Indian question. A practical though slight acquaintance with

many tribes has sufficed to dispel the illusions and
youthful fancies that a severe course of study of Fenimore
Cooper's works, of ' Hiawatha,' and books of that description engendered in my mind. Under the strong light
of personal observation of their filthiness, of their debasing habits and ideas, the halo of romance that at one
period of my life enveloped them has faded considerably,
though it has not entirely disappeared. I have, not unnaturally, acquired a feeling of general hostility towards
them ; for on hunting expeditions they have bothered me
much and have interfered considerably with my pleasure
and comfort, as I am not one of those individuals who
revel, or pretend to revel, in actual danger, and who
delight, or say they delight, in anticipations of a row.
I know too well what a nuisance they become, how inconvenient is their fondness for horseflesh, and their unpleasant
custom of following out the Mosaic law of ' an eye for
an eye and a tooth for a tooth.' If they confined their
attentions to fulfilling the latter part only of the maxim
I should not so much care, for dentistry is practised to
perfection in the States, and a whole set of teeth could
be purchased tolerably cheap, and warranted capable of
cutting through even a boarding-house beefsteak. But,
unfortunately, it is a scalp for a scalp and a life for a life
with them, and they don't care a bit what fellow's scalp
or whose life they take in satisfaction for the loss of one
of their tribe. So I am not disposed to be over·fond
of Indians, or to gloss over their faults and magnify
their virtues. But still I am fond of them ; I respect
their instinct, I admire their intense love of freedom ;
and, while admitting that Cooper's heroes are somewhat
imaginary, I must confess that the ' noble Red man ' is
not altogether such a mythical being as one school of
writers would have us believe. He has some noble and

excellent traits of character, and it must not be forgotten that, although in common with all semi-civilised or totally savage people certain of his natural actions and thoughts are shocking to our ideas of decency and morality, yet the chief causes that render him obnoxious to us are to be traced directly to the contaminating influence of white men.

Indians, though sometimes mean and treacherous, yet often exhibit a grand simplicity and nobleness of character of which we should be envious. As a rule, they exercise great self-control, though now and then they break out in wild orgies and excesses of all kinds; and, if they are frequently unsavoury, they are always picturesque.

Their misfortunes too, and the mere fact of their being a doomed and a disappearing race, enlist one's sympathies in their favour.

Had I been able to remain at the Mission, I could not have hoped and should not have attempted to do more than gratify my own curiosity; but it is a great pity that some one sufficiently well-versed in ethnological subjects to know what inquiries to make, and in which direction to push his researches, does not devote a little time to the North American Indians; for although late in the day, yet many scraps of valuable information might still be gleaned from that field before the sun for ever sets upon it. Though Indian bibliography is extremely voluminous, it does not, as far as I know, contain any work treating seriously and sensibly of their religious observances, their medicine-men, their ceremonies, their fasts, feasts, and festivals. It is true that the golden opportunity for collecting materials has been lost, and can never return; but still something might yet be done. When white men first commenced to mingle much among the aborigines, and indeed among the Western tribes, until about twenty or thirty years ago, they were almost invariably treated with kindness and courtesy. Confidence was placed in them; they were admitted to the solemn dances and religious ceremonies, and heard the legends and traditions of this strange race; and without doubt a great mass of matter extremely interesting to the student might have been gathered together. Unfortunately, most of the travellers and traders who visited the wild tribes in those days were too much occupied with their own business to bestow time or labour upon the affairs of others. A great many of the white men who were intimate with the natives in former days, or who now dwell among them, were and still are incapable, through lack of knowledge, of acquiring any useful information. Some are mere worthless outcasts of society, and those who by nature and education were fitted for the task seem to have considered the absurdities of the native priests as beneath the notice of Christians, and to have taken for granted that the ceremonial of their solemn occasions was a tissue of mere meaningless mummeries and impudent charlatanism, and as such unworthy of investigation. They may be quite right; but they have always argued on an assumption, and have never taken the trouble to prove or even to examine into the truth of their premises. A subject so important as the religion of a people, whose social and religious lives are interwoven so closely as to be indistinguishable one from the other, should not be approached in such a frame of mind. Neither ought the most trivial forms, the most grotesque and senseless ceremonies, to be dismissed as unworthy of attention; for, if carefully sifted and laboriously analysed, there is no doubt that the mass of absurdity would yield some little grain of knowledge for which a place is waiting somewhere in the scientific fabric of the world.

Now, unluckily, most of the savage tribes have learned to so utterly distrust all white men that they will not communicate to them anything that they esteem sacred or worthy of respect. Years of ill-treatment have done their work, and have turned the native, formerly friendly and confiding, into a hostile and suspicious foe. He cannot believe in a pale-face having any disinterested motives for visiting or questioning him; he continually fears lest some mean advantage should be taken of his trust; he jealously hides from a contemptuous eye the mysteries which to him are very dear and sacred; and he refuses his confidence to a people who have so frequently abused it, and upon whom he looks with aversion and contempt.

A problem in many respects are the Red Indians to this day, and a problem they are likely to remain to the end; and, when they have passed for ever from this earth, ethnologists will puzzle themselves vainly over a great mass of literature describing accurately enough their surface life, but not searching sufficiently deep among the hidden springs of action to afford reliable data upon which to found a theory of the origin, history, and position, among creatures, of an extinct race of men.

No better specimens of the aboriginal stock than the Mountain and River Crows can now be found. They are, I believe, fast diminishing in numbers, as are all the other tribes; and although the Red Indians are still numerous in the States and will not be extinguished for many years to come, yet they are rapidly deteriorating, and any one who wishes to form a just estimate of their character and of the value of their career in the world has but little time to lose. There is good evidence that when the States were first settled the native race was already in its decadence, and since that time its degradation has been terribly quick. Too close a contact with civilisation is hurrying them down hill with ever increasing rapidity. As may naturally be supposed, the tribes dwelling remote from our malignant influence are morally and physically the best, and are the most worthy of observation. But when you get very far to the north, climatic influences begin to tell; a too rigorous winter, intense cold, and insufficiency of food operate injuriously, and preclude the inhabitants from attaining to any great degree of excellence in body or mind. Hence it is that at the present day those Septs are probably the finest representatives of the race who range about the north-western limits of the United States and the southern portions of that vast district in British possessions commonly known as the North-West territory or the Great North-West, far away from the centres of our civilisation, yet inhabiting a country well adapted to support a scanty population living by the chase; a country endowed with a climate severe but not at all unfavourable to human life.

The tribes exclusively inhabiting the United States have suffered more than their brethren who partially or altogether live in British possessions, for they have come more into collision with the superior race.

We northern folks in Canada have been very fortunate, and have had little difficulty with our Indians as yet; while the United States, on the contrary, have been in constant trouble with the aboriginal inhabitants of their territories and States. The international boundary line is not respected; its existence probably is not known or acknowledged by the north-western tribes, many of whom roam across it at pleasure, and pass their time sometimes

in one country, sometimes in another. The owner-
ship of the soil is, in their opinion, vested in them alone.
Their hunting-grounds are not limited by the 49th
parallel, and they attach to the territorial arrangements of
Great Britain and the United States about the same
amount of importance that the parochial or diocesan
authorities in this country would consider it necessary
to bestow upon the boundaries of the Roman Catholic
parishes and bishoprics throughout it. This year their
principal village may be south of the line; next season,
scarcity of game, lack of grass, insufficiency of water or
wood, an extensive prairie fire, or some similar cause, may
induce them to move it far to the north. Generally they
deal with the Hudson's Bay Company; sometimes with
American traders on the Missouri. While possessing,
therefore, but very hazy and indistinct notions of the line
of demarcation between the two peoples, they have
acquired at the same time strong general opinions as to
the characteristics of the two white races that dwell, the
one to the north and the other to the south of the line,
and they entertain towards them very widely differing
feelings.

The same tribes may, speaking generally, be described
as being friendly on the north side and hostile on the
south side of the boundary. The white servants of the
Hudson's Bay Company, or their half-bred employés,
whether of French or Scotch extraction, wander securely among Sioux, Black Feet, Crees, and Assiniboins,
who would rarely lose a chance of attacking an American
party.

At Fort Garry is a document signed by certain
chiefs, in which they intimate the assurances of their
friendship for the Canadians. In it they say that they
can generally tell by various signs the difference

Doubtful Friends.

between British subjects and citizens of the United States; but to avoid all accidents it would be well for British subjects to hoist the national flag when near the boundary line.

It would be tedious to go into the subject of the mistakes and mismanagement by which the United States have made themselves so obnoxious. There is no doubt that to their faults of administration, and to the much fairer system of government adopted and carried out by the Hudson's Bay Company is attributable, to a great extent, the difference of sentiment entertained toward the two countries by the Red man. Other and unavoidable causes, however, have aided to bring about this result, and we should be very wrong to attach too much blame to the United States, or to congratulate ourselves too freely upon the success that has hitherto attended our administrative efforts. We have as yet scarcely come in contact with the wild prairie tribes at all; but the States are in constant collision with them, and have been for years driving them out of the way of their settlers and miners, and shifting them about to suit the requirements of the prodigiously rapid growth of their country.

The Indians of Lower Canada, such as the Hurons, Abenakies, Mic-Macs, and the Iroquois of Caughnawaga,— sole remnant, these last, of the once formidable, ferocious, and dreaded league of the seven nations—a combination of tribes that at one time held almost at their mercy the settlements of the Canadas and New York; whose mandates issuing from their great council-house in Onandaga were looked for with apprehension by the Dutch and English; whose warriors when only partially united with certain of the northern tribes under Pontiac, himself a chief of the Ottawas, an offshoot of the Algonquin race, captured, with one exception, the whole chain of British forts which protected the commerce of the great lakes and the highways from them to the Mississippi and the West, and defeated in regular engagements several bodies of troops ; these *sauvages*, as the French *habitants* call them—Indians, as they are designated by the English—are in truth Indians and savages only in name. They have intermarried for so many generations with white men and women, that only in occasional instances do they betray their native origin even in their physiognomies.

The Montaineux and others further down towards the Labrador and in the unsettled interior of Quebec are a quiet, peaceable, half-starved people. But to the west and north-west we come upon quite another class of tribes. Scattered in small parties, fishing and hunting cariboo on the shores of Lake Superior ; dwelling in villages and large camps across the ' height of land ' about Rainy Lake, Lake of the Woods, and Lac des milles lacs ; on both banks of Rainy River, on the shores of the Winnipeg, on the plains about the Red River Settlements, will be found the Saulteaux, Chippeways or Ojibways of the lakes, as they are variously called, a very fine race, brave, and well-disposed to the whites. Westward of Red River, on the great plains, in the valleys of the north and south forks of the Saskatchewan and the Assiniboine, and their tributaries, along the upper portion of Milk River, in the sheltered parks among the foot-hills and spurs of the mountains, roam all the divisions of the Black Feet—such as the Black Feet proper, Bloods, and Piegans ; together with Crees, Assiniboins, and a few Sioux, who took refuge across the line after the great massacre of settlers in Minnesota. These tribes are composed of bold, bumptious, buffalo-eating men. They feed almost entirely on meat, and are strong, brave, audacious, and untamed ; but up to the present friendly to us.

Hitherto they have been scarcely interfered with; their lands have not been wanted for settlement; their hunting grounds have not been turned into pasturage for sheep and cattle. On the contrary, their natural tastes, their love of hunting, their skill in trapping—an art which, by the way, they have learned entirely from the whites— have been fostered and developed to the utmost by the Hudson's Bay Company.

It was to the advantage of this great organisation to keep the country in its primitive state, to discourage immigration and settlement, to maintain the Indians in their normal condition as hunters and trappers, to keep the lands as a great preserve of fur-bearing animals, and as a breeding-ground for the herds of buffalo, upon the flesh of which lived their trappers and hunters, their boatmen, clerks and traders; and it was a very long time before the secret of the rich tillage-lands and valuable pasturage of the North-West oozed out and became generally known. Very little attention has been paid by the English public to this, one of the richest portions of its domains. The popular mind indeed entertains the vaguest and most inadequate ideas respecting the whole territory. British North America is looked upon by many as a sort of frozen, barren waste, whence beaver-skins and bear-skins come; and even now I daresay there are few people in this country who have ever noticed or commented upon the extraordinary curve northward which the isothermal line makes about the centre of the continent. The freezing influence of those internal seas, Lake Superior and the other 'great lakes,' of those vast bodies of fresh water scarcely inferior to them in size, namely, Lakes Winipeg and Manitoba, and of James's Bay, the most southern portion of Hudson's Bay, an arm of the ocean penetrating with its burden of winter ice far into the continent, together with the innumerable lesser sheets of water that constitute so large a portion of Prince Rupert's Land, makes itself very widely felt. But, as soon as you have passed beyond, that is to say to the westward of that influence, you emerge from a country distinguished by a sub-arctic flora of moss, lichens and stunted pines into a region of luxuriant grasses, warm breezes, and hard-wood trees. And the climate improves as you near the mountains, being affected by those great heat-radiating masses, and tempered also by the soft winds from the Pacific Ocean.

Highly favoured indeed by Nature has the North-West been. Speaking in general terms, it is safe to say that from the Rio Grande to the international boundary line is spread, over the central portions of the continent, an almost arid plain. There are exceptions, of course, but the usual character of the country is that of a desert —a desert susceptible of cultivation only by constant irrigation. But no sooner have you struck the tributaries of the South Saskatchewan than you enter upon a region of rich deep alluvial soil abundantly watered, which spreads away on all sides for thousands of square miles. This region is now thrown open to the world, and from it have for ever departed the days of exclusive hunting and trapping. At some time or other, near or distant, all that fertile soil will be tilled and grazed, and where wild tribes now wander settlers will plough and sow, make hay and reap.

When the country begins to be 'settled' up, then our moment of difficulty with the natives will also arrive. In fact it has arrived, for already treaties have been made and lands acquired. And not long ago I heard that the prairie tribes had remonstrated against the existence of the mounted police force organised in Manitoba. They could not understand the objects of this force, and looked upon it with considerable suspicion.

Is it possible so to manipulate the process of extinguishing a race of men that they may neither suffer in themselves nor cause annoyance to the operator? Some mutual pain and inconvenience are unavoidable, but with care we might perhaps succeed, in this case at least, for there are exceptional agencies working in our favour. The colder and more rigorous the climate the better and more valuable is the fur of the animals inhabiting it, and to the north of the districts capable of colonisation lie immense tracts of barren miserable land, inhospitable in the extreme, but still capable of supporting a scanty population of trappers. Thus there is a sort of natural outlet for the native population which will not be driven out suddenly, for the settlement of the North-West will be gradual and slow.

But it behoves us to be exceedingly careful and cautious in our future dealings with our Indians. The department having charge of them should be thoroughly conversant with their modes of life, thoughts and habits; accurately informed as to their numbers, necessities, and the geographical disposition of the various bands; and 'posted' in all matters connected with their hunting-grounds, both those which they hold in common with other tribes and those that they consider exclusively their own. Great attention, too, should be paid to their customs, their vanity, their superstitions, their laws, and estimates of right and wrong. Their moral code is entirely different to ours. As exemplifying this, I am tempted to quote a prayer which I chanced to read the other day. It is thoroughly characteristic of the race in general, and gives one an insight into the feelings and longings that stir their savage minds. It is a prayer to the Great Spirit by a Crow Indian :—

'I am poor ; that is bad.

'Make me a chief; give me plenty of horses ; give me fine clothing. I ask for good spotted horses.

'Give me a large tent; give me a great many horses ; let me steal fine horses; grant it to me.

'Give me guns by cheating; give me a beautiful woman ; bring the buffalo close by.

'No deep snow ; a little snow is good.

'Give me Black Feet to kill or to die ; close by, all together.

'Stop the people from dying, it is good.

'Give instruments for amusements; blankets too, and fine meats to eat.

'Give the people altogether plenty of fine buffalo, and plenty to eat.'

Due allowance for views of morality differing so radically from those we claim to be guided by must be made in dealing with these people.

In the United States we have an example before us well worthy of our study. To put the matter very practically, it is worth while to find out why the appropriations for the Indian Bureau at Washington attain such formidable proportions, and why the Indians in the States cost infinitely more per head than our Canada Indians do. The principal cause is the fact I have first mentioned—namely, that the States have acquired much more land from the Indian tribes than we have; but there are other very important reasons also.

There are three great principles that should guide one in dealing with Red Indians. First of all, make it a criminal offence to sell whisky to them, and take the utmost pains to see that no infringement of this law goes unpunished, and that it is not evaded by whites or half-breeds buying for themselves and handing it over to them. The small private traders will always try to convey spirits to them by fair or foul means, for a glass of whisky will make an Indian drunk, and a drunken Indian will sell his peltry at any price to anybody who will make him a little more drunken, forgetting his obligations to the legitimate traders who have advanced him goods and fitted him out.

Secondly. Treat them with great consideration and respect, hear all their grievances, and listen to what they have to say about their lands. Show a sufficient amount of strength and force to awe them; but, at the same time, conciliate them by numerous presents. It costs but little to please them immensely. Give them a fair price for their lands. I do not mean a fair price according to the agricultural value of the soil, but make as just an estimate as possible of the actual loss to them in respect of hunting, trapping, and deprivation of liberty; and give them an equivalent in annuity goods. See that every jot and tittle of the treaty is properly carried out on both sides; and be sure that the goods delivered to them are of the best quality and represent the full value. Consult their tastes, too. If they like blankets with certain combinations of stripes, let them have that pattern. If they are passionately fond of blue beads, give them beads of that colour. Remember that they are but children. Never try to take them in, or overreach them, for though children in many respects, they are by no means fools, and will find you out to a certainty. Do not attempt to force them upon a reservation, but let them wander

at will, with full rights of hunting, fishing, and trapping, even over the ceded lands; provided of course that
they do no harm, do not trespass upon cultivated portions, don't frighten or stampede sheep or cattle, or in
any way annoy the settlers. They will do scarcely any
damage by trespassing, and they will get accustomed to
the settlers, and the settlers to them.

Thirdly. If depredations are committed, if an Indian
steals anything, or wounds or murders anybody, pursue
the individual who has done the wrong—whatever it may
cost in time, labour, or money—pursue him relentlessly,
bring him to justice, try him, and punish him with seve-
rity. Mete out equal justice to white men and red-skins.
Let it not be murder for an Indian to kill an Englishman,
and justifiable homicide for the settler to slay the savage.
Above all, never make reprisals upon the tribe or family.
Get the man or men implicated, and try them; run them
to ground wherever they may be; even if they fly
hundreds of miles to the fastnesses of the mountains, let
them feel that the arm of the law is long enough to reach
them—strong enough to pluck them from their hiding-
place, and bring them, if necessary, to the gallows. Never
allow a blood feud to originate between the settlers and
the Indians. If a white man kill an innocent Indian in
revenge for some relative or friend slain by a native, try
that white man, and, if convicted, punish him as you
would a savage for the same offence. Abandon at
once the old idea of blood for blood—the scalp of any
white man in atonement for the life of any Indian; the
blood of any Indian in expiation of the murder of any
settler. The old men and chiefs, who are nearly always
for peace and quiet, will help you and bear you out, and
the savages will gradually become amenable to the law.

The two races, not being deterred by mutual dread of each other, will freely mix together, and the weaker will in time be absorbed and assimilated by the stronger, as has been the case in the Lower Provinces of Canada.

There exists, ready-made to our hand, a corporation capable, if anything is, of successfully carrying through this difficult work, and without violence depriving the rightful owners of their possession in the land. The organisation of the Hudson's Bay Company is very complete. Its ramifications extend throughout the whole country, from the Atlantic to the Pacific, from the Saskatchewan to the Arctic Sea. It has been uniformly successful in its dealings with the natives. Its members thoroughly understand the peculiarities of an Indian's character and all the subtle complexities of his brain; and the tribes look up to them with respect and affection.

If this institution be turned to our advantage, its services made use of, its officers consulted and the advice of its members adopted, then we shall have but little trouble and be put to small expense in the North. But if, when in future years settlers pour in in numbers, and in consequence business relations with the natives become complex and voluminous, we allow ourselves to fall into the same error which so much troubles our cousins in the United States, and keep up, as a political engine, a great and expensive Indian Department, employing numerous agents and other officers, and affording nice little titbits of fat patronage, why then, in that case, there is likely to be a plentiful expenditure of blood and money.

Above all things, it is to be hoped that we shall avoid the absurdity involved in a continual change of policy. The disadvantages of such a course are manifest in the States, where at one time the natives are under military control, and at another are, without warning, turned over to the tender mercies of Quakers and men of peace. Had the Indian Bureau been worked entirely and continuously by the soldiers, it would have been far better for both whites and Indians.

A PAPOOSE.

CHAPTER IV.

THOUGH we had determined over-night to leave early in the morning, so as to have plenty of time to reach Boteler's Ranch before dark, and though we were ready at the appointed time after bidding farewell to hospitable Dr. Wright, yet it was late before we did get away. A ' squaw man' was coming part of the way with us, and he, as is the custom with those semi-Indians, fiddled about the store for ever so long, and then had to go to camp to say good-bye to his wife; and then his sister-in-law wanted a lift on the road, and jumped up behind him on the pony; and then a brother-in-law rode after him, and insisted upon having his rifle in case the Sioux should attempt to run off any of the horses during his absence; and then we passed the outlying picket of civilisation, a dissipated-looking whisky shop, and we must needs take a drink with him; so that the sun was pretty high when we at last turned our horses' heads south and started off at a swinging gallop across the dusty plain.

The ' squaw man' was a very jolly fellow, and en-livened the journey, when our pace permitted it and we were forced to walk through cañons or over rocky grounds, with endless anecdotes and highly-flavoured jokes, not very easy to digest. Like most of his kind, he was light-hearted and happy, and galloped along across the level, swinging his whip, his felt hat on the back of his head, his long hair flapping on his shoulders, whooping, yelling, and singing at the top of his voice, out of sheer exuberance of animal spirits. These ebullitions, which were very cheering both to us and our horses, were not indulged in during the early part of the journey. On the contrary, we proceeded cautiously, and kept a bright look-out on either side until we were well through the first cañon. A predatory band of Sioux from the plains had not long before run off with some cattle and horses from close to the walls of Fort Ellis, and had killed two men near the Mission. The Crows reported that their young men, lying out in the passes watching, had detected a large war party of the same tribe coming up from the eastward. The Crow scouts had lost touch of them somehow, and nobody seemed to know whether they had retreated on finding the Crows encamped in force about the Agency, or whether they had dispersed and scattered themselves among the mountains. It was the choke-cherry season; numbers of the Crow Indians were wandering about gathering fruit, and it would have been difficult for any hostile band to approach the Agency undiscovered, a fact which was very reassuring; but still there was a feeling of uneasiness in the air. Dr. Wright told us to be very careful, and, until the first gorge in the range had been placed between us and our possible enemies, we kept our ' eyes skinned ' and all our senses on the alert.

The tribes of the Dakotah, horsemen by nature, men bred upon the plains, are out of their element entirely in the woods or among the hills. On the broad prairies is their home, and they rarely venture far from those congenial wastes. They hang about the passes and make a dash occasionally into the Gallatin Valley, but have never, I believe, been known to extend their forays down the

"*Elk or Indians?*"

valley of the Yellowstone. The ranges on either side of the river would prove impassable to their ponies; the entrance could be easily blocked up by a few men, and into such a trap the Sioux warriors are much too experienced to enter.

The trail has a course nearly due south, following the direction of the river. At a few miles from the Mission it enters the lower cañon, and, passing through it, emerges into a fine plain of about thirty miles in length and eight or ten in breadth. Near the head of this valley is Boteler's Ranch.

The lower cañon is a channel cut by the river for three miles, through a solid limestone ridge at right angles to the line of upheaval.

The second cañon, which forms the upper or southern boundary of the valley, has been worn out of metamorphic rocks. On the east side of it rises a huge granite dome-shaped mountain for 2,500 feet above the river, and the other side is formed by two or three round naked granitic masses of about 1,500 feet in height. Between these two gorges lies a valley which has been at one time a lake basin. This theory holds good of all the valleys that exist between the various cañons on the river, which must therefore, before it carved out these deep channels and freed the imprisoned waters, have formed a chain of lakes. The surface is composed entirely of lacustrine deposit, over which a covering of basalt has been formed. This lava cap has been removed by erosion and denudation from all but a few localities, and the vestiges now remaining are comparatively insignificant; but originally it must have overflowed a very large tract of country, for it is found in detached masses all over this district, and in the Snake River Valley it occupies in fragments an area of some hundred miles in length by sixty in breadth. That the action which produced the outpourings of basalt was not confined to one epoch is evident, for there are several clearly-defined layers of lava; and between the different beds of clay, gravel, or sand layers of various thickness are found, showing that the basalt was ejected by several distinct eruptions and at irregular intervals of time. The plain is for some distance on either side of the river perfectly level, and then rises with a gentle slope and rests upon the mountains. This slope has been moulded by the action of wind and weather, and by the mountain streams cutting their way through it into a range of low rounded foot-hills. The whole is clothed with a thick garment of succulent grass, affording admirable pasture for stock. The land is besides capable of producing heavy crops of wheat and all other grain. The ripening of maize is the crucial test in this country, and at the house of my squaw-man friend we dined sumptuously on very fair green corn. As to potatoes, in no country can they be more successfully grown.

The mountain chain to our left as we rode, that is, on the right or east bank of the river, is very fine. Symmetrical and grand, it rears its huge bulk above the grassy slopes of the foot-hills, a dark-blue mass gashed and seamed with black cañons and torrent-beds, rents of 2,000 or 3,000 feet in depth, gloomy, black with timber, and extending far into the heart of the range, opening up vistas of most forbidding but gamey-looking country. The peaks are chiefly composed of limestone, or of very hard close-textured granite—rocks which have so well resisted the weathering of ages that their angles and edges stand out singularly clear and sharp, giving a hard, cruel look to the mountains, whose summits are entirely bare of vegetation, and are too steep to allow of the lodgment of much snow or of fallen rocks and débris.

These mountains extend down to the Big Horn, and give birth to many important tributaries of the Yellowstone, such as Big Boulder, Rosebud, Clarke's and Pryor's Forks. On the other side of the Yellowstone River the range is principally composed of stratified volcanic conglomerates and breccia. This deposit is of enormous thickness. These mountains are not so high, bold, or impressive as the opposing chain, but they are very extraordinary and worthy of examination, for the softer material of which they are formed has weathered into the most grotesque, fantastic shapes, forming castles, peaks, pinnacles, and buttresses, of infinite variety and strange form.

That ice has played an important part in the formation of these valleys is shown by the deposit of marl and coarse gravel, by the heaps of small rounded stones— evidences of old moraines—by the smoothly polished surfaces of the basalt in certain places, and by the huge boulders of foreign material which are found stranded on the foot-hills and plains.

On the whole, the scenery between the first, or lower, and the second cañon, is decidedly fine. The most remarkable feature in it is Emigrant Peak, a fine volcanic cone rising 10,629 feet above sea-level and 4,704 feet above the waters of the river which wash its base. It forms one of the portals of Emigrant Gulch, a deep narrow gorge eight miles in length, cut by a torrent through the gneiss and quartzite rocks. In the mouth of the gorge there formerly existed a settlement containing some 200 or 300 inhabitants, who were engaged on the placer workings in the gulch and on its confluent streams. About $100,000 to $150,000 worth of dust was washed out, and a Company was formed to work the lodes said to exist at the head of the ravine. A great deal of money was spent in sinking on the bed rock, but no ore was found rich enough to pay for excavation; and nothing but a few chimneys now remain of Yellowstone City.

Teetotalism may be a very fine thing for certain persons and under certain very peculiar circumstances, but occasionally the desire to indulge in the cup that cheers and does inebriate may prove one's salvation. In the present instance it was of great service to us, for if Kingsley and I had been total abstainers we should have lost the whole military chest, and been obliged to put back to Bozeman, and procure fresh funds to carry on the campaign. It happened in this way. Towards evening we got somewhat tired. A little rill chattering and laughing down the hill-side looked so provokingly cool, so invitingly clear, that we could not resist the temptation to take just a 'wee drappie,' and spontaneously and simultaneously pulling up we invited each other to drink. Kingsley, who kept the flask, dismounted, and, kneeling down to blend in just proportions the two fluids, felt in the pocket where the flask ought to have been. A shade of anxiety passed across his countenance as he withdrew his hand empty, succeeded by an expression of blank despair, as, after rapidly trying the remaining pocket of his jacket and other garments, he made the awful discovery that through a hole in his pocket not only had the flask disappeared, but the note-book also which contained all our available funds. There was nothing for it but to turn round and examine the trail, swearing the while the most emphatically. Four or five miles back we were fortunate enough to find the money all correct, and half a mile beyond we discovered the flask. If it had not been for our whisky-drinking proclivities the pocket-book would not have been missed until night, perhaps not till morning. By the time we could have returned to the spot many honest citizens might have passed, and our dollars might have gone 'where the woodbine twineth.' We then and there poured out a libation, and determined never to join any Temperance society, except that excellent one recently started in San Francisco, where it is ruled that 'nothing stronger than wine, beer, or cider shall be drunk on the premises, unless any member be suffering under a sense of discouragement, in which case whisky is allowed.'

While we were recovering our treasure and fortifying ourselves with the consoling cup, evening was drawing on apace, and the scenery was being glorified with sunset effects. The level rays of the sun lit up most brilliantly the Eastern Mountains, striking full upon the sharp angular masses of limestone, bringing out in bold relief against the sky background the cruel jaggedness of their forms, which contrasted strongly with the smooth softness of the plain beneath, penetrating and searching into the deep rifts and gorges, and defining in detail all the savage grandeur of the range.

But, while we gaze, the shadows have crossed the plain, and are climbing the eastern foot of the hills; night is at hand, and there is no time to be lost in looking at the view; so, drumming with moccasined heels on our ponies' ribs, we start on the 'dead jump' and follow at a rapid pace the trail, which we can scarcely distinguish in the increasing gloom. Without drawing rein we galloped steadily on, but not till long after dark did we see the red twinkle of our fire, and the white gleam of our tents, and hear Jack's hearty voice welcoming us to camp.

We lay two days at Boteler's, hiring pack animals, and manufacturing packing-straps, hooks, and girths (or cincts, as the Americans call them); and we secured the services of Fred Boteler to act as guide. Active, strong, willing and obliging, a keen hunter, always in good humour, capable of enduring great hardship, and a capital hand at making you comfortable in camp, I can confidently recommend him to any one visiting these parts.

While the others worked, Campbell and I went out hunting to supply camp, and a nice mess we made of it. We started out into the hills at the back of the house, not knowing exactly where to go, and the first thing we came across was a dead bear. He was too far gone to skin (which was a pity), so we went on till we passed out of the region of foot-hills altogether, and struck a beautiful-looking country for black-tail deer, among the first ridges of the mountains. Great masses of pine timber alternating with spurs striking out from the mountains, wooded on the top but grass-covered on the sides, and valleys bisected by little streams trickling through belts of poplar and aspen, made a perfect feeding-ground for deer. And in fact so it turned out to be, for we had not gone far before we started three does, but failed to get a shot. Not knowing the nature of the ground, we had gone out in boots, and among the withered leaves and dead sticks that littered the earth we had no chance whatever of getting near a deer. Snap would go a dry stick under foot, followed immediately by a crashing among the branches in the distance, and on stooping down we would just catch a glimpse of a brown shadow bounding through the trees. We tried it in our stockings, but either our feet were not hard enough, or the ground was too hard, too thickly covered with prickles and littered with sharp stones; so we were altogether beat, and, tired and disgusted, after starting several deer without getting a shot, we turned our backs to the setting sun and made for camp.

On the way we found a herd of twenty antelope, and Campbell made a beautiful stalk, taking me up to them over almost level ground, the only cover being tufts of coarse grass, a few sage-bushes, and nearly imperceptible irregularities in the surface. It was a very long crawl, and, like the serpent, on our bellies we had to go all the way. But patience was rewarded, and at length, with hands and knees full of cactus spikes and spicula of grass, we got right among the herd, and lay watching them for some time.

I had never been so near to antelope before, and was glad of the opportunity of observing their actions. There was only one buck among them. He had such a splendid head that I determined to take him first, and chance getting a doe—which would be the better venison of the two—with the second shot. The old buck was lying broadside on, not twenty-five yards from me ; he took no notice whatever, but the does were uneasy all the time. At last I gently with my gun-barrel put aside the coarse stems of the grass behind which I was lying at full length, and, sighting for his shoulder, fired. At the report the whole herd bounded to their feet, and with a snort or rather whistle of surprise and terror made off at a pace that only an antelope can keep up. I was so surprised and annoyed at seeing the buck galloping off with the others, and evidently unhurt, that I forgot the second barrel altogether, and stood gazing in open-mouthed astonishment. How I missed that antelope I cannot even now make out. I must have fired clean over his back, I suppose. Campbell *ought* to have consoled me after the manner of stalkers, and made excuses, and said the beast was five yards further than he had guessed him to be, or that a puff of wind had come just as I pulled, and that at the same moment the sun had suddenly glinted out ; but he merely observed that it was 'most extrornary, a great peety, and a vara bad shot ; ' and I relieved my feelings by asserting that it was all his fault, as he had loaded ' Twilight,'[1] and he must have put in too much powder.

And so we went home, and were laughed at and chaffed by our own folk and by the whole family of Botelers. The cook said there was no meat, and muttered that we could not hunt ' no how ; ' and Jack supposed that he would have to go next time; and Kingsley pointed to a fine dish of fish, and said it was lucky *some-body* could get *something* to eat; and finally we had to go penitentially, armed with dollars and our knives, and ask leave to buy, catch, and kill one of Mr. Boteler's pigs, which we did, and ate some with our humble pie.

Campbell and I, abandoning sport, spent the next day in assisting the others to get things into ship-shape and dividing the baggage into bundles of a size and weight suitable for packing ; for though the trail from Fort Ellis, by which our impedimenta had been transported by waggon, continues up to the Hot Springs of Gardiner's River—forty miles beyond Boteler's—yet we were obliged to transfer the loads to pack-mules here, there being no chance of obtaining animals at the other end.

The following morning we made a start, and a most peculiar start it was. It were tedious to note the petty particulars of every day's progress. In place thereof, I will try to impart to the reader, once for all, some idea of the pleasures and miseries, the comforts and inconveniences, attendant upon ' packing.'

Nothing is so abominably temper-trying as journeying with pack animals. Some of the beasts will not feed if

---

[1] The name of a favourite muzzle-loading rifle.

Mule Packing.

they are picketed ; and, as it is essential they should eat well, you picket one or two only, and turn loose the rest. You have a long way to go, we will suppose, and get up early in the morning determined to make a good day's march, and, while the cook is getting breakfast, send a man off to drive in the stock. The rest of the party strike the tents, make up the bundles, eat their breakfast, and then begin to wax impatient, and wonder what has become of the man and the beasts. Presently he comes in with the pleasant intelligence that three-fourths of the stock have left, that he cannot see them anywhere, and that the ground is so hard he cannot trail them. Off you all go, some on foot, others mounted on the remaining horses, and in two hours' time or so the runaways are found and driven in. It is needless to say that they had abandoned very fine pasture and wandered many miles to find grass not half so good.

Well, this delay has not tended to improve your temper, and then the beasts have to be caught, and that is no easy job, and a good deal of kicking and cursing takes place. At last they are all secured, and you proceed to pack.

A man stands on each side of the mule to be operated upon ; the saddle, a light wooden frame, is placed on his back and securely girthed ; and a long rope is looped into proper form and arranged on the saddle. The side packs are then lifted into position on each side of the saddle and tightly fastened ; the middle bundle is placed between them, a few spare articles are flung on the top, a tent is thrown over all, and the load is ready to be secured. The rope is so fixed that the fall, as it were, is on one side and the slack is taken in on the other. Each man places one foot against the pack or the animal's ribs, and, throwing the whole weight of his body into the effort, hauls with all his strength upon the line ; one pulling on the fall, the other gathering in and holding all the slack, like two sailors sweating down the jib-purchase. At each jerk the wretched mule expels an agonised grunt, snaps at the men's shoulders, and probably gives one of them a sharp pinch, which necessitates immediate retaliation. The men haul with a will, squeezing the poor creature's diaphragm most terribly ;—' nothing like clinching them up tight,' as they say. Smaller and more wasp like grows his waist ; at last not another inch of line can be got in, and the rope is made fast. ' Bueno,' cries the muleteer, giving the beast a parting spank behind which starts it off, teetering about on the tips of its toes like a ballet-dancer. The unfortunate beast has assumed the appearance and proportions of an hourglass, large at each end and exceedingly small in the middle. The apparent sufferings of that mule arising from undue compression of its digestive apparatus are pitiable to behold ; but it is all ' kid;' the heart of a mule is deceitful altogether, and in an hour's time that pack will require tightening again.

Having done with one animal, the packers proceed to the next, and so on through the lot. While you are busy with the others, Nos. 1 and 2 have occupied themselves in tracing mystic circles in and out, among and round and round several short, stumpy, thickly branching firs, and, having with diabolical ingenuity twisted, tied, and tangled their trail-ropes into inextricable confusion, are standing there patiently in their knots. No. 3, on whose back the brittle and perishable articles have been entrusted, he being regarded as a steady and reliable animal of a serious turn of mind, has acquired a stomach-ache from the unusual constriction of that organ, and is rolling over and over, flourishing all four legs in the air at once. No. 4, who carries the bedding, a pack bulky but light, and measuring six feet in diameter, has thought to run between two trees only five feet six inches apart, and, hopelessly jammed there, is trying vainly to back out stern first. She is a persevering creature, and will in time back herself out of the pack altogether. Nos. 5 and 6, fidgeting and twisting about as only mules can do, come into violent and unexpected collision with each other behind, and with ears laid back and tails tucked between their legs are squealing and letting fly, as if they never expected to have another chance of kicking in this world. It is no use interfering; nothing will stop them. You may use language strong enough to split a rock, hot enough to fuse a diamond, without effect; you may lay hold of the trail-ropes and drag as hard as you like, but you might as well catch the tail end of an express train and expect to stop it. It is wiser to refrain from all active intervention, for possibly you may be kicked; certainly you will be knocked down and dragged about the place in a sitting posture, to the great destruction of your pants. You may, and of course you do, curse and swear your 'level best'; but it does not do a bit of good. Go on they will, till they kick their packs off; and then they must be caught, the scattered articles gathered together, and the whole operation commenced afresh.

At last things are all fixed. Boteler leads off on his riding-horse, old 'Billy,' for the mules know him and will follow him anywhere; and the pack animals straggle after. We take a careful look over the place lately occupied by our camp, to see that nothing is left behind; coil up our lariats, tie them behind the cantle, take our rifles, swing into the saddle, and spread out in open files, some behind, some on the flanks, to keep the cavalcade in order. All goes very nicely for awhile; the beasts are plodding along, very slowly it is true, for some will wander, while others will stop to graze; when suddenly Satan enters into the heart of the hindermost animal. A wild ambition fires his soul; he breaks into a trot, and tries to pass to the front. A tin bucket begins jangling on his back; he gets frightened at the noise, and breaks into a canter. The bucket bangs from side to side; all the small articles in the pack rattle and shake; an axe gets loose, and the handle drops and strikes against his ribs; he fancies that there must be something alive upon his back hurting and belabouring him—something that must at any price be got rid of. A panic seizes him, and, wild with fright, he breaks into a mad gallop. Yells of entreaty, volleys of oaths are hurled at him; two of us try to cut him off, and only add to his terror and make matters worse. The pack begins to slip over his tail; mad with ungovernable fear, blind with terror, he kicks, squeals, and plunges. A saucepan flies out here, a lot of meat-cans there; a sack of flour bursts open and spills its precious contents over the ground; the hatchet, innocent cause of all the row, is dangling round his neck; a frying-pan is wildly banging about his quarters; until at last he bucks himself clean out of the whole affair and, trembling and sweating with fear, stands looking on the havoc he has wrought, and wondering what on earth the noise was all about.

After a few days things settle down into their places, and everything works smoothly enough; but, at the best, travelling with pack mules is a slow and weary process. To keep up about fifteen miles a day for any length of time is good work; and a great deal of time is wasted every morning in getting the animals in and fixing their loads. Mules are proverbially obstinate, and the specimens with which I have had the honour of being acquainted have not belied their reputation. ' To exhort the impenitent mule ' is a fashionable attainment in the territories ; and, to become a good driver of ox or mule teams, a man must learn the art of hard swearing. Such a man as that Pike, mentioned by Clarence King in his delightful book, 'Mountaineering in the Sierra Nevada,' commands high wages. The scene is so well described that I cannot refrain from quoting it :—

' The great van rocked, settled a little on the near side, and stuck fast.

' With a look of despair the driver got off and laid the lash freely among his team ; they jumped and jerked, frantically tangled themselves up, and at last all sulked and became stubbornly immovable. Meanwhile a mile of teams behind, unable to pass on the narrow grade, came to an unwilling halt.

' About five waggons back I noticed a tall Pike, dressed in a checked shirt, and pantaloons tucked into jack-books. A soft felt hat worn on the back of his head displayed long locks of flaxen hair, which hung freely about a florid pink countenance, noticeable for its pair of violent little blue eyes and facial angle, rendered acute by a sharp long nose.

' This fellow watched the stoppage with impatience, and at last, when it was more than he could bear, walked up by the other team with a look of wrath absolutely devilish. One would have expected him to blow up with rage; yet withal his gait and manner were cool and soft in the extreme. In a bland, almost tender voice, he said to the unfortunate driver, " My friend, perhaps I can help you," and his gentle way of disentangling and patting the leaders would have given him a high office under Mr. Bergh. He leisurely examined the embedded wheel, and cast an eye along the road ahead. He then began in rather an excited manner to swear, pouring it out louder and more profane, till he utterly eclipsed the most horrid blasphemies I ever heard, piling them up thicker and more fiendish till it seemed as if the very earth must open and engulf him.

'I noticed one mule after another give a little squat, bringing their breasts hard against the collars and straining traces, until only one old mule, with ears back and dangling chain, still held out. The Pike walked up and yelled one gigantic oath; her ears sprang forward, she squatted in terror, and the iron links grated under her strain. He then stepped back and took the rein, every trembling mule looking out of the corner of its eye and listening at *qui vive*.

'With a peculiar air of deliberation and of child-like simplicity he said in every-day tones, "Come up then, mules."

'One quick strain, a slight rumble, and the waggon rolled on to Copple's.'

Getting into camp in the evening is not nearly such a lengthy operation as getting out of it again in the morning;—in this respect it resembles getting in and out of the bed of civilisation. Men soon get used to it, and learn instinctively to undertake each a separate job, and not to interfere with one another. One of us, Jack for instance, would ride ahead, and pick a suitable place with plenty of grass, wood, water, good shelter from the wind, and a nice level soft place for the tents. Having fixed upon a spot, he would await our arrival. The mules, as soon as they catch sight of his pony unsaddled and cropping the grass, would know that the end of their troubles was near, and would press forward, each animal trying to get in first and be relieved of its heavy burden. 'Where will you have the tents?' I ask, riding up in front of the outfit. 'There is a nice place,' says Jack; 'dry, sheltered, and level. I think they will do very

Making Camp.

well there with the backs to the north.' 'All right;'
and the animal bearing the tents and bedding is led to
the indicated place. 'Where shall I put the fire, sir?'
inquires the cook. 'There, in that little hollow,' replies
Jack; 'there is plenty of dead wood close by, and the
wind will blow the smoke clear of the tents.' 'Not much
of a place that for a fire; they seem to think I can cook
anywhere; how the devil do they expect me to manage,
I wonder?' grumbles Maxwell to himself. He is sure to
develope some sort of grievance. It is either too far from
water or not far enough; the wood is all wet, is bad in
quality or insufficient in quantity; something or other
is the matter; but, all the same, he conducts his mule to
the place, lights a little fire, and busies himself in ar-
ranging his *batterie de cuisine*. Two men attend to each
animal as he comes in, loosen the ropes, and ease down
the pack. The tired beast walks off, has a good refreshing roll, and proceeds to graze. I take the axe,
walk down to the creek, and speedily return with six
long straight saplings for tent-poles, and a lot of short
stout sticks for pegs. These I throw down, and go off to
cut firewood. Dr. Kingsley puts his rod together and gets
a dish of trout for supper and breakfast. Boteler takes
care of the stock, leads them to water if necessary, drives
them into good pasture, and pickets some of them.
Campbell and Jack set up the tents, pitch out all the stones
and fir-cones, cut down the stumps and roots with a
shovel or axe, and stamp the surface smooth with their
feet; then cut a lot of long dry grass, spread it evenly
over the ground, and unroll the buffalo robes and
blankets. Each man places his bag or bundle at the
head of his bed, and lays his rifle, cartridges, and pistol
beside it; rummages out his tobacco-pouch and pipe, a
pair of dry moccasins and socks, or anything else he

requires to make himself comfortable ; then goes down to the creek with a lump of soap and a coarse towel, and removes in its icy cold waters the dust and travel-stains of the day's march. Somebody suggests a drink ; the keg is produced, and a little old Bourbon at the bottom of a tin pannikin, very slightly diluted with water, gives just the amount of stimulus to the system that is required, freshens you up, and makes you feel ready for the supper which your nose ascertains is nearly ready for you.

After dinner all hands are pretty tired and soon go to rest, for late hours are not fashionable in these parts. But there are two or three things to be done first, and some necessary precautions to be taken.

If it is cold we shall have pitched the three tents on the circumference of a circle, the centre of which would be a point about four or five yards in front of them, and two or three large trunks of fallen trees must be rolled and lugged into camp, cut into twelve-foot lengths, and a large bonfire made that will radiate heat through the canvas and keep us warm all night. If there is any chance of rain a prudent man will dig a little trench round the tent, for nothing is more disgusting than to wake and find yourself and your bedding soaked through, and a gradually increasing flood invading the floor of your abode. It is not amusing to spend a long night sitting on your saddle, with your knees tucked up, in the middle of a muddy sea, wishing for the day.

By the time all this is done it is getting late. Campbell and Maxwell have finished their supper and washed up the things, and are now quarrelling about who shall have the best side of their tent. The Doctor lies flat on his back by the fire, his head supported by a saddle, a smile of ineffable content stealing over his countenance under the soothing influence of the divine weed. Jack, who is of course also smoking—he always is smoking, except when he is eating, and the few minutes he is obliged to devote to mastication are grudgingly given—is holding forth to the rest of us, telling us some thrilling tale of cattle raids away down by the Rio Grande on the Mexican frontier; graphically describing some wild scurry with the Comanches on the plains of Texas; or making us laugh over some utterly absurd story narrated in that comical language and with that quaint dry humour which are peculiar to the American nation. Boteler is lying on his stomach, toasting on a willow-wand a final fragment of meat. He does not use tobacco, and eats all the time that others smoke. He is greatly relishing Jack's story, except when some not over-complimentary allusion to the Yankees comes in; for Boteler served in the Federal Army during the great Civil War, while Jack, Virginian born and raised in Texas, naturally went in for the Southern side. I am squatting Indian fashion, wrapped in my blanket, for it is getting chilly; and Wynne is reclining on his elbow, warming on the embers his last pannikin of tea.

Pipes are let out; men begin to yawn. Wynne and Kingsley say ' good-night,' and go to their tent. Jack also prepares to go to bed; and, after pondering awhile whether he will take off his leather breeches or not, finally decides not to do so. I linger somewhat, gazing into the embers, reluctant to leave the pleasant warmth of the fire; then, after turning the logs and rolling on a fresh chunk of wood, I call up Tweed, and together we creep into the little tent where I find Jack already in the land of dreams. The dog turns round and round three or four times, and with a long sigh of satisfaction curls up at my feet. I double up my coat on the saddle and place it under my head for a pillow, tie up the door, roll up in my blanket, and lie down and feel more comfortable than in the most luxurious bed. For a little while I lie blissfully awake, listening to the sighing of the pine-trees, the whisper of the night wind to the aspens, and the low murmuring of the little stream; watching through the thin canvas the moving shadows of the branches, cast by the broad full moon sailing overhead through a cloud-flecked sky; or blinking drowsily at the red and faltering flicker of the firelight; until in sweet slumber I wander imperceptibly across the borders of reality and fact, and revel in the delicious incongruities of a pleasant dream, or glide into the utter oblivion of sound death-like sleep.

About one or two in the morning I awake (probably Tweed has got cold and, leaving his nest at my feet, has tried to get nearer to my body) and find the fire burning brightly, and Jack sitting up in bed smoking, for he is of a wakeful disposition, and has been out to look about and put on some fresh fuel. We have a smoke and a talk, see what time it is, get sleepy and curl up again. The next time consciousness invades me I hear Jack outside, yawning, stretching, stamping on the ground, and making all manner of strange Indian noises. The morning star is high, the east is getting white, and it is time to get up. A muttered damn from the other tent, grunts and growls from Campbell and the cook announce that the camp is awake. One by one the inmates crawl out of their beds; toilets don't take long, consisting as they do of a shake and a stretch and a little eye-rubbing. The fire is freshened up. Jack, after the manner of his race, takes a good square honest drink of whisky 'straight,' while hot coffee dispels the vapour of the night and clears the cobwebs from the brains of the rest of us. The stock is driven in, and while breakfast is preparing we make ready for the work of another day.

A Yellowstone Highway.

A start very like that which I have attempted to describe above was made on leaving Boteler's Ranch on Tuesday morning. It was a cold sleety day, enlivened by occasional hailstorms. The animals were all chilly and out of temper—a state of things which was somewhat shared in by the men. Boteler led the way, followed by the pack mules; then came Campbell on a diminutive pony, his long legs almost trailing on the ground, accompanied by the cook, sulky as all niggers are in cold weather, hung round with baskets, cans, buckets, jars, and all sorts of kitchen impedimenta, which he could not stow away; and the Doctor, Jack, and I brought up the rear. Many mishaps we had during that day's march of eight miles, and right glad we were to get into camp at the end of it.

Though the weather was still disagreeable, we got along much better on Wednesday, making a very fair march, and camping comfortably on a little creek (the name of which I forget) that discharges itself into the Yellowstone.

Being very unwilling to go to the Geysers without Wynne, whom I now expected every day, I determined to leave a permanent camp there, and, taking one pack mule and a spare horse, to go up into the mountains for a few days' hunt. Accordingly, the next morning four of us, taking only the two light mosquito bars and a blanket apiece, started up the creek. We at first experienced some difficulty in making our way. The creek bottom was quite impracticable, and 200 or 300 feet above it the slopes were so steep that the animals could scarcely retain their foothold on the slippery grass. We might have left the valley altogether by ascending one of the spurs that led out of it up to the mountains, and following along the crests; but it was doubtful whether we could have descended further on. We therefore made the best course we could below, and, by carefully picking the way, we got along safely enough, and after a few miles struck a strong deer-trail leading in the direction we wished to go, and followed it.

Towards the lower end of this valley the sides are composed of washed-down deposits, detritus, and fallen débris, forming hillocks, water-worn by numerous little rills, covered with short slippery grass, and sloping very steeply towards the creek that brawls along below, fringed with poplars, alders, and aspens. The middle portion is quite different; the stream flows with a more steady current through pine woods; the ground slopes gently upwards, covered on one side by dense forest, on the other broken into little parks and glades, till it abuts on a long impassable scarp, above which the mountains tower in successive slopes and cliffs. A little further on the valley closes up somewhat, leaving only a narrow strip of comparatively level ground near the creek, from which the mountain rises very steep, but still practicable for a height of about 2,000 feet or so. At that elevation a sort of plateau exists, tolerably level, well timbered and covered with good grass. It gradually rises towards the east, and extends quite to the head of the ravine, where it terminates among the mountains. At the opposite side to us, that is to say, on the south, this plateau leads up to a sheer precipice, which forms the northern crest of another valley. The upper part of the gorge is very marshy; and just at the head, where the creek, dividing into numerous little forks and branches, takes its rise, it forms a circular basin, the bottom and sides of which are made of mud-heaps washed down from the peaks. This soft deposit is cut by numerous little rills into deep dykes, wet, slippery, and full of dead trunks of dwarf junipers and cedars. The mountains themselves, constituting the rim of the basin, are composed of or coated with thick tenacious clay. This substance, wet with the constantly falling and quickly melting snow, is indescribably slippery, and forms about the most dangerous ground that it has ever been my lot to walk over.

Two or three tributaries discharge their waters into the principal creek, through small gulches and valleys; and in one place a great circular break occurs in the mountains, rimmed round by steep broken cliffs. Up this principal stream we wound our way towards the head of the valley, half asleep, for the day was very hot —one of those blazing 'foxy' days (as sailors would say) that frequently occur in the middle of a cold stormy spell, and indicate worse weather to come—when all of a sudden, skip! jump! away went three deer leaping through the trees, flourishing their white tails after the manner of their kind. ' G—d Al—ty d—n,' says Jack, ' there goes our supper ! Why the h—ll don't you fellows in front look out ? ' Well, we fellows in front did look out after that, and before long I jerked my horse on to his haunches and slid quietly off. The others followed my example without a word, for they too had caught a glimpse of the dark-brown forms of some wapiti feeding quietly in the wood. Boteler, in his enthusiasm, seized me violently by the arm and hurried into the timber, ejaculating at every glimpse of the forms moving through the trees, ' There they go! There they go! Shoot! Now then! There's a chance.' All the time he was dragging me along, and I could no more shoot than fly. At last I shook myself clear of him, and, getting a fair easy shot at a large fat doe, fired and killed her.

Wapiti are the stupidest brutes in creation; and, instead of making off at once, the others all bunched up and

stared about them, so that we got two more before they
made up their minds to clear out. There was a fine stag
in the herd, but, as is usually the case, he managed to
get himself well among the hinds out of harm's way, and
none of us could get a chance at him. Boteler and I
followed his tracks for an hour, but could not come up
with him; and, finding that he had taken clear up the
mountain, we returned to the scene of action. There we
found the rest of the party busily engaged in gralloching
and cutting up the huge deer. One of them was a yeld
hind, in first-rate condition and as fat as butter. We
were very glad of fresh meat, and, as the ground was
very suitable, determined to camp right there, and send
some of the flesh down to the main camp in the morning.
Accordingly, having skinned and hung up the quarters
and choice pieces of venison, we pitched our lilliputian
tents at the foot of one of a hundred huge hemlocks, lit
a fire, and proceeded to make ourselves comfortable for
the night.

We were all smoking round the fire—a most attentive
audience, watching with much interest the culinary feats
which Boteler was performing—when we were startled
by a most unearthly sound. Jack and Boteler knew it
well, but none of us strangers had ever heard a wapiti
stag roaring before, and it is no wonder we were astonished at the noise. The wapiti never calls many times
in quick succession, as his little cousin the red stag
of Europe frequently does, but bellows forth one great
roar, commencing with a hollow, harsh, unnatural sound,
and ending in a shrill screech like the whistle of a locomotive. In about ten minutes this fellow called again,
a good deal nearer, and the third time he was evidently
close to camp; so Jack and I started out, in the company of 'Twilight,' and, advancing cautiously, we pre-

sently through a bush distinguished in the gloom the dark body and antlered head of a real monarch of the forest as· he stalked out into an open glade and stared with astonishment at our fire. He looked perfectly magnificent. He was a splendid beast, and his huge bulk, looming large in the uncertain twilight, appeared gigantic. He stood without betraying the slightest sign of fear or hesitation ; but, as if searching with proud disdain for the intruder that had dared to invade his solitude, he slowly swept round the branching spread of his antlers, his neck extended and his head a little thrown back, and snuffed the air. I could not see the fore sight of the little muzzle-loader, but luck attended the aim, for the bullet struck high up (a little to the back of) the shoulder ; and, shot through the spine, the largest wapiti stag that I had ever killed fell stone-dead in his tracks.

It was early in the season, and his hide was in first-rate condition, a rich glossy brown on the sides and jet black along the back and on the legs ; so Jack and I turned to, cut off his head and skinned him ; and, by the time we had done that and had packed the head and hide into camp, it was pitch dark, when we were ready for supper and blankets.

That night the carcasses were visited by two grizzly bears. We could hear them smashing bushes, clawing up earth, and, to use the vernacular, 'playing hell generally.' Every succeeding night they came, sometimes as many as four of them together, generally arriving after dark and leaving before light.

It was impossible to get a chance at them at night, for there was no moon, and the sky was invariably cloudy and overcast ; and during the day they stowed themselves away among the crags, defying detection. We were very unlucky with them indeed, for though bears were plentiful

in the valley, and the members of our party had inter-
views with them, we got only one, a middling-sized beast,
weighing about 800 pounds. Had we been provided
with a dog to track them, we should have obtained many
more.

These bears behaved in a very singular manner.
They scarcely ate any of the flesh, but took the greatest
pains to prevent any other creature getting at it. I had
hung a hind-quarter of one of the does on a branch, well
out of reach, as I supposed, and had left the skin on the
ground. To my great astonishment, on going to look for
it in the morning, I found the meat had been thrown
down by a bear, carried about 300 yards, and deposited
under a tree. The brute had then returned, taken the skin,
spread it carefully over the flesh, scraped up earth over the
edges, patted it all down hard and smooth, and departed
without eating a morsel. All the carcasses were treated
in the same way, the joints being pulled asunder and
buried under heaps of earth, sticks, and stones. The
beasts must have worked very hard, for the ground was
all torn up and trampled by them, and stank horribly of
bear. They did not appear to mind the proximity of
camp in the least, or to take any notice of us or our
tracks. A grizzly is an independent kind of beast, and
has a good deal of don't-care-a-damnativeness about him.
Except in spring, when hunger drives him to travel a
good deal, he is very shy, secluded in his habits, and hard
to find ; very surly and ill-tempered when he is found,
exceedingly tenacious of life, and most savage when
wounded or attacked. Few hunters care to go after the
grizzly, the usual answer being, 'No, thank you ; not
any for me. I guess I ain't lost no bears ;' thereby implying that the speaker does not want to find any.

One day, while camped in the same place, Jack came

in quite early, looking rather flustered, sat down, filled his pipe, and said, 'J—s! I have seen the biggest bear in the world. D—n me if he didn't scare me properly. Give me a drink and I'll tell you.' He then proceeded :—— ' I started out to try and strike some of those white-tail we saw (if you remember) coming up, for I am getting pretty tired of elk meat ;—ain't you ? Well, the patch of timber is quite small there, and beyond it is nothing but rocks. So when I found there was no fresh sign in the wood I took the back track for camp. When I got near where the first elk was killed I saw something moving, and dropped behind a tree. There, within sixty yards of me, was a grizzly as big as all outside. By G—d, he was a tearer, I tell you. Well, I had been walking fast and was a little shaky, so I lay still for some time to get quiet, and watched that bear, and I'll be dog-goned if ever I saw such a comical devil in my life. He was as lively as a cow's tail in flytime, jumping round the carcass, covering it with mud, and plastering and patting it down with his feet, grumbling to himself all the time, as if he thought it a burning shame that elk did not cover themselves up when they died. When he had got it all fixed to his satisfaction, he would move off towards the cliff, and immediately two or three whisky-jacks,[1] that had been perched on the trees looking on, would drop down on the carcass and begin picking and fluttering about. Before he had gone far the old bear would look round, and, seeing them interfering with his work, would get real mad, and come lumbering back in a hell of a rage, drive off the birds, and pile up some more earth and mud. This sort of game went on for some time. Finally I got a fair broadside shot, and, taking a steady sight, I fired. You should have heard the yell he gave ; it made me feel sort of kind of queer,

---

[1] Whisky-jack, or Camp-robber ; a very important species of magpie.

I tell you. I never heard any beast roar like it before, and hope I never may again; it was the most awful noise you can imagine. He spun round at the shot, sat up on his haunches, tore the earth up, and flung it about, boxed the trees with his hands, making the bark fly again, looking for what hurt him, and at last, having vented his rage a little and seeing nothing, turned and skinned out for the rocks, as if the devil kicked him. No, Sir! You bet your life he didn't see me. I lay on the grass as flat, by G—d, as a flap-jack until he was out of sight. Well, all right; laugh if you like, but wait till you see one, and then you'll find out how *you* feel. *I* don't want to have any more bear-hunting alone, anyhow. It's all well enough with the black bears down south; I don't mind them; but I ain't a going to fool round alone among these grizzlies, I tell you. Why, with one blow of the paw they would rip a man and scatter him all over the place; you just look at the marks of his claws on the trees, and the furrows he has torn in the hard ground.'

We went to survey the scene of action, and there, sure enough, were the marks of the bear's claws on the trees and on the ground, marks most unpleasant and edifying to behold. We followed that bear for a whole long day, up the mountain side, trailing him very quickly when we got to the snow on the top. After crossing the plateau to the next valley, and descending that for some distance, we turned back, and at last arrived at a great mass of fallen cliffs and rocks, close to where Jack had shot him, and there of course we lost him: but he was killed some days afterwards at the very same carcass where Jack had wounded him. Jack had fired low, and beyond cutting a deep score in the skin and flesh the bullet had done no damage.

Dr. Kingsley also had a private audience. He was out one day armed with a little Ballard rifle looking for deer, when he espied a grizzly, ' as big as a bull,' coming towards him. The doctor walked on, and the grizzly walked on; and as the latter did not appear to 'scare worth a cent,' or to have the smallest intention of giving way, the former, concluding that his gymnastic acquirements might not be equal to swarming up a tree with a bear close in pursuit, adopted a more prudent course. He determined to climb first and shoot after. Accordingly, he ensconced himself in a comfortable fork of a tree, under which the bear should pass, and waited chuckling to himself at the prospect of the nice, safe and easy shot he was about to have: but Bruin, evidently thinking that that was taking a mean advantage of him, would not play any more, but went off in another direction, and Kingsley, coming down disconsolate, returned to camp in the condition of Artemus Ward's poor Indian, who, ' though clothed before, yet left his bear behind.'

Campbell too had an adventure; which, as I am on the subject of bears, I may as well mention, though it did not occur in the same place. Lying out one fine day by a little pond, not many miles from Fort Bridger, with a small muzzle-loader of mine, waiting for deer, he hears a great pounding and crashing among the trees, when out walks a bear not five yards from him. With more pluck than prudence Campbell fired at him, striking him in the shoulder. The bear gave a hideous yell, and sat up on his haunches looking for his assailant; upon which Campbell slapped the other barrel into his chest, and, jumping up, ran for his life, and the bear after him. Fortunately for the man, he was provided with a pair of very long Scotch legs, of which he made great use, and the bear, sickened by two mortal wounds, and not feeling up to a vigorous pursuit, made only two or three jumps after him, or there would have been one of the party wiped out. As it was, he fled without looking back for 200 yards, and then, running up the sloping trunk of a fallen tree, ventured to throw a glance over his shoulder, when to his great relief he saw the beast making off. He had had sufficient bear-hunting for one day, however, and did not pursue. By the time he got back to camp it was too late to do anything; but the next day we all went out to look for Bruin.

We had some difficulty in finding the pond, for Campbell's mind was so full of bear on the preceding evening that he had not very accurately noticed the appearance of the woods. So we all separated and hunted about for it, and finally Jack, Campbell, and I got together at the right pond. We saw the impression in the grass where the man had been lying and the marks that the beast had left where he made his spring, and had no difficulty in following the trail, for the ground was literally soaked with blood pouring from both wounds. It was evident by the colour of the blood and by other signs that the poor beast was mortally wounded, and we followed in high hopes. We had not gone far before we noticed that the bear had become so weak as to be obliged to crawl under, instead of climbing over, the fallen trunks; and we expected to come across him, savage and desperate, at any moment. After a mile or two the trail led into a little swamp, and as we could not find any tracks going out it appeared evident that he had remained in there.

We were all most civil to each other. Such was our modesty that no one seemed anxious to put himself prominently forward, to claim the post of honour; and this diffidence continued until Jack, breaking the ice of restraint, volunteered for the forlorn hope, and taking off his coat, and leaving behind him all weighty articles except his gun, divesting himself, in short, of everything that could interfere with quick movement, cautiously entered the swamp. Highlander and I stationed ourselves on a slight eminence, from which we could see well into the willow-bushes, ready to warn Jack of the smallest sign of danger and to turn the bear. Lord! what a state of anxiety (I don't like to say funk) I was in. My mouth was just as dry as a lime-burner's breeches; and my eyes ached with peering into the long grass and brush, expecting every moment to see the great brute bounce out. However, we drew the cover blank, and, after carefully re-examining the swamp, discovered the trail leaving it on the other side. The bear, who had probably stayed in the water several hours, had completely stanched his wounds with mud. There were no longer any blood-stains to guide us, and it was with much difficulty that we could distinguish his tracks on the hard ground. It is very tedious work puzzling out a blind trail. But Jack, with his nose almost on the ground, kept deciphering it step by step, while Campbell and I made casts ahead, and occasionally hit it off some distance in advance, where his feet had pressed upon some softer patch of earth, or where we had trodden upon sand or among leaves; and by this means we got along tolerably fast.

After a while blood stains became frequent again; exercise had caused his wounds to break out afresh, and with renewed hopes we rapidly pursued the quarry. Another two or three miles passed, and by the signs we judged that we must be very close to him. 'Say!' whispers Jack; 'go slow now, he is right heresome where; he has only just managed to drag himself over this trunk. See there! how he has reeled against that tree; look how wide his footmarks are! Why he has almost fallen here, and by Jove! see, there he has fallen altogether. Look out, boys! First thing, you know, he will be on the top of us; never you mind the trail. I'll take care of that: you just keep your heads low and your eyes skinned, and look well under the bushes, and, when you do see him, give him fire.'

We went very cautiously now, expecting every moment to put him up or find him dead; but we were disappointed. After falling three or four times in fifty yards, the bear, unable to walk any further, had dragged himself through the long grass into a little run. There he had rolled in the clay and water until he succeeded for the second time in stopping the flow of blood. When we reached the spot the mud was just barely commencing to settle in the water; he could not have left more than a few minutes, and we listened, expecting to hear him forcing his way through the brush. In all probability we had ourselves scared him out of the place, and we felt satisfied that we were bound to come up with him before long.

But alas and alas for all our hopes and all our trouble! The watercourse led into a large swamp, several miles long and half a mile broad, made up of old beaver dams, full of deep holes and stagnant streams, and thickly covered with a tangled and almost impenetrable cover of willow and alder. There we lost our bear, and there we left him. A heavy shower came on and obliterated all trace and trail, and in the face of a blinding, pelting, pitiless rain we were forced to give up the search and make the best of our way home. And a first-rate land-fall we made, considering that we had neither sun nor compass to guide us, and had to guess a straight course through the same woods that we had so crookedly traversed in the morning while following the devious windings of the trail. What an

awful ducking we did get! I had on new buckskin
trousers, too, and what misery those garments caused me!
They stretched about twelve inches at least, got under
my feet and threw me down, and hampered my legs with
their cold, clammy stickiness to such an extent that I
could scarcely walk. We were all thoroughly drenched,
and did not take long to change, in spite of the guide, old
Man Smith, asking us whether we wanted to catch our
deaths of cold, shifting our wet things in that way. He
stood, smoking like a volcano, by the fire that evening
till he was well warmed though still wet; then rolling
himself up in his dripping blanket, he slept out in the
rain under a tree, and the next morning arose from his
lair steaming,—looking like Venus in dirty buckskin
breeches emerging from a hot bath.

The next day we all went back again to the scene of
action, riding through and through the swamp on our
horses, but could see nothing of the dead beast, for dead
by that time he must have been. We were much vexed,
for the bear, to judge by his footprints, must have been an
enormous animal and it was just the time of year when
their fur is in best condition. But to return to our tents.
On the morning succeeding that of the big wapiti stag,
we all 'slept in,' the previous day having been an
exhausting one, and we, moreover, not having gone to
bed—if a blanket on the ground can be dignified with
such a name—till very late. We had barely got our
eyes and ears open before we heard wapiti roaring up
the valley not far from camp, and Boteler and I immediately started in pursuit, hoping to overtake them on the
low grounds. Our laziness proved adverse to sport. If
we had been out only an hour earlier, we should have
experienced no difficulty in getting up to them in the grey
dawn; but by the time we reached the place where

they had been feeding they had taken to the mountains in search of a secluded spot to lie down in, leaving a broad trail, showing by the numerous tracks that a large band had passed by. We followed at our best pace, but the ground was very steep, and the deer were moving so fast that it was some time before we could get near them. At last we came in view of the herd—some forty or fifty hinds and four stags. They had stopped for the moment, and were feeding when we first caught sight of them ; but, before we could approach, the stags had moved the hinds on again, and were driving them up the mountain at a pace that we could not keep up with.

Walking, or trying to run fast up an extremely steep hill-side, when the ground is rendered wet and slippery by melting snow, may be a very fine exercise, but, at an altitude of 8000 feet or so, certainly it is awfully trying upon the muscles and lungs. Boteler no doubt, if alone, would soon have overtaken the game, he being very strong, hardy, and in first-rate condition ; but I, soft as I was, and unaccustomed as yet to mountain walking, made rather a poor hand of it. However, I did my best, and ran till I was sea-sick. The work—to my great joy— was telling heavily upon Boteler also, for his nose began to bleed violently; and we would both willingly have given up the chase had not the sight of an unusually fine herd encouraged us to proceed.

Every now and then, when open spaces favoured the view, we could see the whole band straggling up the mountain before us. The hinds would walk on fast for awhile, then, stopping to snatch a mouthful of grass, would wander off on either side. They even showed a disposition to loiter or stop altogether, which was not encouraged by the stags, who, roaring at intervals of ten minutes or a quarter of an hour. kept behind and on the flanks of the herd and drove them steadily onward. At last they all stopped again, and we thought we might make a stalk upon them; but to our great annoyance an old stag lay down in a little coulé or run of water on a piece of ground so exposed that we could by no means circumvent him. There he lay, the brute! long after the others had gone on, rolling himself about in the water, every now and then stretching out his neck and throwing his head up with a hoarse bellow. At last he got up and followed the band, and we, as soon as he was out of sight, resumed the pursuit. The deer had got a long way ahead by this time ; but after about an hour's very hard work, for the snow was getting deeper and deeper as we ascended, and our progress was proportionately slow and laborious, we came upon them in some timber, which gave us the long-wished-for opportunity of crawling up to within about 150 yards. After infinite labour, much shifting of position, and crawling and grovelling in the snow, we got a pretty fair shot at the master-stag. We both fired, but were so shaken by our exertion that we missed him clean. However, he took no notice whatever, beyond looking round inquiringly, and we had time to load again and fire : this time more successfully, for he wheeled at the shot, and after running about 200 yards pitched on his head down a slope into a deep drift, and lay there doubled up in the snow. We were not sorry that the chase was ended. When we got up with our knives ready to perform the necessary operations, our disappointment was keen to find that we had greatly overrated the size of his head. The peculiar condition of the atmosphere had deceived us, and we found, to our disgust, that the antlers which had appeared huge in the morning mist, and as viewed from a distance against the white background of the snow, dwindled and diminished most scandalously on close inspection, becoming smaller and smaller as we approached. They proved on examination to be much inferior to those of the stag we had killed on the preceding day. However, it was by no means a bad head, so we cut it off, stuck it up in a conspicuous place, and left it 'to be called for another time.'

During the last two days the weather had turned very coarse and disagreeable ; snow fell in considerable quantities, and melted almost immediately everywhere except on the tops. It rained, too, very heavily at times, and our light mosquito bars afforded but a poor shelter from the elements. The bottom of the valley was completely flooded ; streams of muddy water descended the hills from all sides ; the ground was wet and sloppy, and, when it was neither raining nor snowing, a thick fog alternating with Scotch mist and drizzle enveloped all the lower portions of the vale. The outlook was very far from cheerful, and our eyes turned somewhat wistfully towards the comforts of the permanent camp below. But we had to wait somewhere for Wynne ; game seemed tolerably abundant in the valley ; and, hoping constantly for a change of weather, we, on the next day, moved our little camp right up the head of it to try for mountain sheep. We made a pretty good camp, among the stunted and rapidly expiring fragments of the forest ; but the damp cold was very trying, much more disagreeable than the dry severe cold of winter.

That same afternoon Boteler and I ascended the mountains forming the rim of the basin, which, as I have previously stated, encircles the upper end of the valley, and after a very fatiguing tramp discovered a band of sheep feeding in a little open glade about half way down the other side of the ridge. We made a scientific stalk upon the only two good-sized rams among the band, but we were in too great a hurry and made a mess of it. The ewes got our wind or heard us—I maintain that it was entirely Boteler's fault — and before we could say 'knife,' or much more get a shot, the whole herd were scampering up the mountains at a pace marvellous to see. How they did make the stones rattle down as they bounded from crag to crag! They would gallop for four or five hundred yards, then suddenly stop on some projecting point to look back, and off again as hard as they could go.

In about ten minutes they gained the summit, an undertaking that took us two hours' hard walking to accomplish. There they all gathered together and stood still for several minutes, clear against the sky line (the big horns of the rams appearing most provokingly· large), looking back to see what had disturbed them; and then having made up their minds that, as far as we were concerned, 'distance lent enchantment to the· view,' they fell into single file, galloped for several miles along the crest, and finally disappeared over the other side. So Boteler and I, our hearts full of mutual recriminations, but with no other burden, had to climb up, over, and down the ridge, and struggle back to the camp through the melting snow and the greasy, slippery, treacherous clay. The walking was both unpleasant and dangerous.

All day long the sky had been very lowering, bending as it were under the weight of vapour, and about sunset the accumulated masses of cloud sank down, enveloped all the hill-side, and broke. During the night about twelve inches of snow fell.

The following morning Jack, Boteler, and I went out to try our luck, and speedily found some sheep feeding on the ends of the long dry tufts of grass that protruded through the snow. They were all ewes, but, as we wanted fresh meat very badly, we were not proud, and determined to try and get one of them. It was necessary to make a very long round to get down wind of them, and unfortunately, while doing so, we exposed ourselves to the view of a magnificent band of old rams fourteen in number, some of them carrying splendid heads. It was unlucky; but we had no just cause to blame ourselves. We could not see the rams from where we started, because, like the Spanish fleet, they were not in sight; there was little shelter to be got; we were obliged to make a long détour through the snow, and against that white background our bodies appeared very black and distinct. But it was nevertheless most annoying to see our supper tearing up the hill-side, and our prospective trophies ' putting out ' at their best pace for the most inaccessible part of the mountains.

The sheep ran in two bands until about midway up the hill-side, and then all joining together proceeded to walk so leisurely that we thought it worth while to pursue them, particularly as they were going straight up wind. Patiently we followed their trail all day over the most infernal ground. The mountain was very steep, and naturally quite bad enough; but on this occasion it was rendered unusually dangerous by the loose wet snow which covered the smooth surfaces of rock, and filled up all the interstices between the broken fragments of cliff, hiding the untrustworthy places, deceiving the foot and eye, glossing over little chasms, giving a false appearance of stability to tottering stones, and converting a difficult but feasible hill-side into a most dangerous and well-nigh impracticable slope.

We crawled along one behind the other, forming when necessary a chain with our guns, the leading man taking every advantage of the stunted pines and jutting crags of rock, and making each foothold good and secure before venturing on another. If he faltered or slipped, the next man held him up—very little support is sufficient to restore the balance—and he tried again until he got his foot on to some little ledge, or jammed into some crevice that would support his weight, and the others then followed, treading carefully in his footsteps. Thus we toiled on painfully and slowly, our feet (which were protected only by wet and flabby moccasins) pinched and sore with being jammed in between loose stones; our bones aching from repeated falls; wet to the skin with the thick drizzle, half rain and half snow; until tired and in very bad temper we were obliged to abandon the pursuit, and descending to the creek followed it up to camp.

I awoke tolerably refreshed, though very stiff and sore about the legs, and, by way of variety, went out all by myself, and hunted over and across the Divide, and down the plain on the other side nearly up to the West Madison River. It was a fine day for a wonder, and the sun, bright and warm, shone beautifully through the dripping foliage, diffusing a most grateful glow through my aching limbs, and reviving my drooping spirits. The country about there is very pretty, and at some seasons of the year must be full of game, for the little prairies and woodland glades, the slopes of the foot-hills, and the bare ridges jutting out from the mountains like promontories into a sea of forest, were covered and intersected in all directions with the paths and trails of mountain buffalo, wapiti, and deer. The signs of bear also were very numerous.

Near the foot of the mountains are two picturesque little lakes; and several streams—confluents of the West Madison—wander sparkling in the sunshine through meadows and parks dotted with stately spruce and firs, or plunge into the dark recesses of the forest. All around rose in endless billows a great surging mass of peaks—unnamed, unknown, untrodden—tiresome in their lack of distinctive character, all very similar in general appearance and shape, with the exception of one very remarkable flat-topped mountain in the distance which reared itself above the general level of the range. It is said to be quite inaccessible, and this allegation seems likely to be true, for the side exposed to my view was entirely surrounded by a sheer wall of cliff.

But, though pretty scenery and fine weather partially repaid me for my exertions, I was disappointed at the results of my walk; for, as is very often the case, though indications were abundant, they were all old, and not a single living thing did I see all day long. I smelt a band of sheep, it is true, so distinctly that they could not have left the ground very long; but their trail led over some very rocky ground, across which it was impossible to follow it; and, though I searched very diligently, I failed to find the quarry.

Bear signs were so very abundant, and the tracks of one or two animals were so fresh, that I looked forward with a good deal of anxiety and some trepidation to an interview with Bruin; but it was not to be, and—as usual —I returned home with a whole skin, empty hands, a loaded rifle, and a clean knife.

I became so wearied and discontented with this continual bad luck that at our council fire that night I formally abdicated all right to command. It was evident that I had made bad medicine, and that no good fortune would attend my efforts; so I handed full control over to Jack, and under his leadership we returned next day to our first camp; and in the evening, acting on his suggestion, I rode on to our permanent camp below, and from there into Boteler's Ranch, to see if there were any letters, and to ask for news of Wynne.

As I rode I had the pleasure of witnessing some very peculiar, thoroughly local, and quite indescribable effects of colour.

The day cleared suddenly for a short time just about sundown, and the gorgeous flaunting streamers of bright yellow and red that were suddenly shot out across a lurid sky were most wonderful to behold. If the vivid colours were transferred to canvas with a quarter of their real brilliancy, the eye would be distressed by the representation, and the artist accused of gross exaggeration and of straining after outrageous effects; but the critic would be mistaken, the fact being that nothing but actual eye-proof can reconcile one to the belief that such effects could be produced at all, much less produced with harmony, even by Nature herself.

These stormy American sunsets are startling, barbaric, even savage in their brilliancy of tone, in their profusion of colour, in their great streaks of red and broad flashes of yellow fire; startling, but never repulsive to the senses or painful to the eye. For a time the light shone most brilliantly all over the Western hemisphere, breaking through a confused mass of dazzling purple-edged clouds massed against a glowing burnished copper sky, darting out bright arrows through the rifts and rents, and striking full upon the mountain tops. But not long did this glorious effulgence last. The soul of the evening soon passed away; as the sun sank the colours fled; and the now snow-white mass of the Yellowstone range filling the centre of the valley, down which I looked as through a tube, assumed a most peculiar aspect, caused by the reflection of the cloud tints on the snow and the reflection of the snow colour on the sky. The mountains became of a ghastly, livid, greenish colour; and, as the faint rose light paled, faded slowly upwards and vanished, it really looked as though the life were ebbing away, and the dull grey death-hue spreading over the face of a dying man.

I found that Campbell had killed a couple of antelopes, and he would no doubt have killed many more, but that Maxwell, the black cook, was so fearful of bears and Indians that he would not on any condition stay in camp alone; and consequently, as the camp could not be left to take care of itself, Campbell was obliged to remain with him. Somebody at Denver had persuaded Maxwell that Indians had a special aversion to coloured gentlemen, and he firmly believed that there was not a red man in America but would travel half across the continent to get his woolly scalp. If there were no Indians about he was in dread of bears, and if there were no bears he made shift to be terrified at snakes. The state of his nervous system was a great nuisance to us, for there was no use in telling him that he must stay in camp. He simply would not do it, but would ' fork his pony,' and make for the nearest settlement or shanty if left to himself.

No intelligence of any kind awaited me at Boteler's, and early next morning I returned to our camp up the valley.

That night our animals stampeded, and came galloping by the tents, tails out, picket-ropes flying, making a tremendous clatter. We never found out what started them, though we examined the ground carefully for signs of Indians or other wild beasts. Probably the disturbing cause was a mountain lion, or puma, as it should more properly be called. It gave us a long day's work to find them again, for instead of going down the valley towards home, as any sensible beasts would have done, they turned straight up the mountains and made a short cut for Bozeman. Late the next evening Boteler discovered them miles away in the direction of that town. One of the mules we did not get for four days, and we suffered much anxiety on his account, for it sometimes happens that animals stampeding get hung up by their picket-ropes twining and knotting round trees, or the stake to which the rope is attached gets jammed in some crevice of a rock, and the unfortunate beast, if he has gone over hard ground and left no trail, perishes miserably by starvation. I need scarcely say that the mule we lost was the best of the lot, and we were much afraid that such had been his fate; but, to our no small satisfaction, he turned up eventually in good condition at Boteler's Ranch.

We spent two more very uncomfortable days in the valley—wet, cold, and badly off for food. One of the party became quite ill and unable to work from constant cold and exposure; and indeed the weather was too coarse and the state of the ground too treacherous and dangerous to allow of any of us hunting with comfort, safety, or even a moderate chance of success.

The last evening was an exceptionally stormy one. The rain poured down in torrents; the wind blew fiercely; and it was with difficulty that we could keep our huge camp-fire burning. Great roots of fir trees, and knots and logs of pitch pine we heaped on, and made at last a regular bonfire of it; but it was of little service to us, for the gusts of wind eddying round the tree-stems drove the smoke and ashes in our faces and forced us to fall back as we crowded round the flame in a vain attempt to keep ourselves warm. There are some people in the world who always get the smoke in their faces, even in fine weather, on whichever side of the fire they sit, and whichever way the wind blows. Others, again, seem to have made some compact or arrangement with the Spirit of the Flame, for when they sit down to toast themselves the smoke always curls gracefully in the opposite direction, or ascends straight up to heaven. It is said that, in consequence of the murder of Thomas à Becket, 'the Traceys have always the wind in their faces;' and perhaps it is as a punishment for some former sins or crimes, that the smoke pursues some of us with such diabolical persistence. But on this occasion we were all in the same fix; equal sinners we appeared to be; and if we wished to be warm we were obliged to submit to being fumigated and scorched also.

The Indians say that white men are fools, and don't know how to keep themselves warm—building such fires that they cannot get near them. The first assertion undoubtedly is frequently true; and there is much sense, I allow, in the whole remark. Your red man kindles a few sticks, and crouches over them, covering the little flame with his blanket, and by that means conveys to himself, I daresay, more caloric than the white man can do by alternately scorching and freezing before the shifting, roaring flame of a fire large enough to roast an elephant. Yet there is comfort in the *appearance* of a big bright flame, and much may be said for both methods. On the evening in question, however, neither big fire nor little fire, neither white man's plan nor red man's plan, would have availed to keep us shivering wretches warm. I shall not very quickly forget that afternoon and night. How snug the recollection of it makes me by contrast feel as I pile a fresh log on the fire at home, stretch out my slippered feet in post-prandial ease, warm my hands and toast my shins at the cheerful blaze, and convey hot liquid comfort to the inner man, or as I turn round in

bed, comfortable, warm and cosy, and listen half asleep —only just awake enough to realise how comfortable one is—to the driving of the rain and wind, and thank my stars that I am not out in it! Kingsley, Jack, and I had been wandering disconsolately about the sloppy valley all day long, sitting down violently and unexpectedly on the slippery wet grass, our feet flying from under us on the smooth rounded surfaces of the fallen tree-trunks, dislocating our bones and our tempers by many and violent falls. About an hour before dark, and about 100 yards from camp, we parted from Kingsley, who persevered in the pursuit of game with a persistency worthy of better results, and returned to our fire. A thick fog was rising from the inundated marshy borders of the creek, and, gradually rolling up the valley, filled it with dense white vapour, rendering obscure and indistinct all our well-known landmarks, such as isolated clumps, solitary trees, bare cliffs, or jutting headlands. We found camp easily enough, but the Doctor, who had wandered on some distance, came very near being lost.

When Jack and I got in we found camp in a sorry plight, everything soaked through—tents, bedding, and all, and our prospects for the night looked anything but cheerful; but by extending the hide of the wapiti stag between four trees, and hauling it out taut with ropes, we managed to make a tolerable shelter; and, taking from out of our *cache* some dry birch bark and splinters of fat pine, we lit a huge fire, and sat down to make some tea for supper. About dusk we heard a shot, and visions of fresh venison steaks floated before our eyes. About half an hour passed, but no venison and no Kingsley appeared, and then we heard another shot, and two or three minutes afterwards yet another.

By this time it was getting quite dark, and we were

puzzled to know what Kingsley could be firing at—unless, indeed, he was treed by a bear. After a short interval we heard the sound of his rifle again, evidently further off, and then it suddenly occurred to us that he was lost and making signals. We fired our rifles, and whooped, and yelled, and shouted, but all to no purpose. The sound of his rifle became fainter and fainter;—he was going in the wrong direction.

To be left out on such a night might cost a man his life, for it would have been hard for even an old experienced mountain man to have found material dry enough to make a fire; so Jack and Boteler started out into the blackness of the night and the thick fog to look for him, leaving me behind to heap logs on the fire, and occasionally emit a dismal yell to keep them acquainted with the whereabouts of camp.

For some time I could hear the responsive shouts of the searchers, but after awhile they ceased, and nothing broke the horrid silence except the noises of the night and of the storm.

The heavy raindrops pattered incessantly on the elk-hide; the water trickled and splashed, and gurgled down the hill-side in a thousand muddy rills and miniature cascades. The night was very dark, but not so black but that I could dimly see white ghost-like shreds of vapour and great indistinct rolling masses of fog driving up the valley in the gale. The wind rumbled in the caverns of the cliffs, shrieked and whistled shrilly among the dead pine-trees, and fiercely shook the frail shelter overhead, dashing the raindrops in my face. Every now and then the fire would burn up bright, casting a fitful gleam out into the damp darkness, and lighting up the bare jaws and white skulls of the two elk-heads, which seemed to grin derisively at me out of the gloom; and then, quenched by the hissing rain, it would sink down into a dull red glow. My dog moved uneasily about, now pressing close up against me, shivering with cold and fear, nestling up to me for protection, and looking into my face for that comfort which I had not in me to give him—now starting to his feet, whimpering, and scared when some great gust smote the pine-tree overhead, angrily seized and rattled the elk-hide, and scooping up the firebrands tossed them in the air. The tall firs bowed like bulrushes before the storm, swaying to and fro, bending their lofty heads like bows and flinging them up again erect, smiting their great boughs together in agony, groaning and complaining, yet fiercely fighting with the tempest. At intervals, when the gale paused for a moment as it were to gather strength, its shrill shrieking subdued to a dismal groan, there was occasionally heard with startling distinctness, through the continuous distant din and clamour of the night, a long, painfully-rending cr-r-r-rash, followed by a dull heavy thud, notifying the fall of some monarch of the woods, and making my heart quake within me as I uneasily glanced at the two tall hemlocks overhead that wrathfully ground their trunks together, and whose creaking limbs were wrestling manfully with the storm. Strange and indistinct noises would come up from the vale: rocks became detached, and thundered down the far-off crags; a sudden burst of wind would bear upon me the roar of the torrent below with such clearness that it sounded as though it were close at hand. It was an awful night, in the strictest sense of the word. The Demon of the Tempest was abroad in his anger, yelling down the valley, dashing out the water-floods with his hands, laying waste the forest, and filling with dread the hearts of man and beast and every living thing.

There was not a star or a gleam of moonlight. It was

very gruesome sitting there all alone, and I began to feel, like David, 'horribly afraid.' I do not know how long I was alone; probably it was only for a short time—a couple of hours or so, at most—bnt the minutes were as hours to me. Most dismal was my condition; and I could not even resort to the Dutch expedient for importing courage, to supply my natural allowance of that quality which had quickly oozed out of my cold finger-tips. I had poured into a tin pannikin the last drain of whisky from the keg, and had placed it carefully to settle. I knew that Kingsley would really want it, so I could not seek consolation in that way. I could not find even a piece of dry tobacco wherewith to comfort myself; I began to feel very wretched indeed; and it was truly a great relief when I heard the shouts of the returning party.

They brought in the lost man pretty well exhausted, for he had been out a long time exposed to the weather, had walked a great distance, and had fallen about terribly in the darkness. He had tried in vain to make a fire, and was wandering about without an idea of the direction in which camp lay. He was indeed in real need of a stimulant, and when, in answer to his inquiring glance at the keg, I said that there was half a pannikin full, his face beamed with a cheerful smile. But alas! a catastrophe had occurred. A gust of wind or a falling branch had over-thrown all my arrangements, and when I arose to give him the pannikin, behold, it was bottom upwards and dry!

If it be true that 'the effectual fervent prayer of a righteous man availeth much,' I suppose that it must be equally true that the effectual fervent swear of a despairing mortal will penetrate far. If so, I know that a responsive echo must have been awakened somewhere by the vehemence of the monosyllable that greeted this discovery.

So we had to make the best of matters, and put up with hot, strong, green tea, which consoled us a little; but we spent a very uncomfortable night, sitting by the fire as long as we could keep our eyes open—four unhappy human beings in their wet shirt-tails and damp blankets, trying to dry their socks, underclothes, and trousers, and to get a little warmth into their chilled limbs.

It was on this occasion that the following verses were, with many others, produced by a short-sighted member of the party, and dolefully sung to the tune of 'Ten thousand miles away' :—

> I am wet, and cold, and hungry, and there's nothing here to eat ;
> Take up your gun, for goodness sake, and bring in some fresh meat;
> Oh ! I'm hungry and I'm thirsty, I'm very cold and wet;
> Take up your gun or rifle, and get up, Sir, and get.[1]
>
> Kill a cabre or an antelope, a rocky mountain sheep,
> A wapiti or bounding elk, the meat to dry and keep ;
> A white-tail or a black-tail, a partridge or a hare,
> Or a squirrel or a gopher, or a badger or a bear.
>
> It snows, it blows, and rains, and then begins to freeze ;
> All sodden is the ground, and all dripping are the trees ;
> The hill-tops are all shrouded in impenetrable fog,
> The creeks they are all flooded, and the valley is a bog.
>
> I have wet breeches on my legs, a wet shirt on my back,
> I've lost my hat and spectacles, and busted my shupack; [2]
> The horses have stampeded, the mules are gone astray,
> My own dog snarled and bit me, and then he ran away.
>
> My tent is full of holes, and my bedding it is damp ;
> The ground is quite a puddle, it's a miserable camp ;
> The fires won't burn, but are betwixt and likewise are between,
> Half flame, half smoke are they, for the wood is much too green.

---

[1] To get up and get signifies, in Western parlance, to set off about your business without delay.

[2] *Shupack*, a stout moccasin made of cowhide.

Our tea is now expended, the salt is left behind ;
The sugar's a dissolving view, but that I do not mind ;
And the cook has burned the coffee, unmitigated scamp,
And the whisky keg is dry too—it's the driest thing in camp.

I could not find a match when I thought to take a smoke,
And when I got my pipe, behold it was broke ;
My knife was very blunt, and we'd lost the whetstone,
Yet, in cutting some tobacco, cut my finger to the bone.

I wandered down the valley and slipped upon the ice,
I tried to climb the mountain, but fell down a precipice ;
The ground it was so slippery, I could not stand or walk,
And my gun missed fire at the end of the stalk.

I cannot find a mountain sheep, I cannot find a bear,
Or a deer, or a gopher, or a badger, or a hare ;
Corn bread and trout our diet still must be,
With no pepper, sugar, salt, and no whisky and no tea.

Oh, Montana, it is beautiful ! the Yellowstone is fine,
Game it is abundant, leastways the sign ;
But when living in the wilderness, and dwelling in a tent,
On its climate and its weather I don't pan out[1] a cent.

The next morning we four unhappy individuals,
stiff-jointed and rheumatic, blear-eyed, unshaven, dirty
and unkempt, assembled round the fire, and without much
discussion arrived at the conclusion that this sort of thing
was all very well for a picnic party, but that a little
went a long way, and that we had enjoyed quite enough
of it. The 'Greenwood Tree,' we thought, *sounded*
nice, but a warm dry tent appeared to us to be the right

---

[1] To 'pan out' is a most eloquent expression derived from the vocabulary
of gulch mining or gold washing. The quantity of gold dust remaining at
the bottom of the pan or shovel is what you 'pan out' of the particular
stream ; and so the value you get out of an individual, occupation or thing
is what you 'pan out' of it. To say that a man 'pans out badly' or 'does
not pan out a cent' implies that, having sifted him thoroughly and with
the greatest care, you find there is no residue of sterling metal in him at all ;
nothing but valueless dirt.

sort of place in a September storm; and so, soon after daybreak, we packed up, left our elk-heads where they were, and moved down to permanent camp.

MEXICAN SADDLE

CHAPTER V.

THE HOT SPRINGS ON GARDINER'S RIVER.

WE arrived early and lay in camp all day, weathering out as best we could the fearful storm that still continued. At night one of the tents blew down, nearly frightening Tweed into fits. Jack and I tried with all the calmness of desperation to think that the wet clammy folds of the canvas were rather pleasant and warm, but we could not keep up the delusion, and had to drag ourselves out, and in the face of the wind and rain set up the tent again. It is intolerable to have one's tent blown down on a drenching night, as I am sure will be allowed by any one who has had experience of that calamity ; and it put the finishing touch to our misery. But, as often happens, matters began to mend soon after they were at their worst.

Towards morning a few stars began to peep through long ragged rifts in the clouds, and the day broke finer than it had done for weeks. The dawn revealed detached masses of vapour driven in by the fierce rays of the attacking sun, like outlying pickets of the storm, rolling up the wet shining sides of the mountains, and concentrating their forces in ominous columns about the higher peaks. As the light grew brighter, the leaden sky broke up, showing two or three patches of·blue ; and, as the sun rose higher, the fog melted and, curling up from the low grounds, floated round the summits of the range. The clouds, losing their torn, tormented appearance, became softer and more rounded in outline. Everything betokened fair weather; and in somewhat better spirits we broke camp, and marched that day to the Mammoth Hot Springs on Gardiner's River.

The road passes through the second cañon, which, as I have before stated, has been cut by the river through metamorphic rock, and, after traversing two or three miles over rough broken spurs of the foot hills, descends and pursues a level course along what may be termed the second valley of the Yellowstone till it reaches the mouth of Gardiner's River. Here the Yellowstone takes a sudden turn to the east, entering a great gorge in the mountains which forms the third cañon; and the trail turning to the west follows the direction of Gardiner's River, and does not again strike the waters of the Yellowstone until just before its entrance into the Grand cañon.

We saw nothing very worthy of notice on this day's march, the most important object being 'Cinnabar Mountain,' apparently so called because there is no cinnabar there. A very peculiar broad band of red clay that traverses the mountain was at one time thought to be composed of that mineral, and to this circumstance I suppose it owes its name. It is a fine ridge of about a mile in length, rising some 2,000 feet above the river, but is remarkable only on account of the rich colour of these clay bands, and for two very noticeable trap dykes which traverse it from top to bottom. Of these the one furthest to the north is composed of greyish-coloured quartz, while the other is of greenish trachyte or basalt. These walls are in some places 200 feet high, and about 50 feet in thickness. The space between them is about 150 feet broad at the top, and tolerably smooth throughout; but the sides slightly diverge, and the slide would be about double that width at the bottom. This is locally called the Devil's Slide.

Before proceeding any further, I should like to clear the ground a little, and try to convey to the reader in a few words a sort of general notion of the geography and geology of that portion of the Rocky Mountains with which we have to deal. It must be essentially a vague impression, for I am neither a geographer nor a geologist; and the country is so vast, so little known and understood, and has been up to the present time so poorly mapped, that it is impossible even for one who has visited it not to feel somewhat 'mixed' on the subject. But I will endeavour to make myself clear.

I will therefore try briefly to sketch out a sort of skeleton of this part of the continent, showing the principal mountain ranges and river systems, and merely indicating the great depressions, valleys, and plains. In taking a mental survey of the Western portions of the United States, the first operation is to disabuse one's mind of the notion that the words ' Rocky Mountains ' are used to designate any particular chain. I know of no belt, on the continent, so called by the natives. An inhabitant of Denver speaks of the great barrier that raises itself above the Colorado prairies as ' the Range ' or ' the Snowy Range '; while in Wyoming your inquiry as to the Rocky Mountains would be answered by pointing to the great bulk of Laramie Peak and the lesser summits of the Black Hills. The name ' Rocky Mountains,' then, is applicable, though it is not applied, to numerous ranges having various local names; and it indicates generally all that vast and broad upheaval which traverses the entire length of the continent from north to south.

The Rocky Mountains, if they be measured from their eastern flank in Colorado to the western slopes of the Sierra Nevada in California, would be found to occupy an area of about 700 miles in breadth. In some places they contract to about half that width, and they extend the whole length of the continent, but by no means continuously. On the contrary, like waves of the sea, which, though they appear to be very persistent, yet are in reality constantly subsiding and fresh ones arising in their place, the mountain ranges which we are about to examine continually sink into the plain, being succeeded by other belts, distinct, but having the same trend, direction, and characteristics.

But we shall not need to take such a greatly extended view. It will answer our purpose better to glance over the country lying between the northern borders of New Mexico and the boundary line dividing the British possessions from the United States, and between the eastern flanks of the range in Colorado and the Wahsatch Mountains to the west.

This great elevated portion of the globe which divides the solid ocean of the eastern prairies from the liquid plains of the Pacific, and which longitudinally splits the continent in two, contains on a great scale three distinct features in physical geography—high plains or prairies, depressed basins, and river valleys. The plains and depressions seem to occur promiscuously, without method or order; but the valleys are arranged systematically and according to law. If small, they have a direction nearly north and south; and, if large, a general tendency to run east and west. The reason of this is obvious. The ranges all trend more or less due north and south, but the waters they contain must find an outlet somewhere at right angles to this direction. The smaller streams therefore are compelled to follow the course of the mountains, gradually converging until they gather suffi cient strength to burst through the barriers and carve an outlet towards either sea. Hence it follows that, while the great watersheds strike north and south, all the smaller divides have their longer axes lying east and west.

The prairie gradually rises from the Missouri River, where it is less than 1,000 feet above the sea, till it attains, where it abuts upon the Colorado range, a height of from about 5,000 to 6,000 feet above the sea-level. Buried to their middles in this deep deposit the mountains stand, heaving out their broad shoulders and thrusting up their heads to an additional height of some 6,000 or 8,000 feet ; forming a barrier that from a distance looks im- passable ; but it is not so, for in some places the prairie billow has overlapped the range, and flowing completely over depressed portions of it, has poured itself down the other side in an unbroken wave.

The principal plateaus are the flat country lying near the head of the Missouri, between the Maria and Milk Rivers ; Laramie Plains and North Park, taken together, as one plateau ; Middle, South, and St. Louis Parks, and the upper valley of the Arkansas.

The depressions are the great basin of Salt Lake and the Colorado Desert.

Among the river systems may be mentioned the val- leys of the Upper Missouri, of the Yellowstone, the Green Snake, Bear, and Grand Rivers.

To speak in very general terms, the summits of the mountains are granite or limestone, usually the former, protruding through sandstones which are overlaid with drift. In some places the sandstones are tilted completely on their edges, and, running in long lines across the foot-hills or breaking in detached masses through the super-incumbent drift, are very noticeable on account of their bright colouring, which vividly contrasts with the dark-green foliage of the stunted oaks.

Perhaps the most remarkable feature, geologically, is the vast extent of the drift formation.

After that the region I am speaking of had been through infinite ages formed in the depths of ocean and upheaved, and after that the cycles during which tropical forests flourished, died, decayed, and formed the coal-measures, had unrolled their interminable length, it must have passed through a long geological period submerged, if not entirely, at any rate with the exception only of the highest peaks. During this period Nature was fearfully convulsed. Volcanoes blazed and smoked, casting out the molten entrails of the earth, pouring floods of lava into the hissing evaporating seas, levelling the hollows of the ocean-beds, smothering the inequalities in the lake floors, and filling up the valleys with a soft covering of sifting ashes.

Evaporated from the higher mountain masses, the waters during this fiery epoch must have subsided and grouped themselves into more modern seas. The present great watersheds and the principal geographical features must then have been roughly hewn out while the land was all covered with ice, rending and tearing slowly but irresistibly down the valleys and grinding up the surface of the rocks. Great boulders, large deposits of drift, gravel and marls, vast accumulations of fine sand, clay, and loess—the result of all this grinding and disintegra-tion—must have been left stranded near the summits, cast in huge heaps by the mighty hands of swirling ocean currents on the slopes of the mountains, spread out over the bases and flanks of the hills by the rushing floods of mountain torrents, and sprinkled gently through the quiet depths of placid lakes.

At 10,000 or 12,000 feet above the sea large boulders may now be seen, and the mountain-sides and foot-hills are covered with drift becoming smaller as you descend. The further you go from the mountains the finer becomes the deposit. It may be said that the greater portion of the country from the Missouri to the Rockies is composed of this drift. Occasionally large tracts of fine gravel and coarse sand will be met with in isolated places, as if these heavy materials had been swept far out into the ocean by the current of a great river, and precipitated at some bend or eddy. All the plains and parks in the mountains are made of it, and it covers the greater portion of Minnesota, Dakotah, and the prairies, 'bad lands,' and deserts of Montana, Wyoming, and Colorado. The celebrated plateau of the Côteau du Prairie is a huge gravel ridge. In Nebraska occurs an extensive deposit of fine sand, in which are found the remains of multitudes of extinct animals; and the unstratified clays or loess extend to the lower Missouri, possibly even to the Gulf.

The district under consideration is contained in the State of Colorado and the territories of Utah, Wyoming, and Montana, and is approximately bounded by the 105th and 113th meridians on the east and west, and to the north and south by the 37th and 49th parallels.

The Great or Salt Lake Basin is only partially situated within these limits. It is a vast hollow contained by the Wahsatch, the Sierra Nevada, and their offshoots. Its waters have no outlet whatever, and have been and probably still are receding, owing to the great excess of evaporation over condensation. It is remarkable that the points of greatest depression are placed, not in the centre, but near the edges. The Colorado Desert forming the upper portion of the Green River system ought, perhaps, not to be called a 'basin,' for it is drained by Green River, which bursts through the Sierra Escalante, an eastern arm of the Uintah range. The greater portion of it is a broad, irregular, treeless depression, bounded to the north and south by the Wind River and the Uintah Mountains, to the east by an imperceptible divide, and to the west by the Wahsatch. The valley of the Upper Arkansas partakes so thoroughly of the character of a park that it should be placed in that category. If it be possible to assign any definite limits to a district when its borders are broken, detached, and fragmentary, I should say it was bounded by the Wet Mountains, which are merely a continuation of the main range extending south of Pike's Peak, and by the Sangre de Christo and Raton Mountains.

Laramie Plains are girdled to the north and east by the black hills of Wyoming, which almost unite with the Colorado range, leaving, however, a broad sloping gap through which the Union Pacific railway passes. These plains form a sort of elevated eastern bay of the great Green River Basin, and they cannot be said to be actually divided from the North Park.

The North, Middle, South, and St. Louis Parks are the four largest among numberless level depressions or basins which lie nestled among the mountains, and by their singular beauty make Colorado the most picturesque State of the Union. They are properly described as 'Parks,' for I know of no other word that so well conveys an idea of their peculiar beauty and characteristics.

Of all sizes, from a few acres to many hundreds of square miles in extent, they lie, fertile, clothed with grass, decked with flowers, sparkling with silver streams, lovely oases amid the savage barrenness of the mountains. They are not only beautiful but useful, and answer a very wise purpose in the economy of Nature, for, acting like huge reservoirs, they collect the thousand rills that steal out from under the everlasting snows, and uniting them in one perennial stream launch it out into the world to bear fertility to the arid plains below.

These four principal parks are entirely cut off from each other by lofty ranges.

This great district is partially bisected by Green River, and Nature has also divided it into quarters. Traversing it longitudinally, runs the Great Divide of the continent, that sheds the waters either to the Pacific or to the Atlantic. As might be expected, it follows generally the main range and has a north-west and south-east direction, but occasionally it leaves the mountains, and its course, curving and bending to the east or west, is determined by an almost imperceptible ridge. Cutting this divide nearly at right angles runs a transverse 'height of land,' scarcely noticeable above the general level, which, starting from the north-west corner of Nebraska, curves northward round the Green River Basin, and enters the south-west angle of Nevada. Thus four minor watersheds are formed, sloping to the north-east, south-east, south-west, and north-west; the two former discharging their waters into the Atlantic through the Missouri and its confluent the Platte, while the Columbia and Colorado carry the drainage of the latter to the Pacific.

The principal mountain chains are, first and most important, the Wahsatch range on the west, which for about 400 miles forms the rim of the Salt Lake Basin. With several breaks and flexures this range continues northward under the names of the Wind River Mountains, the Tétons, Salmon River, Big Hole, Bitter Root, and Flat

Head Mountains. East of these chains, and in about the same latitude, rise those detached belts that divide the head waters of the Missouri, namely, the Jefferson, Madison, and Gallatin rivers, from each other and from the Yellowstone. These belts connect with the Big Horn Mountains, which, continuing south with many breaks of continuity, join the Black Hills; and these last strike out towards and almost touch the main range in Colorado.

By the belts above enumerated this region is girt about, and the contained area is, with the exception of the plains, valleys, parks, and basins already mentioned, a great confused mass of mountains and peaks. The northern half is filled up by the Yellowstone, Gallatin, and Jefferson Mountains; by the Tétons, the Wind River, Big Horn, Rattlesnake, Sweetwater, Medicin Bow ranges, and other spurs and offshoots. The elevations are lower, and the country in general more open than in the southern division, where occurs the most densely packed and heaviest mass of mountains in the United States. A little south of the lateral divide, the Uintah range, a great offset from the Wahsatch, strikes out due east or at right angles to the trend of the parent chain. Its eastern extremity goes by the name of the Sierra Escalante, and between this extremity and the Uintahs, Green River finds a channel. Near the southern limits of the territory in question the Raton Mountains, giving birth to the Cimaron and Purgatory Rivers, are stretched out towards the east like an arm from the main range. Between these two principal chains are crowded and pressed together a vast multitude of independent belts and spurs. Their general direction is north and south, but occasional offshoots strike out at various angles from this line.

The nomenclature of these various chains is derived

from a mixture of many languages. In the south the melodious Spanish or Indian names have been retained, and we find the Sierra San Miguel, Sierra de los Pinos, Uncompagre Mountains, Sierra San Juan, and the like. Further north the less tuneful Anglo-Saxon tongue prevails, and the chains and peaks either are unnamed, or are called *the* range, the snowy range, *the* divide, or somebody or other's peak.

If the rivers rising in this region be followed up in the map, it will be seen at once that the sources are grouped into three principal centres, points of division, or watersheds ; one situated in the north-eastern quarter, the other two in the south-eastern. The most southern and least important centre is just south-west of the South Park in Colorado. From it radiate several streams, the chief among which are the Rio Grande, the Grand, the Arkansas, and the South Platte. In the chain forming the barrier between North and Middle Parks lies the second apex, a very important watershed, inferior to only one, or at any rate two, on the continent. Around it are the sources of the Blue River, White River, Bear River, the North Platte, and several branches of the South Platte.

But the culminating point of the whole system—the Great Divide of the United States, the nucleus of the continent—lies in the north-eastern quarter, in the girdle that encircles the district containing the Geyser Basins and the Yellowstone Lake. I have previously enumerated the rivers that have their sources there, and hope a little further on to revert to them ; there is no occasion to mention them now.

Having thus in a very few words endeavoured to portray the general features of this portion of the Rocky Mountains, and to dispel the mists of ignorance which, because in my own mind they shrouded the peaks of that mysterious range, I (probably erroneously) consider must also exist in the minds of others, I will ask my readers to turn their attention more particularly to the north-eastern section of the region I have attempted to describe, for to that quarter our wanderings will for the future be confined.

Let us take, as an eastern anticlinal line, a continuation of the Big Horn Mountains, running north and south, forming the divide between the Yellowstone and the Gallatin, crossing the former river at the lower cañon, and extending as far as the 'Gate of the Mountains' just below the Grand Falls of the Missouri. This is the Yellowstone range, and its summits are composed principally of limestone.

Although detached mountains and chains occur on both sides of the Yellowstone River as far as below Tongue River, yet it may be said, speaking in general terms, that the cretaceous and tertiary deposits of the plains reach clear up to the eastern flank of this chain. Whether a true western anticlinal exists I do not know. I should look for it in the Big Hole and other mountains west of the Madison extensions of the Wind River and Téton Range. The synclinal of this valley would run in a south-east direction from the 'Gate of the Mountains,' through the place of meeting of the three forks of the Missouri, between the West Gallatin and Madison, and through the comparatively level depression containing the Yellowstone lake and the basins and valleys of the three forks, and extending indefinitely towards the south.

The principal secondary chains embraced in this area with which we have to deal are the Madison and West Gallatin Mountains, and the range on the west of Yellowstone River. These have a tendency to spread out towards the south, and converge towards the junction of the three forks. Through all these belts torrents have cut deep gorges at right angles to their axis of upheaval, exposing fine vertical sections of the material composing them.

The Yellowstone and Gallatin Mountains, which are part of one and the same range, show, as before mentioned, a good deal of sedimentary rock. Peaks of very hard limestone tower from 1,000 to 1,500 feet above the silurian deposits, which rest upon quartz, mica-schists, and gneiss. The variety in texture, form, and colour of the meta-morphosed rocks is infinite. The West Gallatin Mountains, and those on the west bank of the Yellowstone, are largely composed of conglomerates and breccia, and the peaks are of volcanic origin. These ranges, as also that of the Madison, sink down towards their point of union at the three forks, and in that vicinity are largely made up of lake deposits and silurian shales. As you ascend the rivers the metamorphic rocks and carboniferous lime-stones become frequent. No doubt all these valleys have been scooped by the action of the water and weather out of originally homogeneous masses, for the signs of erosion and the effects of ice are universal; and there is abundant evidence that the entire country must have been under water, and subjected to the action of icebergs and glaciers for a very long period of time. Cretaceous and calca-reous strata of considerable thickness are overlaid by vast deposits of clays, and every variety of tertiary formation; and the ranges are everywhere begirt with a fringe of foot-hills formed of drift, varying in size from large boulders to fine gravel.

Through all this region volcanic action has been ex-ceedingly vigorous. The effect of fire upon the rocks is plainly visible and widely spread. All the stratified rocks, clays, and slates have been burned, baked, and changed into various forms and substances. Whole mountains of volcanic breccia exist. Inequalities of the surface have been smothered and covered under many hundred feet of ashes. Trachyte protrusions are numerous; trap dykes are common; and several great overflows of basalt have at different times occurred.

The last feeble evidence of this gigantic force, the expiring effort of the power that once shook the round world to its very foundations, is to be seen in the hot springs on Gardiner's River and on many other streams, and in the strange phenomena of the Geyser Basins, to which we will now proceed.

Gardiner's River heads in three forks among some bold basaltic peaks. At the sources of the western branch is situated—at least, so it is said—a remarkable group of springs. Below the forks the river has a course of about twenty miles through a formation generally composed of calcareous and tertiary strata, which it has cut through and exposed to a depth of 1,200 feet. From these beds the vast quantities of lime deposited by the hot springs have, I presume, been derived. In these cretaceous strata occur occasionally intruding outflows of basalt. The lower portion of the valley is covered and littered with volcanic débris, lying on and mixed with the clays, and the surface resembles the slag-heaps round old furnaces and smelting works. In two or three places occur small deep ponds, looking like old volcanic craters, filled now to the brim with water.

Over this dismal country the road passes for about three miles with a gradual ascent ; and, after traversing a small level grass-covered plateau, it descends suddenly by a steep pitch, crosses a small, perfectly level, and snow-white plain, and lands you at the door of the little shanty which is dignified by the name of hotel. This plateau is about 1,000 feet above Gardiner's River.

Standing outside the hotel door, and facing the river, the traveller will see before him this white plain, abutting on the left upon the grassy slopes of the hills, bordering to the right on a remarkable mound of about 200 feet in height, composed entirely of calcareous deposit from the springs. On the plateau are the remains of two geysers, one of which must have been rather small, as the cone remaining is only three or four feet in height. It is called, from its appearance, ' The Bee Hive.' The other certainly was once gigantic, for it has left a cone about fifty feet high, by twenty in diameter at the base. Professor Hayden calls this the Liberty Cap; locally it goes by another name. On the right edge of the plain are several springs of water of various temperatures, which have been artificially conducted into three rude huts answering the purpose of bathing-houses. They are neither elegant nor luxurious, consisting only of a few rough boards temporarily nailed together. The water flows into deep wooden troughs formed of rough deals, which the deposit from the water has covered with a white enamel, perfectly smooth and pleasant to the touch, thus converting these makeshift troughs into marble basins. The temperature of the water varies irregularly at different times throughout the day, which is very annoying, for it is impossible to tell exactly when the water will be warm enough and not too warm to bathe in. It retains its heat, too, in the most marvellous manner, for I have on several occasions, finding the water too hot, plugged up the orifice by which it flowed into the bath and stopped the supply; but after waiting half an hour the water in the bath showed no appreciable difference of temperature.

The water is not unpleasant to the taste, and the

bathers who flock to these springs to cure their rheumatic
affections think it necessary to imbibe great quantities. I
swallowed a good deal of it myself, but could not notice
that it had any effect whatever. If it deposits in a man's
interior as it does in the baths, it would be invaluable for
supplying a new coating to the worn-out integument of an
ill-used stomach; and if only two eminent physicians, one
on either side of the 'Herring Pond,' would make discovery of this fact, the fortunes of Montana and Wyoming
would be for ever made. It is very pleasant to the skin,
soft and mollifying in its effects; and, instead of having a
debilitating tendency, as is usually the case with very
warm baths, it seems to brace and invigorate the system.
If the reader will kindly imagine us comfortably camped
hard by the springs, ourselves in the occupation of a
deserted shanty, and our horses picketed in a small
grassy plain not far distant, we will, after breakfast, a
bath, and two or three tin pannikins of hot water, which
we must drink because it is fashionable—and we must be
fashionable even in the wilderness,—ascend the white hill
of which I have spoken, and take a survey of the country.
This elevation is about 200 feet high, and is built up in
steps or successive layers somewhat after the fashion of
an Egyptian pyramid, only the steps are generally not so
high, and the intervening ledges are much broader.
Some of the terraces are many feet in breadth; others
are quite small. In some cases they are separated by little
cliffs of six, eight, or ten feet in height; in others, again,
the steps are only an inch or two high. The top is perfectly level, and about 150 yards in diameter; on it occurs
the largest hot spring at present in activity. It consists of a
basin forty feet in length, by twenty-five feet in breadth,
and contains three centres of ebullition. The water at
the edge is only 162°; it is probable, however, that, in

those places where it appears to be boiling and bubbling very violently, it would reach boiling point, which at this height is 194°; but the principal cause of the disturbance in the water is the quantity of carbonic acid gas that is discharged. The water is exceedingly clear, clearer than anything I had ever seen before, and of a blue colour, marvellously beautiful to see. The smallest fleck of cloud floating in the sky is reflected in it, and the most minute tracery at the bottom of the pool can be distinctly seen. The little waves or undulations, radiating from the boiling spring in the centre of the basin, and refracting the sun's rays, give a shifting opalesque lustre to the rounded beads and nodules that adorn the sides and transform into varied beauty their comparatively dull hue.

From various places in the rim of this basin a moderate quantity of water flows out over the sides of the hill, forming on the steps and terraces a most beautiful series of pools, varying in depth from an inch to two or three feet. Where the slope is very gentle and the flow of the water consequently slow, these basins are minute, and are separated from each other by rims of no more than an inch or two in height, and the lace-work and bead-work ornamentation is most delicately beautiful, and almost microscopically minute. Where the stream has been rapid much larger basins have been formed, having sides six or eight feet high, over which the water has poured, forming fantastic stalactites and stalagmites. It looks as if a stream, pouring over some gigantic staircase, had been suddenly congealed. Most of the basins are oblong in shape, the curves are very graceful, and the edges scalloped. The crust, composed of a solid scum of deposit, extends over the water, getting gradually thinner and thinner, until on the very verge it is scarcely thicker than paper; and it is necessary to use caution in approaching the edge to avoid the penalty of an involuntary plunge into hot water which might repay the curiosity of a too venturesome observer. The rims are frequently bordered with round, pearl-like ornamentation, the pearls varying in size from a pin's-head to a hazel-nut. The general colour of the bottom and sides of the basins is that of rich cream, occasionally deepening into bright sulphur yellow, with streaks and patches of vivid red, as bright and clear as our brilliant modern mineral dyes ; and yet so harmonised and blended together that the general effect is by no means harsh or disagreeable. The water gradually cools as it falls from terrace to terrace, so that the bather can accommodate himself to any temperature he pleases. In the cooler pools grow quantities of very fragile hair-like vegetation, which, becoming encrusted with lime, forms a most delicate lace-like fabric, in some cases almost as fine as cobweb.

After falling down the hill the water finds its way to Gardiner's River through several channels, the largest of which is about six feet broad and two deep. The sulphur, iron, and lime in solution have formed in the bed of this stream a most beautiful mosaic-like substance. It is full of bright green confervæ, which contrast strangely but very beautifully with the reds and yellows. The lime deposited is, when fresh, perfectly and most dazzlingly white ; after awhile it gets brown and discoloured, becomes hard and dry, and gives out a hollow cavernous sound as you walk over the surface. In some of the dry pools the delicate apple-green fading into yellow of the sulphur tinge is very lovely, and the sulphur crystals are both lovely in colour and beautiful in form.

Below the level plateau the ground slopes quickly down to the river. It is composed almost entirely of old deposit. Close to the margin of the stream are several active springs much frequented by invalids. The whole area occupied by the calcareous deposit of these springs is about two square miles. It appears as if the whole mass were moving down the mountains, for it has in many cases covered the pine-trees to a depth of six or eight feet, and left them standing erect, but dead and looking very sad and dreary. On a lower level other trees are growing in the old deposit, which creates an erroneous impression that the mass of white lime is bodily descending and encroaching on the forest. On the bank of the river, and also on the sides of the slope, are many springs of various temperatures, the full particulars of which will be found in the following tables, compiled by Mr. A. C. Peale, to which is added an analysis by Dr. Endlich :—

SPRINGS AT THE LEVEL OF THE RIVER.

Time of Observation, 8.30–8.40 A.M., July 29, 1872. There was no perceptible gas given off.

No.	Size of spring	Depth	Temperature of air	Temperature of spring	Elevation above sea-level
	Inches	Inches			Feet
1	12 × 12	3	70° F.	104° F.	5750
2	30 × 30	12	70	104	5750
3	... ...	...	70	111	5750
4	24 × 24	...	70	114	5750
5	} Artificially {	...	70	112	5750
6	} enlarged {	...	70	94	5750
7		...	70	132	5750

'As we go from the river up the hill towards the main springs we meet with a large pool of hot water, about 100 feet in diameter. It is 230 feet above the level of the river, and on its edge there are several springs. Of two I took the temperatures, and found them both to be 140° F., the temperature of the air being 65° F., and the time of observation 8 A.M. A short distance farther up we came to the main mass of springs, arranged on a series of terraces at different levels. The first terrace is 528 feet above the level of the river. The principal springs are on the first ten terraces, and as we go up the valley we find that, although there were once many springs here of a most active character, at the present time they have nearly all died out. The first four or five have the hottest springs, the boiling-point at which varies from 190·5° to 200·9°.' I give the temperatures and other particulars in tabular form on the next two pages, with the intimation that the observations were all made on the 28th of July, 1872.

AN INDIAN VILLAGE.

Number	Position of Spring	Time of Observation	Size	Depth	Gas given off	Temperature of air in Fahrenheit	Temperature of spring in Fahrenheit	Elevation above the sea in feet
1	First terrace	8.40 a.m.	5 ft. × 7 ft.	6 in.	Sulphuretted hydrogen	70	150	6278
2	,,	8.40 a.m.	Fissure of 30 ft.	...	,,	70	152	6278
3	,,	8.40 a.m.	Fissure of 14 ft.	...	,,	70	160	6278
4	,,	8.40 a.m.	Fissure of 6 ft.	...	,,	70	158	6278
5	Second terrace	9.0 a.m.	20 in. × 20 in.	12 in.	,,	69	144	6304
6	,,	9.10 a.m.	15 in. × 35 in.	12 in.	,,	69	162	6304
7	,,	9.20 a.m.	40 in. × 50 in.	16 in.	,,	69	162	6304
8	Fourth terrace	9.25 a.m.	29 in. × 20 in.	36 in.	,,	72	152	6412
9	Fifth terrace	9.30 a.m.	50 in. × 60 in.	24 in.	,,	74	152	6465
10	Sixth terrace	12.30 p.m.	...	...	,,	80·5	150	6491
11	,,	12.30 p.m.	...	...	,,	80·5	148	6491
12	,,	12.30 p.m.	...	...	,,	80·5	148	6491
13	,,	12.30 p.m.	...	...	,,	80·5	142	6491
14	,,	12.30 p.m.	...	...	,,	80·5	152	6491
15	,,	12.30 p.m.	...	...	,,	80·5	148	6491
16	,,	12.30 p.m.	...	...	,,	80·5	152	6491
17	,,	12.30 p.m.	...	...	Carbonic acid	80·5	152	6491
18	Seventh terrace	10.0 a.m.	150 ft. × 70 ft.	10 ft.	Sulphuretted hydrogen	72	150	6551
19	,,	10.0 a.m.	100 ft. × 50 ft.	10 ft.	,,	72	154	6551
20	Eighth terrace	9.45 a.m.	9 ft. × 13 ft.	3 ft.	,,	72	122	6556
21	Ninth terrace	10.10 a.m.	20 in. × 2 in.	6 in.	,,	74	157	6591
22	,,	10.12 a.m.	100 ft. × 25 ft.	5 ft.	,,	74	162	6591
23	,,	10.14 a.m.	4 ft. × 7 ft.	18 in.	,,	74	162	6591
24	,,	10.14 a.m.	2 ft. × 3 ft.	3 ft.	,,	74	162	6591
25	,,	10.15 a.m.	2 ft. × 3 ft.	1 ft.	,,	74	162	6591
26	,,	10.15 a.m.	2 ft. × 3 ft.	6 in.	,,	74	120	6591
27	Tenth terrace	10.30 a.m.	2 ft. × 3 ft.	1 ft.	,,	74	162	6596
28	,,	10.30 a.m.	3 ft. × 3 ft.	6 in.	,,	74	154	6596
29	Eleventh terrace	10.35 a.m.	6 in. × 6 in.	7 in.	,,	74·5	148	6603
30	,,	10.40 a.m.	6 in. × 2 in.	6 in.	,,	74·5	150	6603

No.	Locality	Time	Orifice	Size	Depth	Gas	Air temp.	Water temp.	Elevation (ft.)
34	,,					,,	78·5	162	6681
35	,,					,,	78·5	160	6681
36	,,					,,	78·5	162	6681
37	,,					,,	78·5	160	6681
38	,,					,,	78·5	162	6681
39	,,					,,	78·5	160	6681
40	Thirteenth terrace	12.20 p.m.				,,	78	160	6681
41	,,	12.25 p.m.	Fissure of 3 ft.			,,	78	142	6758
42	,,	12.25 p.m.	Fissure of 3 ft.			,,	78	140	6758
43	,,	12.26 p.m.				,,	78	142	6758
44	,,	12.26 p.m.	Geyser-like tubes			,,	78	142	6758
45	,,	12.28 p.m.	Geyser-like tubes			,,	78	108	6758
46	,,	12.28 p.m.	Geyser-like tubes			,,	78	130	6758
47	,,	11.0 a.m.				,,	78	144	6758
48	,,	11.0 a.m.				,,	78	144	6758
49	,,	12.5 p.m.	Geyser-like tubes on mounds			,,	78	148	6758
50	,,	12.5 p.m.	Geyser-like tubes on mounds			,,	78	146	6758
51	,,	12.7 p.m.				,,	78	130	6758
52	,,	12.7 p.m.				,,	78	140	6758
53	,,	12.10 p.m.				,,	78	140	6758
54	Fourteenth terrace	11.11 a.m.		12 in. × 12 in.	8 in.	Carbonic acid	74	142	6779
55	,,	11.11 a.m.		3 in. × 4 in.	12 in.	,,	74	96	6779
56	,,	11.12 a.m.		6 in. × 6 in.	4 in.	,,	74	92	6779
57	,,	11.12 a.m.		1 ft. × 2 ft.		,,	74	108	6779
58	,,	11.13 a.m.		1 ft. × 1½ ft.	2 in.	,,	74	102	6779
59	,,	11.13 a.m.		8 ft. × 3 ft.	3 ft.	,,	74	110	6779
60	,,	11.15 a.m.		4 ft. × 3 ft.	2 ft.	Sulphuretted hydrogen	74	112	6779
61	,,	11.40 a.m.				,,	74	108	6779
62	,,	11.40 a.m.	Fissure 60 ft. long			,,	74	145	6779
63	,,	11.45 a.m.	Fissure 60 ft. long			,,	74	145	6779
64	,,	11.50 a.m.				,,	74	140	6779
65	,,	11.50 a.m.				,,	74	130	6779
66	,,		Fissure 54 ft. long			,,	74	116	6779
67	,,		Fissure 54 ft. long			,,	74	118	6779

The elevation of the ridge just above the Fourteenth terrace is 7,035 feet.

	Per Cent.
Loss at 110° C. 1·75 } Loss at ignition, 30·35 }	32·10
Lime	57·70
Silica	3·32
Ferric Oxyd	3·62
Alumina	3·31
Magnesia	Trace
Soda[1]	Trace
	100·05

Altogether these hot springs of Gardiner's River afford a novel, beautiful, and very marvellous sight. The only other instances, that I am aware of, of a spectacle equalling or surpassing them in size, and of a similar character, exist in New Zealand, in the terraced formations of Te Tarata and Otukapuarange. These remarkable groups of springs are situated on the borders of Lake Taupo, the former being at the north-east end, while the latter is on the opposite shore, 'Te Tarata;' which being translated signifies 'Tattooed Rock,' and is thus described by Hochstetter :—

'First of all is Te Tarata at the north-east end of the lake, with its terraced marble steps projecting into the lake, the most marvellous of the Rotomahana marvels. About 80 feet above the lake, on the fern-clad slope of a hill, from which in various places hot vapours are escaping, there lies the immense boiling cauldron in a crater-like excavation, with steep, reddish sides, 30 to 40 feet high, and open only on the lake side towards the west. The basin of the spring is about 80 feet long and 60 wide, and filled to the brim with perfectly clear, transparent water, which in the snow-white incrustated basin appears

[1] By spectroscopic examination.

of a beautiful blue, like the blue turquoise. At the margin of the basin I found a temperature of 183° F., but in the middle, where the water is in a constant state of ebullition to the height of several feet, it probably reaches the boiling-point. Immense clouds of steam, reflecting the beautiful blue of the basin, curl up, generally obstructing the view of the whole surface of water; but the noise of boiling and seething is always distinctly audible. Akutina (Augustus), the native who served me as a guide, asserted that sometimes the whole mass of water is suddenly thrown out with an immense force, and that then the empty basin is open to the view to a depth of 30 feet, but that it fills again very quickly. Such eruptions are said to occur only during violent easterly gales. . . . . The reaction of the water is neutral; it has a slightly salt, but by no means unpleasant taste, and possesses in a high degree petrifying, or rather incrustating qualities. The deposit of the water is like that of the Iceland springs, silicious, not calcareous, and the silicious deposits and incrustations of the constantly overflowing water have formed on the slope of the hill a system of terraces, which, as white as if cut from marble, present an aspect which no description or illustration is able to represent. . . . . The flat spreading foot of the terraces extends far into the lake. There the terraces commence with low shelves containing shallow water basins. The farther up the higher grow the terraces; two, three, some also four and six feet high. They are formed by a number of semicircular stages, of which, however, not two are of the same height. Each of these stages has a small raised margin, from which slender stalactites are hanging down upon the lower stage; and encircles on its platform one or more basins, resplendent with the most beautiful blue water. These small water basins represent as many natural bathing basins, which the most refined luxury could not have prepared in a more splendid and commodious style. The basins can be chosen shallow or deep, large or small, and of every variety of temperature, as the basins upon the higher stages, nearer to the main basin, contain warmer water than those upon the lower ones. Some of the basins are so large and so deep that one can easily swim about in them. In ascending the steps, it is of course necessary to wade in the tepid water, which spreads beside the lower basins upon the platform of the stages, but rarely reaching above the ankle. During violent water eruptions from the main basin steaming cascades may occur; at ordinary times but very little water ripples over the terraces, and only the principal discharge on the south side forms a hot steaming fall. After reaching the highest terrace there is an extensive platform with a number of basins, five to six feet deep, their water showing a temperature of 90° to 110° F. In the middle of this platform there arises, close to the brink of the main basin, a kind of rock island about twelve feet high, decked with manuka, mosses, lycopodium, and fern. It may be visited without danger, and from it the curious traveller has a fair and full view into the blue, boiling, and steaming cauldron. Such is the famous Te Tarata. The pure white of the silicious deposit in contrast with the blue of the water, the green of the surrounding vegetation, the intense red of the bare earthwalls of the water crater, and the whirling clouds of steam,—all together presents a scene unequalled in its kind.'

Judging by this account, and by the descriptions contained in other narratives, it would appear that the Mammoth Hot Springs and Te Tarata, though differing a good deal in size, yet very closely resemble one another in many respects, the producing causes being in both cases identical. The formations are much the same in general appearance and characteristics, though, owing to an important difference in composition, they are not precisely alike in matters of detail. But the latter is certainly the more remarkable group of the two. It enjoys the privilege of being surrounded by very picturesque scenery; it has the advantage in point of size; and, thanks to the prevalence of silica in its constituent parts, it stands pre-eminent in beauty.

The deposit which during ages it has formed occupies a space about one-third larger than that covered by the sediment brought to the surface by the other spring. While the principal mound at Gardiner's River is higher than the summit of the Te Tarata terraces, yet the platform that crowns it is considerably smaller; and in the latter case the level surface of the top is occupied by several springs, the principal one of which has a huge orifice measuring 80 feet by 60, quite eclipsing in point of size the basin of the former. It is a true geyser also, and plays at rare intervals, occasionally expelling the whole mass of water contained in it. At the Mammoth Hot Springs, on the contrary, there is no sign whatever of any recent eruption. The central spring merely bubbles constantly, and the overflow of water from it is moderate, and does not vary much in the quantity at different times discharged.

That enormous geysers have at one time existed in activity on Gardiner's River, is evidenced by their remains; and I have no doubt that formerly the central fountain on the summit of the white hill was a spouting geyser of the first class. Geysers are very provident. From the moment of their birth they commence to build up their own tombs; and, as the specimen in question at present shows signs of great exhaustion, I expect that the days of its hot youth are over ; that its life's work is nearly done ; and that before long, geologically speaking, it will have closed up altogether and have joined the ranks of its companions already dead and buried.

From the signs of past activity and the evidence of present want of energy, and from the fact that a great portion of the deposit on Gardiner's River has decomposed and crumbled away, I should surmise, after making due allowance for the more perishable nature of the secretion, that the system of Te Tarata is the more recent of the two. The peculiarities of both groups are similar in character and description, but they are most strongly marked at Te Tarata, where the steps and terraces are broader, more perfectly formed, and more regular in shape, and where the pools are deeper and larger. In strangeness and variety of colouring, however, Gardiner's River bears off the palm. But the New Zealand group must be by far the more picturesque. Its superior attractions are to be attributed partly to the pleasing effect produced by the terraces descending into and extending under the waters of the lake, and partly also to the verdure and the beauty of the surrounding scenery ; but principally they are owing to the fact that the deposit contains silica very largely in excess of any other material. The consequence of this is that, whereas at the Mammoth Hot Springs the deposit, which is principally composed of lime, is soft and crumbly, and has in many places decayed and turned brown, presenting a somewhat dirty, ragged, and used-up appearance, at Te Tarata the formation is as beautifully white and undefiled as Carrara marble, and is hard and brittle, breaking into clean lines of fracture like porcelain. This quality must greatly enhance the beauties of the place.

Otukapuarange must be exceedingly lovely. It also appears to have originated later in the world's history than its American rival, and perhaps on that account it excels that rival in beauty, though not in general interest. The pure white of Te Tarata is here replaced by a delicate pink, which pervades the whole mass of deposit. The principal crater or cauldron exceeds in magnitude anything at Gardiner's River, being forty or fifty feet in diameter. It is situated on a circular platform one hundred yards in breadth. Silica enters largely into the composition of the deposit here also, and it is consequently hard, brittle, and flinty, like china. The terraces are very regular, but are not as remarkable in construction and form as those across the lake at Te Tarata.

In Iceland there is no deposit equalling in size or rivalling in interest those mentioned above.

The accommodation at the Mammoth Hot Springs Hotel was in an inverse ratio to the gorgeous description contained in the advertisements of the Helena and Virginia newspapers. No doubt the neighbourhood of these springs will some day become a fashionable place. At present, being the last outpost of civilisation,—that is, the last place where whisky is sold,—it is merely resorted to by a few invalids from Helena and Virginia City, and is principally known to fame as a rendezvous of hunters, trappers, and idlers, who take the opportunity to loiter about on the chance of getting a party to conduct to the geysers, hunting a little, and selling meat to a few visitors who frequent the place in summer; sending the good specimens of heads and skeletons of rare beasts to the Natural History men in New York and the East; and occupying their spare time by making little basket-work ornaments and nicknacks, which, after placing them for some days in the water so that they become coated with white silicates, they sell to the travellers and invalids as memorials of their trip. They are a curious race, these mountain men, hunters, trappers, and guides—very good fellows as a rule, honest and open-handed, obliging and civil to strangers if treated with civility by them. They make what I should think must be rather a poor living out of travellers and pleasure parties, doing a little hunting, a little mining, and more prospecting during the summer. In the winter they hybernate like bears, for there is absolutely nothing for them to do. They seek out a sheltered cañon or warm valley with a southern aspect, and, building a little shanty, purchase some pork and flour, and lay up till Spring opens the rivers and allows of gulch mining operations being recommenced. If you ask a man in the autumn where he is going and what he is going to do, ten to one he will tell you that it is getting pretty late in the season now, and that it won't be long before we have some heavy snow, and he is going ' down the river or up the cañon.'

For a week we lay at the hot springs on Gardiner's River, unable to move on account of illness in the camp, and waiting for Wynne. The weather was beautiful ; the storm had entirely subsided, and was succeeded by bright, warm, sunny days, softened and beautified by the dim autumnal haze. It was very aggravating to lose such fine weather for travelling, and we chafed impatiently at the enforced delay. Some of us went out hunting, and brought in good store of fat antelope ; others amused themselves with the trout which abound in Gardiner's River and the Yellowstone. However, at last, on a Sunday, Wynne arrived, with a large and very welcome packet of letters from home. We had plenty to do all that night reading and answering letters, and on the next morning we made a start.

The trail, after crossing one of the forks of Gardiner's River, follows up the main stream, which makes near its head a very pretty little fall. The cañon is there about 500 hundred yards across at the top, and narrows at the bottom to a width of thirty or forty yards. The top is densely covered with small pines, which also grow on the precipitous sides wherever they can find room to strike their roots. Flowing out of these pine-trees the river rushes down a precipitous cliff for about 300 feet, leaping over a sheer fall in one place of 100 feet in height. The volume of water is small, but the fall is full of grace and beauty. In the sides of the cañon above the fall occur some interesting and remarkable instances of structural basalt, the different outflows being divided by intervening bands of clay. The columnar forms are very distinctly shown, and the strata look at a little distance exactly like ramparts of masonry.

The path—if so vague an indication of former travel can be called a path—after winding most picturesquely along the sides of the ravine debouches into a sort of upland prairie country, composed of low, rounded, grass-covered hills, concealing in their hollows many still, sedgy, reed-fringed ponds. By ascending any of these little hills you will see spread out all around a great black mantle of forest rolling in successive waves to the horizon, apparently without limit, save that in the distance the range of the Yellowstone and the mountains about the sources of the Madison break through its dark uniformity; while far away to the south is shadowed the dim outline of the three Tétons.

In the afternoon we passed quite a patriarchal camp, composed of two men with their Indian wives and several children ; half a dozen powerful savage-looking dogs and about fifty horses completed the party.   They had been grazing their stock, hunting and trapping, leading a nomad, vagabond, and delicious life—a sort of mixed existence, half hunter, half herdsman, and had collected a great pile of deer-hides and beaver-skins. They were then on their way to settlements to dispose of their peltry, and to get stores and provisions ; for they, too, were proceeding to look for comfortable winter quarters, ' down the river or up the cañon.'

Encountering people in these solitudes is like meeting a suspicious sail at sea when your country is at war, and you are uncertain as to the character, nationality, intentions, size, and strength of the stranger.   The latter point is the most important to clear up.   Man is the most dangerous beast that roams the forest, and the first idea that enters the mind on meeting him or seeing his traces is one of hostility ; you take it for granted that he is an enemy and to be guarded against, until you ascertain that he is a friend and can be trusted.   It is therefore advisable in such cases to heave-to and reconnoitre, and make signals.   The number of horses staggered us at first, but we soon discovered that the strangers were white, and, moreover, that there were only two men in camp ; and without more ado we rode in and made friends.   What a lot of mutually interesting information was given and received !   We were outward bound and had the news, and the latitude and the longitude.   They were homeward bound, had been wandering for months, cut off from all means of communication with the outside world, and had but the vaguest notion of their position on the globe.

But, though ignorant of external matters and what was going on in settlements, they had not lost all desire

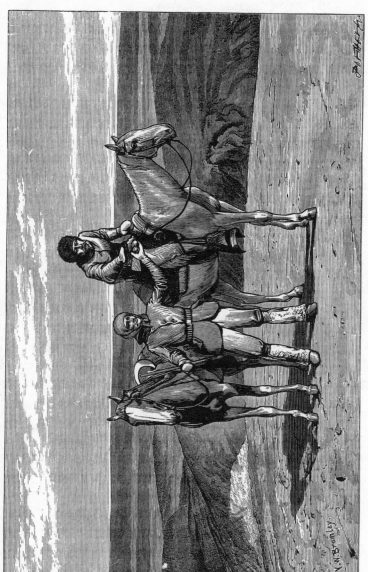

"Indians, by Jove!"

for information. It seems natural to suppose that a man condemned to a long sojourn in the wilds would become quite careless of everything but the wants and necessities of his daily life. But with United Stateans, at any rate, this is not the case. An American, although he lives with an Indian woman in the forests or on the plains, never quite loses his interest in politics and parties; and these two squaw-men were very anxious to hear all about electioneering matters, and to know whether anything important had taken place on the great question that was convulsing their world—that is, the few detached settlements in Montana; namely, whether Virginia City should continue to be the capital, or whether her mantle should be taken from her shoulders and transferred to the back of her more prosperous rival, Helena. They wanted to know also how far it was to Bozeman, and how the place lay by compass.

These men looked very happy and comfortable. Unquestionably the proper way for a man to travel with ease and luxury in these deserts is for him to take unto himself a helpmate chosen from the native population. No amount of art, industry, and study can rival the instinct displayed by savages in making themselves comfortable, and in utilising for their own benefit all the accidents of Nature. Nobody can choose a camp as they can; nobody knows how to make a fire so quickly or so well; nobody can so wisely pick a shady cool place in summer heat, or choose one sheltered from wind and storms in winter. With an Indian wife to look after his bodily comforts, a man may devote himself to hunting, fishing, or trapping without a thought or care. He may make his mind quite easy about all household matters. His camp will be well arranged, the tent-pegs driven securely home, the stock watered, picketed, and properly cared for, a good supper cooked, his bed spread out, and everything made comfortable; his clothes and hunting-gear looked after, the buttons sewn on his shirt— if he has got any shirt or any buttons; and all the little trivial incidents of life which, if neglected, wear out one's existence, he will find carefully attended to by a willing and affectionate slave.

They had a lot to tell us also about their travels and adventures, about the wood and water supply, and the abundance or deficiency of game. So we sat down on bales of beaver-skins and retailed all the civilised intelligence we could think of; and the women came and brought us embers for our pipes, and spread out robes for us and made us at home; and the little fat, chubby children, wild and shy as young wolves, peered at us from behind the tent out of their round, black, beady eyes.

Soon after leaving their camp we crossed the low divide between the valley of Gardiner's River and that of the Yellowstone, and camped very late on Tower Creek, a little above its junction with the former river.

The falls, and also a portion of Tower Creek, are well worthy of a visit. The cañon of the river is exceedingly precipitous and rugged, and is so black, savage, and forbidding in its aspect that it has, with the strange aptitude evinced by the human race to attribute everything strange or horrible to the Evil One, been called the Devil's Den. Through this narrow gorge the river foams and rushes with great velocity; and about 200 yards above its entrance into the Yellowstone, which occurs just where that river debouches from the Grand Cañon, it shoots over an abrupt descent of 156 feet, forming a very picturesque fall.

In the sides of Tower Creek and in the walls of the lower end of the Grand Cañon near the mouth of the creek are, I think, the most perfect instances of basalt to be seen anywhere along the trail. The plain, composed of volcanic breccia, rolls steeply to the edge of the precipice, and then occurs a long escarpment of perpendicular basaltic columns arranged with perfect regularity. Below, at a little distance, is another wall of similarly constructed basalt, and below that again is a third row, terminating in a stratum of reddish clay, which tops a sheer precipice of the primitive rock. The three different lines of basalt are separated by thick layers of a whitish substance, resembling the deposits of the hot springs, and with bands of red and brown clay or marl. The débris of this calcareous formation seems to rest loosely upon the trachyte beneath it, as it forms pyramid-shaped heaps on the prominent buttresses of basalt.

We saw to-day on the opposite side of the river the gloomy forbidding gorge of Hell Roaring Creek, its entrance guarded by a bold promontory or mountain blessed with the same euphonious name. We also passed THE bridge, the only bridge across the Yellowstone, and therefore an object of some interest. It is situated close to the junction of the east fork with the main stream, is constructed of stone, and was made at a great expense for the accommodation of miners on Clarke's Fork. Few there be that cross over it now.

The next day (Tuesday) we broke camp early, and about noon met another party, consisting of three men, out prospecting. They had but the haziest notion of their whereabouts in the world. They had wintered in the mountains, and had only once been into settlements, down somewhere on Snake River, early in the spring. We gave them all the information we could, and bought some flour from them, giving them an order on Boteler's brother for some groceries in exchange.

The country traversed on this day's march was not

very interesting. The trail, soon after leaving Tower Creek, passes to the west of the Yellowstone, and crosses at an easy gradient the northern rim of the basin of that river, about a mile west of Mount Washburne. The ascent and the descent were very long and tedious, but there was a fine view from the summit of the pass. A heavily-timbered, flattish, but uneven plain lay beneath us, broken with occasional open spaces or parks; to the south the jagged outlines of the Tétons burst through the forest; in the east, the range in which Clarke's Fork has its rise was glowing in the setting sun, as our jaded horses slowly climbed the steep incline; and to the west the Madison Mountains were darkening into night. The snow must be awfully deep on this path sometimes, for near the top we noticed some pine-trees which had been cut down, fully twenty feet above the ground, by a party two or three years ago.

Mount Washburne is the highest peak in this range, and, like most American mountains, is very easy of ascent. You can ride to the very top, and the view from the summit is magnificent; but the day being very cloudy I did not then attempt to go up.

We camped at a late hour on the south side of the mountain; and what a supper I did eat! It may seem strange, and it may be very shocking to think and talk about one's material comforts and gross appetites : but, as I am writing from memory whatever comes uppermost, the recollection of antelope-steak is very fresh and distinct just at present, savouring in my nostrils and bringing moisture to the lip, and overpowering all other thoughts. In fancy I can scent the odour of it afar off. Would that I could do so in reality! Bearing in mind that I had lived for a week at the hot springs on burnt flour and water, you will perhaps pardon my gastronomic enthusiasm. If people deny that one of the greatest enjoyments of life is eating when you are famishing, then those people either are devoid of the first principles of morality or have never been hungry; and they had better learn to speak the truth, or live on spare diet for a week, then get into vigorous health, and so know what a good appetite really means.

If a man wishes to be comfortable in camp, once for all, let him give up the idea of being *too* comfortable. If he tries to carry out his preconceived ideas as to cleanliness and dry changes of clothes; warm things for cold weather and cool garments for hot; boots for riding and boots for walking, and all the rest of the appliances of civilised life, he will find himself constantly worried and continually disappointed. Encumbered with a large kit, he will never be able to find anything he wants, for the needed article is sure to sink out of sight into the bottom of the bag. If he comes in hot and exhausted—in the condition that at home would call imperiously for a bath and a change—and sets to work to rummage out another suit and flannel shirt, he will only succeed in making himself ten times hotter than before. He will be irritated by hopping about on one leg and tripping up in his efforts to scramble out of and into his trousers; and probably they will prove hairier than the last pair and will tickle his legs. His shirt will certainly have a grass-seed or a little bit of stick or something sharp and disagreeable sticking in it, that will scratch him every time he moves; or the collar will have shrunk at the last washing to half its natural dimensions; or his boots will pinch his swollen feet; and altogether he will find himself at the end of his exertions much more uncomfortable than he was at the beginning. No, no; reduce yourself to primitive simplicity; one suit, and a change of under garments. If it is cold, put on your change and extra shirt; if it is very hot, go without your coat or waistcoat—or breeches, if it pleases you.

As with dressing so it is also with cooking. The same principle obtains in both cases; the simpler and less pretentious the style of your cook the better pleased you will be with the result of his efforts. There is nothing between the high art of a *cordon bleu*—the supreme flights of genius which result in such dinners as one gets only in a good English house, a first-class London club, or an A 1 Paris restaurant—and a steak toasted on a stick. I love not the greasy luxuries of the frying-pan, the hollow mockery of plates and things set out as if for a civilised dinner, napkins folded, and all the rest of it. Maxwell tried it on at first, and was indignant that his neatly-folded cockades and solidifying fat were not appreciated.

If you like to sit at a cloth spread and arranged in imitation of a dinner-table and to eat of fried meat, very good; I don't mind. Those two candles which dimly illuminate you are very hard and solid; they are made of elk-fat; and before you have done supper you will have several of those candles in your inside. It is all a matter of taste.

Let me tell you the other way. First of all, make yourself a cake of flour and water, a little sugar, salt of course, and a pinch—a most minute pinch—of baking-powder. It does not matter if you put none of the last ingredient in; the bread will be wholesomer without it. Roll this out extremely thin like a biscuit, score it with your knife, put it on a tin plate, and prop it up with a short stick before the embers to bake. It will be crisp, brown, and digestible in a few minutes. Put another plate near the fire, and let it get nearly red-hot. Then with a sharp knife cut yourself a portion of meat from the best part of the animal, cutting it at least an inch and a half thick. Beat it with your knife-handle to break up the fibre, unless it is very tender indeed. Then divide it into several small fragments, one of which you will, after carefully salting and peppering it, impale upon a stick and plunge momentarily into a bright clear flame. Then toast it slowly over the embers. The sudden immersion in the fire glazes the surface of the meat and cakes the salt over it, so that during the after process of cooking scarcely any of the juice can escape, and the result is a kabob—rich, succulent, tender, and fit for any epicure. While you are eating one bit you toast another. Your plate is hot, your meat hot, your bread crisp and hot, and your tea hot; and, if that won't satisfy you in the wilderness, nothing will. This was my style and Boteler's; and we would lie side by side in front of the fire, toasting a little bit, and yet still another little bit, long after the others had bolted their hot soft rolls and fried meat.

We had a most lovely camp that night on the edge of a prairie, in a little cozy grassy bay that indented the forest shores. The sun sank in a quiet sky; the stars shone clear, bright, and steady with unwavering light; the universe rested and was at peace. The wind talked to the trees, and the pines in answer bowed their stately heads, and with a sigh of melancholy swept their gloomy branches to and fro. All through the night the mysterious music of the distant falls rose and fell upon the breeze—sometimes borne up distinct and clear, a mighty roar and crash of waters; then sinking to an almost inaudible hum like the tremulous vibration of a mighty but remote harp-string. Not far away stood some bare burnt pine-trees, sadly complaining to the night air when it rose and softly touched their naked boughs, making to it their melancholy moan, and sinking again into silence as the breeze passed on.

We could hear the short comfortable crop, crop, crop of the horses as they nipped the herbage. The day had been very warm, and the air was heavy with the faint odour of autumn flowers and sweet grass, and with the strong fragrance of the resinous firs. It was almost too fine a night to waste in sleep, but slumber comes soon to tired men soothed by Nature's harmony when the elements are at rest; and unconsciousness, casting over us her mantle, quickly wrapped our senses in her dark folds.

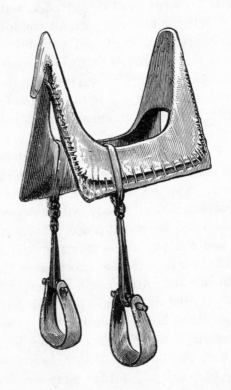

INDIAN SADDLE.

CHAPTER VI.

TO THE YELLOWSTONE FALLS.

WEDNESDAY morning found us up betimes, blowing our fingers and stamping our feet in that chilly ' little hour before day,' pulling up tent-pegs, rolling packs, putting together a few necessaries, and making preparations for a hard day's work. As we intended, if possible, to pitch our tents the same evening beyond the Mud Springs, and as we wished to examine those volcanoes, and also to visit the Falls of the Yellowstone, we had determined overnight to divide into two parties in order to save time, and to send Boteler, Jack, Maxwell, and Campbell straight to the camping-place, while the rest of us made a détour to the Falls and Springs. Both parties having a very long and arduous day's march before them, we all hurried out early in the morning before it was light, and drove in the stock. While looking for them we found wapiti close to camp, and Campbell fired at but missed a stag. Jack killed one later in the day. Wynne, Kingsley and I felt a little ' dubersome ' as to whether we were capable of finding our way unguided; but Boteler reassured our diffident minds by saying it was all right, and that we should be certain to find him without trouble camped about eight or ten miles west of the Springs. We could not possibly miss him, he said, because as far as the mud volcanoes there was a fine plain trail to guide us, and after that we had only to turn due west and follow another track leading in that direction, and right on that track the tents would be pitched. So after seeing everything properly packed and secured, and the mules well under weigh, we turned our horses' heads, and guided by the distant sound of water cantered off, full of expectation, to see one of the greatest sights of the country side ; and after a short ride we arrived at the river's brink just above the Falls.

When the Yellowstone leaves the lake of the same name it flows in a calm steady current for many miles, and then, before charging through the phalanx of the mountains which oppose its passage to the north, it performs a series of gymnastics over rapids, cascades, and waterfalls, as if exercising its muscles and sinews, preparing itself and gathering strength for the mighty effort by which it tears a passage through the granite flanks of the range. A mighty effort truly, or rather a vast expenditure of force, has been employed in cleaving the Grand Cañon, a rent in the mountains over twenty miles long, and of vast depth. Where the river enters the cañon the sides are from 1,200 to 2,000 feet high ; and further down they rise to a greater altitude, an altitude which has never been determined, for the depths of that chasm have not yet been explored or trodden by human foot.

Both the Falls are caused by basaltic dykes or walls, crossing the bed of the river at right angles to its course. The volume of water is not very great, and there is nothing stupendous or soul-subduing here as there is at Niagara ; neither are the Falls very remarkable for their height. But they have a savage beauty all their own, a wild loveliness peculiar to them ; and what they lack in volume, power, and general grandeur is amply atoned for in the pre-eminently distinctive character of the scenery about them, and by the lavish display of colour and strange forms of stratification which distinguish their surroundings. The scene is so solitary, so utterly desolate, the colouring is so startling and novel, the fantastic shapes of the rock so strange and weird, that a glamour of enchantment pervades the place, which, though indelibly impressed upon my mind, is yet quite impossible to describe.

Above the first cascade the river flows in a bold sweeping curve through meadows, its swift green current unbroken by rock or rapid. Presently it begins to break and foam, dashing over several trachyte ledges of eight or ten feet in height. Then the sides close in; the channel contracts rather suddenly; and the river penned in between its converging walls rises to a greater height, and, rushing with vast force through a narrow space, shoots clear out into the air, and dashes down 140 feet. The water must be deep at the brow of the Fall, but it is perfectly white, and does not possess those glorious streaks of colour, purple and green, that are so beautifully exemplified at Niagara. It lodges in a horseshoe basin, the sides of which are rather low, not more than from 150 to 200 feet in height. Just beneath the surface of the water, and directly under the cascade, a sloping ledge of rock projects; and the somewhat narrow and slender column of water strikes the seething waves that barely cover this shelf with such violent concussion that it drives itself forward like a white fan or inverted wedge for some distance along the dark surface of the pool beyond.. Immediately after its leap the river bends somewhat suddenly to the left, and rushes in a series of small rapids over the low ledges and detached fragments of rock of which its bed is composed for the space of about half a mile which intervenes between the two principal dykes. In this half-mile it drops altogether sixty-eight feet.

Above the lower Fall also the waters are compressed and heaped up into a narrow channel; and the Yellowstone entering the gorge with the velocity acquired in its rapid descent from the upper shoot, and pressing tumultuously through, hurls itself bodily out from the edge with a descent of 397 feet, forming a very grand cascade.

After that it goes tearing and tossing, rising in the centre in white surges, and lashing the sides of the chasm in anger, till it is lost to view round an angle of the Grand Cañon.

The upper cascade, though much the smaller of the two, is the most beautiful, being more instinct with life, motion, and variety than the other; but the lower Fall is by far the most impressive.

Along the brink and descending the sides in all directions run many game-trails, which may be safely followed, for though mountain sheep can climb almost anywhere, yet their ordinary paths are quite practicable for man.

There are three points from which good views can be obtained. The first is a sort of ledge, jutting out and affording a fine opportunity for observing the upper cascade, the Horseshoe basin, and the crest of the lower Fall.

The lower Fall itself is best seen from a little promontory, which forms an angle in the cliff, and partially overhangs the brink. The view from there of the river preparing for its leap is very good. The advancing volume of water flows rapidly but solidly to the very edge, then hurls itself into the air suddenly, and falls with a dull thud into a circular foaming cauldron, bounded by steep precipices 800 feet in height.

The dark masses of water casting themselves continuously over the ledge string out into long, perfectly white threads of glistening air-bubbles and foam, and long before they reach the surface beneath seem to be entirely dissolved into fine spray and rain; but it is not so, for at the repeated shocks of their concussion earth and air tremble. From the misty depths below the roar of the waters constantly arises in distinct vibrations like the humming of a harp-string, and the steam floats up for ever in great clouds. The cliff is very bare and naked, but on the western side it is partially covered with a carpet of bright green moss, nurtured by the ever-falling spray.

A little further down is a ledge terminating in a pillar or horn of rock, from which you can see right into the jaws of the cañon, and command a general view of the foot of the Falls and of both cliff faces, far surpassing that to be obtained from any other standpoint.

I left my horse in a clump of trees, and, crawling out upon a projecting rock, sat down at the foot of a pine-tree, leaned back against its ruddy trunk, and surrendered myself to the enchantment of the spot. Looking across the river to the east, I saw in the distance wave after wave of forest, broken now and then by a bare crest, appearing like an occasional breaker in a tumultuous sea. Then came an interval of plain, sloping gently down in graceful undulations, carpeted with short grass, fringed with the forest, and dotted with clumps of pines and solitary trees. This lawn continues to the very edge of the precipice; and then beneath it, and right opposite to me, rose the face of the cliff. This face is composed principally of soft material, clays and conglomerates, with here and there a few intrusions of weather-worn basalt. The clays are dyed (I presume, by the presence of iron, copper, and sulphur) into brilliant and startling combinations of colours, sometimes beautifully blended together, sometimes opposed, with that glaring contradiction to the laws of man of which Nature is so fond, and with that perfect success that always attends her efforts. Every shade of yellow is represented, from a delicate cream colour to glaring saffron; bright reds and scarlets, and most glorious purples, shading off into black, are relieved by occasional patches of vivid verdure, or by the more sombre green of the few audacious pine-trees that cling triumphantly to the cliff. The surface is by no means uniform, being partially composed of basalt, bearing a wonderful resemblance to old masonry, and looking like the crumbling walls of some overwhelmed town, and partly of conglomerates of hot spring deposit and calcareous earths. Breaking through the soft material in lines and buttresses, these harder fragments terminate in or rest upon a steep slope of richly-coloured clay. The whole face of the cliff is thus composed of a series of broken detached sheer precipices, divided by almost perpendicular intervals of variegated conglomerates and clays, on which grow a few scattered and struggling pines.

The easily disintegrated strata, yielding more readily to the action of weather than the harder rocks, have assumed most fantastic shapes; spires, pinnacles, and isolated peaks, round towers, and square castellated masses of indurated clays, alternating with sharp angular fragments of more closely-textured rock, are left standing erect upon the slopes. Some of the springs have formed on the smooth surface crooked horns and protuberances. In some places the precipice is coated with lime, dazzlingly white; in others the deposit is of delicately yellow crystals of sulphur. Springs of water carrying sulphur and sulphate of copper are numerous, and have painted the cliff in long streaks of colour.

To examine and study at all in detail this wonderful cañon and these waterfalls would occupy the attention of a scientific man for a long time, and right well would he be rewarded for his labour. It is a place full of interest even to the most casual and careless observer. His external senses are all appropriately appealed to ; the hidden recesses of his inner self are reached and stirred by the mystery and wild beauty of the scene ; and a man sitting alone and gazing upon it cannot fail to be strongly impressed by so wonderful a view. He becomes saturated with the glories of Nature, stunned with the magnitude of her works. His ear is soothed and his soul awed by the deep, monotonous, everlasting cadence of the Fall, and by the sad sighing of the pine-trees under which he sits. His eye, pleased yet almost bewildered by the infinite variety and voluptuousness of the colouring, rests with gladness on the scattered patches of spray-nurtured moss. His whole being becomes possessed with a feeling of utter littleness, and with the hopelessness of ever thinking to rise to a level sufficiently high to enable him to comprehend in the smallest degree the greatness and grandeur of the Creator's works, mingled with a sense of intense delight and enthusiasm at the manifestation of force, beauty, and persistent strength before him. A feeling of pardonable pride thrills through him—pride that he too forms a part of the same scheme, is a higher manifestation of the same power, a more perfect combination of the same material. He feels at one with Nature ;—the birds that fly, the beasts that roam the forests, the very trees and leaves and flowers are his brethren. For an instant there rushes across his mind a swift shadowy apprehension of the idea of an all-pervading Something, of a great awful Oneness, that, in spite of the jangling discordant jarrings, the dislocations and apparent contradictions of existence, envelopes us in its limitless unanimity, is round about us everywhere, in all things and through all things. For an instant he soars above the shadows cast by the ignorance of mankind, and pierces the clouds of our folly. The harsh grating of the inexplicable problems that haunt us, the hideous inharmonies that harass us, the questions which, because they cannot be answered and will not be evaded, drive men to despair, dimmed in the sudden blaze of intelligence that dazzles him, drowned in the great monotone that thrills him to the core, sound but as the slight creaking of machinery, the necessary rattle of the cranks, the unavoidable friction of the wheels of an engine not yet in thorough working order, yet as perfect as possible, and destined one day to run smoothly without sound, or jar, or jerk. He snatches at the flash of a vision of what the world might be, of what it will be. For one second his eye and mind overleap the barriers of space and time, and for once in his life he understands the statement that when God looked down upon the world, 'behold it was very good.'

The sleep-giving, soothing fragrance of the resinous pine, cleanest, sweetest and most healing of all scents, fills the air. Far up above in the transparent sky two eagles are slowly circling. There is a drowsy, dull, contented hum of insects in the branches. All the senses are hushed and quieted, the nerves soothed, the soul steeped in the infinite beauty of the scene. And in truth a man is so wrought upon, his nerves are so excited, and at the same time so gently calmed—so many conflicting emotions are called up at once, so many different chords are struck and vibrate together, that he scarcely knows what to do or how to analyse and appreciate his feelings. At one moment he could sit for hours in solitude, acutely listening to the whispered messages of Nature, absorbing the life of the forest, drinking in God's glories. At another moment he is almost overcome ; the awful sense of the nearness of Nature is too much for him ; he feels as though he was sitting in the presence of some great Mystery. An unutterable longing to know more seizes his soul, mingled with an instinctive dread that the unfolding of the secret would be too much for mere mortal ears ; and he is possessed with an impulse to rush from the spot and escape from too close a contact with Nature, which he has not spiritual strength enough to bear. He can understand the feeling of Longfellow's Count Arnaldo in ' The Secret of the Sea,' where it says—

> His soul was full of longing,
> And he cried with accents strong :
> ' Helmsman, for the love of Heaven,
> Teach me, too, that wondrous song ; '

or of the poet himself when in the same hymn he sings—

> Till my soul is full of longing
> For the secret of the sea,
> And the heart of the great ocean
> Sends a thrilling pulse through me.

I think that men become half mesmerised when in lonely places they look upon some masterpiece of the great Architect of all things. They become partially ecstatic ; and it is a great and positive relief to break the charm by talking to somebody, and by doing or saying something to bring them back to the realities of ordinary life.

We were very soon hurried out of fairy land by noticing the fact that the pine-trees were casting short shadows, and that it must be getting very late in the forenoon. So we reluctantly went back to our horses, who had been eating all the time, and in nowise thinking of or appreciating the scenic excellences about them; and, tightening up our girths, we swung into the saddle and resumed our way.

I never enjoyed a ride more in my life, and never expect to have so pleasant a one again. The day was very bright and warm, and the hazy autumn atmosphere cast over distant objects a shimmering gauzy indistinctness that greatly enhanced their beauty.

The country was throughout pretty. At every turn in the trail some fresh vista in the forest opened out, or some new distant view unfolded itself before our eyes. Woodpeckers tapped busily on the dead trees; squirrels chattered as they shook down the pine-nuts, and, full of fun and mischief, peeped at us from their homes in the branches; the few song-birds that are met with in American forests were singing, happy in the pleasant warmth of an Indian summer day. We had no pack-mules to bother ourselves about; and with light hearts full of merriment, happy with the exhilaration of animal health, rejoicing in the sheer pleasure of being alive, we cantered over the level plain or wound in single file, our guns lying across the pommel in front of us, through the silent glades of the forest. The hours sped quickly by, for time does not hang heavy when all the senses are occupied with observing and appreciating the various changes of scenery that constantly occur. Sometimes the trail followed the river, which flows, now rapidly and noisily over broad shallows, now with a swift but quiet current, through a deeper channel. Sometimes it turned into the forest and twined and twisted among its dark recesses, or traversed open glades and parks, apparently so well tended and cared for that one was constantly expecting to come in sight of some stately country house.

One very pretty view I remember well. I would have given much to have been able to sketch it. We were riding quietly along, and turning suddenly round a bend came upon a broad reach of the river, glassy, smooth, and deep—on either side the ground, turf-covered, level, and trim like a lawn, rolled upwards in long graceful curves, its open glades interspersed with trees, arranged by a hand more artistic than that of man. The upward sloping ground on either side of the water formed a perfect frame, in which was set in the far, far distance a great solitary scalped mountain, black with ravines and valleys, bright with sunshine, and capped with snow.

Nor were we indebted to scenery alone for the pleasures which we so thoroughly enjoyed this day. Wynne enlivened the road with humorous stories; and many a song, composed and sung by some camp-fire in the Crimea, or in some far-away bivouac of India, rang through the forest and awakened the echoes. We were constantly on the look-out for game also, for signs were plentiful enough to keep us on the *qui vive*, and fish and fowl swarmed in the woods and water. Flocks of Canada geese and ducks rose splashing and flapping from the margin of the river, filling the air with their sonorous cries. When we rode by the brink the great trout wagged their broad tails at us as they slowly sailed from out the patches of green weed. We saw several indications also of deer; and on riding out of a wood on to a little plain covered with grey sage-brush we espied, not half a mile off, a large bull elk. Wynne and I determined to stalk him, so we dismounted, and Kingsley held the horses.

The wind was all right, but, as the ground was very level, we had to crawl for a long way through the brush;

and after making ourselves very hot and dusty we were disgusted to find that the wapiti was on the other side of the river, which is here about 200 or 250 yards broad, and that the sage-brush which concealed us did not grow down to the brink. So we sat down and looked at him, much to the Doctor's astonishment, for he could not see the water, but could see us and the stag, and wondered why on earth we did not crawl up and shoot. While we watched the stag went down to the river, drank a little, and then going back 100 yards or so lay down under a tree. We fired two shots at him; the first one went just over his head, for we could see the bullet strike the dusty ground beyond. He did not take the slightest notice of it; but the second shot struck him fairly in the heart and killed him where he lay.

We wanted meat, and the head appeared to be a large one; so I forded the river, and a very nasty job it was. The water was just of that depth that my horse could keep his feet and no more, and the river-bed was full of patches of quicksand, into which he sank, terrifying both himself and me into fits. The river was full of trout; behind every bit of weed lay a fish of about two to four pounds weight; and very much astounded they appeared to be at my intrusion: but I will warrant they were not a whit more alarmed at finding me among them than I was at finding myself in their society. Either walking or swimming I should not have minded; but my pony's progress was a mixture of both, aggravated by an occasional violent flounder and struggle to extricate his feet from a quicksand. It took me, I am sure, more than half an hour to pick my way across that treacherous river; and when I did get over I found that the stag was utterly worthless for food. He was reduced almost to a skeleton; his hair had all come off, and he presented a most mangy, dissipated, dilapidated appearance; but he carried an exceedingly fine pair of antlers; so I cut off his head, and left it to be called for on our return.

Having rejoined Kingsley we pushed on rapidly, passing several mounds and hills of white deposit, some extinct, others active and smoking briskly.

Among these are the hot sulphur springs of 'Crater Hills,' so called from two detached hills or buttes of 150 and 140 feet in height respectively. They are composed of the usual deposits of calcareous matter, largely impregnated with sulphur and iron. The surface has dried, cracked, and peeled off in scales and loose cinters, which have slid down and littered the base.

The water in these springs contains a strong mixture of sulphuric acid. The table on p. 232 will supply all particulars of the principal springs at Crater Hills.

We also passed, but did not stop at, two little streams flowing together, which Professor Hayden has named Alum and Violet Creeks. In speaking of them he says :—

'The first spring we met with was on the right bank of the creek, in a silicious cone-like mound that rises six feet above the bed of the stream. Its temperature was 126° F., the air being at 70° F. The bed of the creek was filled up with confervoidæ, leading us to suspect that there were springs still further up. After a further ride of about a quarter of a mile we came to quite a large group of hot springs lining both sides of the creek. The first spring I will describe is on the right bank of the creek, in the centre of a white mound twenty feet in diameter, and rising ten feet above the bed of the creek. This mound is formed of the deposits from the water, which consist mainly of various carbonates and silica.

SPRINGS AT CRATER HILLS.

General elevation above sea-level 7,828 ft. ; boiling point 198·2° F.

No.	Size of Spring	Temperature of Spring	Temperature of Air	Remarks
		° F.	° F.	
1		174	59	
2	A collection of	176	59	
3	springs cover-	182	59	The water in this collection of springs
4	ing an area of	186	59	has a milky hue, and the noise made
5	600 sq. ft., and	144	59	by them resembles that made by a
6	varying in size	160	59	number of pots boiling simulta-
7	from 1 to 3 ins.	168	59	neously.
8	in diameter	150	59	
9		160	59	
10	3 ft. diameter .	80	59	White sulphur spring.
11	8 ft. „	148	59	Clear spring.
12	. . . .	176	59	Thick greenish mud spring.
13	2 ft. diameter .	180	59	Yellow mud spring in active ebullition.
14	8 × 2 ft.. . .	90	59	A turbid pool bubbling at the edges.
15	. . . .	162	59	
16	. . . .	166	59	A collection of greenish sulphur
17	. . . .	182	59	springs, each a few inches in di-
18	. . . .	178	59	ameter.
19	. . . .	108	59	
20	. . . .	180	59	This spring was called Foam Spring last year.
21	2 × 4 ft. . . .	170	59	Bluish muddy water.
22	10 × 3 ft. . .	188	59	Both these springs have lavender-
23	2 ft. diameter .	180	59	coloured mud, and No. 2 is in active agitation.
24		150	59	
25		184	59	
26		130	59	
27		170	59	
28		168	59	
29		184	59	
30		106	59	
31		154	59	
32		188	59	
33		160	59	
34		130	59	This collection of springs varies in
35	These springs oc-	162	59	size from a few inches to 4 ft. The
36	cupy a space of	174	59	water in the majority is of a milky
37	about 1,200 sq.	128	59	hue ; in others it is yellow or laven-
38	ft.	120	59	der-coloured, and in some it is trans-
39		106	59	parent.
40		176	59	
41		146	59	
42		186	59	
43		168	59	
44		174	59	
45		178	59	
46		172	59	
47		90	59	
48		158	59	
49		170	59	

The orifice of the spring is circular, and about three inches in diameter, and looks as though it had been artificially punched in the deposit, so mathematically exact is it. The water gives off carbonic acid gas, leaving a deposit of iron. Its temperature was 190° F., the air being 70° F. Spring No. 2 is on the opposite side of the creek, and has a basin measuring four feet by two feet. The temperature of the water was 160° F., the air remaining at 70° F. No. 3 has a circular basin two feet in diameter, which is lined with an abundant deposit of iron; carbonic acid gas bubbles through the water. Its temperature was 158° F. No. 4 is six feet deep, and one foot by three feet in diameter, and has a temperature of 188° F. The next three springs had temperatures as follows: — No. 5, 192° F. ; No. 6, 194° F.; and No. 7, 188° F., the air still remaining at 70° F. All these springs have circular orifices of about six inches diameter, and the water proceeding from them flows over a series of small terraces, resembling those of the Gardiner's River springs on a miniature scale. These basins are lined with a gelatinous form of silica, which has a leathery appearance, and is coated with an iron deposit. The springs are about ten feet above the level of the creek, and all give off carbonic acid gas. No. 8 is very irregular in shape, and almost hid in the grass about forty feet from the creek. There is a slight bubbling in it, and its temperature was 178° F. No. 9 is a small spring two feet in diameter and one foot deep, lined with confervoidæ, and having a temperature of 140° F. No. 10 is a very pretty spring, about four feet above the creek, and has a beautiful scalloped edge, moss-lined on one side. Its temperature was 175° F. The boiling-point at this locality is 198·3° F. None of the springs reached this temperature, 194° F. being the nearest approach. The rocks exposed near these springs are sedimentary, and contain a great deal of obsidian.

'About three-fourths of a mile further up stream we came to the head of the creek, and found that it originated in a most important group of springs. They are situated in a semicircular basin, bounded by a low hill, wooded on the summit. The sides of this hill are perfectly bare, and covered with glaring white deposit, through which steam-jets force their way. Looking down into the basin from the top of the hill is like looking into a volcanic crater. The fumaroles, solfataras, and mud springs scattered through it give it a most peculiar appearance. The general colour throughout the basin is a glaring white, relieved here and there by patches of brick-red iron deposits, and the yellow of sulphur masses that are scattered throughout the basin. The crust extending over the basin is lined with beautiful crystals of sulphur. On the left of this basin is a ravine covered with deposits of the same character, but containing no springs. There are a few fumaroles remaining, the evidence that once the ravine was the site of active springs. A few yards on the opposite side of the basin there is a second ravine similar to the first, and in which also the springs are all dead, nothing remaining but the rust-coloured deposits. I give the different springs in this basin in tabular form (see opposite page).

'Besides the springs enumerated in the table there were many smaller ones and a few large pools, through which the gases bubbled at various points.

'On the way back to camp we came across another group of springs, about a mile south-east of the group given above, and which have an elevation about 200 feet lower. They are situated in a ravine bordering a small

SPRINGS AT THE HEAD OF VIOLET CREEK.

August 10. Time of observation 12.30 A.M.; general elevation above the sea-level 8,059 feet; boiling-point 198·1° F.

No.	Character of Spring	Size	Gas Evolved	Temperature of Spring	Temperature of Air
				° F.	° F.
1	Silicious	8 × 10 feet	Steam	185	72
2	Do.	3 feet diameter	Do.	172	72
3	Do.	2 feet diameter	Do.	194	72
4	Do.		Do.	194	72
5	Sulphur	20 feet diameter	Steam and sulphuretted hydrogen	Not taken	72
6	Do.	30 feet diameter	Do.	165	72
7	Mud Spring	2 × 4 feet	Do.	170	72
8	Sulphur	8 feet diameter	Do.	140	72
9	Blue Mud Spring	6 × 10 feet	Do.	162	72
10	White Mud Spring	1 × 3 feet	Do.	168	72
11	Blue Mud Spring	3 feet long	Do.	188	72
12	Yellow Mud Spring	4 feet diameter	Do.	180	72
13	Blue Mud Spring	2 inches diameter	Do.	190	72

branch of Violet Creek. The following table will show them all at a glance:—

SPRINGS ON BRANCH OF VIOLET CREEK.

Aug. 10, 1872, time 2 P.M.; elevation above the sea 7,873 feet; boiling-point 198·5° F.

No.	Size	Gas Evolved	Temperature of Air	Temperature of Spring
			° F.	° F.
1	3 × 4 feet . .	Carbonic acid and steam	68	160
2	10 feet diameter	,, ,, ,,	68	184
3	5 feet diameter .	,, ,, ,,	68	154
4	5 × 2 feet . .	,, ,, ,,	68	188
5	3 feet diameter .	,, ,, ,,	68	180
6	5 × 3 feet . . .	,, ,, ,,	68	191
7	7 × 3 feet . . .	,, ,, ,,	68	186
8	3 feet diameter .	,, ,, ,,	63	192
9	8 × 1 foot . . .	,, ,, ,,	68	194

The amount of carbonic acid gas given off from these springs is small, and although there is considerable bubbling in some of the springs, it is caused mostly by the escape of steam. This, in some, is enough to cause the ground to tremble beneath. All the springs deposit iron. The first three springs given in the table are on the edge of a pool of water having a diameter of 100 feet by 50 feet, in which the thermometer stood at 120° F. There is also one spring in the midst of this pool which was beyond reach. The bottom of the pool is lined with gelatinous silica, which is coated with oxide of iron. The edge of the pool next the creek slopes to the level of the stream in a series of small basins, over which the water flows. The creek itself is divided into a number of basins formed of the deposits (mostly carbonates), and the water flows from one basin to the other, they being at different levels. These basins are filled with a luxuriant growth of very bright green confervoidæ. The temperature of the water in the creek a short distance below the springs is 140° F.'

It is scarcely necessary for me to say that when we arrived at the Mud Springs we found that the principal geyser had just finished spouting, and that the water in the basin was rapidly subsiding. However, we had three or four hours to spare, so we tethered our horses and sat down patiently to watch. In about an hour's time we were joined by the outfit. This was a very lucky accident, for if they had not passed that way we might have been sitting at the Mud Springs till now. We never should have found camp, for the trail which Boteler said would lead us to it existed only in his imagination. After waiting a little to rest the animals, Boteler went on, telling us to turn sharp to the west and follow his trail.

The principal spring in this group is a basin of about 100 feet in circumference, situated within a larger basin. The sides and surrounding surface are composed of bare smooth mud, baked by the sun, and worn into little channels by the action of the water, which when we arrived was trickling back into the basin from which it had been hurled by the last explosion. While we watched, the water in the inner orifice sank until there was but a little thick muddy liquid left at the bottom, and then it began slowly to rise again.

There we sat for hours, a ludicrous-looking group, three men and a dog gazing earnestly at a lot of mud which slowly, slowly rose, while the sun rapidly sank. I suppose, acting on the principle that a watched pot never boils, this geyser sternly refused to do its duty. It would not get angry. Every now and then a slight spasm would shake its placid, muddy countenance, but it was rather, I think, a smile of derision than a grin of rage that crossed it. We abused that spring in every way in our power. We threw sticks into it and stones, but it was no use ; nothing would rile it ; and at length, when we could count only upon an hour's light, we were forced to leave and look for camp. Very lucky it was that we did not delay any longer, for we had not gone 500 yards before we utterly lost the trail of our outfit. They had turned on to a prairie, baked as hard as iron and covered with perfectly dry wiry grass, on which the animals' feet left no impression whatever. We knew the direction they had gone, and that was all ; but whether they had traversed the prairie, or turned into the forest that bordered it, we could not tell. However, there was no time to waste in hunting the trail ; so, sticking spurs into our horses, we galloped along due west. The sun sank and the night fell ; there was no sign either of trail or camp, and we began to think that we might make up our minds to go supperless and blanketless to sleep that night, when, to our great satisfaction, we saw a little glimmer of light reflecting on the white canvas of the tents, and found camp comfortably placed in a nice sheltered nook just at the edge of the forest. It was the second time I had had a scare that day, for in the morning I somehow got separated from my two companions, and could not find them for a couple of hours.

It is a very mean feeling to be all alone and to fancy one's self lost ; nothing so quickly upsets a man's mental equilibrium. I have been most fortunate (in a good hour be it spoken), and have never yet got out of my reckoning without getting in again pretty soon. The nearest I have ever come to being lost was in the neighbourhood of Fort Bridger. It happened in this way.

Camp was on a creek running into one of the tributaries of Green River, and into this creek flowed several little rills. On the banks of one of these small branches, about half a mile up from its junction with the creek, we had slept on our way to Henry's Fork, where we had been looking for wapiti. We were now on the return journey, and had pitched our tents on the borders of the creek some distance above the old camping-ground I have just mentioned. The country about there is very heavily timbered, and consists of endless ridges, all much the same in appearance. Very few distinguishing landmarks break the uniformity of the forest. Well, our guide, Old Man Smith, and I went out one morning to look for deer, and hunted all the forenoon along a little rivulet, a tributary of the creek. About noon Smith went home, telling me to leave the watercourse and to keep about south. If I did so, he said, I should pass through a good hunting-ground, and could not go astray, as I should strike the springs of the little stream beside which we had camped on the way up. So, acting on his advice, I plunged into a forest so thick that I could barely see enough of the sun to keep my course correctly. After hunting along diligently for an hour or two I came across some dry *coulés*. I followed them down going west, and after awhile came to stagnant pools and then to flowing water. 'All right,' thought I ; 'this is the creek sure enough.' As I descended the stream the banks became very steep and rough, and much encumbered with fallen trees. The water had in many places been dammed up by beavers, and impenetrable marshes had been formed that necessitated tedious détours. I made slow progress, and, as it was getting late, determined to strike into the timber in a north-west direction and so make a short cut to camp. But I came across such an awful windfall that I could make no headway, and was forced to abandon that attempt and return to the stream.

This term 'windfall' is used technically, to describe

those streaks and patches of dense forest in which the trees, by some sudden gust or blast uprooted, have fallen to the ground, or, locked in each other's branches, form a half standing, half falling network of limbs and boughs. It is impossible for a man who has not seen it to imagine the inextricable confusion of a windfall.

The travelling improved a little and I pushed on rapidly, running whenever I could, and expecting at every moment to see in the distance the hills bounding the main creek. But, no ; I was doomed to constant disappointment. Every ridge that I took to be the high bank of the principal stream turned out, on approaching it, to be merely a bend in the rivulet I was descending. From what Old Man Smith told me, I had calculated the length of the little creek from its source to our old camp, and I judged I must have travelled at least twice that distance. Quite blown and out of breath I stopped, and it flashed across me that I was on the wrong creek, and that I was lost. There was no use in my arguing with myself that I had been going in the right direction, and that my course, though very zigzaggy, was in the main correct ; that Old Man Smith had said that the first water was the right one, and that I could not have missed it. I *knew* that a quarter, or at any rate half, the distance I had travelled ought to have brought me out at the main creek, and I felt that I was lost. I reflected a moment. Where could this stream be flowing to? I had no acquaintance with the geography of the country, beyond a vague idea that the little rills all ran into creeks, that united in two or three larger creeks, which in their turn discharged into Green River. Supposing that I followed this down, and then followed the creek it discharged into down to Green River, whereabouts would I strike it? Near the Green River railway crossing, or far below? How long would it take me to get to the railway? For how many days would I have to wander and fast? Besides, was I certain that there was no other watershed? Did all the streams and creeks flow into Green River? Might I not fall upon some tributary which, flowing with a course nearly parallel to the main river, would lead me through hundreds of miles of dismal desert? I tried to think composedly, but could not.

My head turned; my brain became quite bewildered; and an impulse to run straight ahead seized me. I was, to use the vernacular, for the moment completely 'turned round.' It seems to me most absurd, as I sit here writing, to suppose that one could be so easily thrown, even for an instant, off one's balance; but all men, except those who by long custom have acquired habits of complete self-dependence and self-control, are liable to such temporary aberrations—for it almost amounts to that;—and I have even seen very old and experienced prairie men become quite 'turned round' after running elk, and so obstinate in their conviction that they were going right, when in reality the fact that they were moving in a totally wrong direction was clearly demonstrated by compass, that it required a strong effort on their part to force themselves to act according to the needle and not upon their own mistaken judgment.

However, I was not so stupid long; I had sense enough to know that I must on no account leave the water, and I determined to believe that, though I was certainly on the wrong stream, yet no doubt it ran somewhere or other into the right creek. And so, as I did not seem capable of reasoning my way out just then, and as the sun was very low, I made up my mind to camp right there. Accordingly, I shot a squirrel for supper, picked a dry spot to sleep on, gathered a lot of branches together, and, having thus provided food and fire, thought I would take one more good look around. I mounted the highest ridge close by but could see nothing. On the top was a tall pine-tree. I climbed that, and beheld right in front of me a distinct unmistakable ridge cutting at right angles across the direction of my valley. Hooray! I said to myself; the stream runs into something anyhow; and, as it cannot be more than a couple of miles to that ridge, I may as well chance it and go down to the mouth. And so I pocketed my squirrel, left my fire, and made tracks at best pace down stream. I had not gone very far before I saw the impression of a boot-heel in the sand. That's all right, thought I; and chucking away my squirrel I cheerily walked on, for I knew I must be close to the old camp. A few hundred yards further on I found it, followed our old trail into the waggon-track leading to the saw-mill, and plodded along that road till I got to camp.

I had been right enough all the time; the only trouble was that the little stream was much longer, and made a great deal more southing than, judging by Smith's description, I had supposed it did.

Of course, when they said in camp that they had been getting anxious and had thought of looking for me, lighting fires, firing guns, and all the rest of it, I laughed the idea to scorn. I wasn't going to get lost, not I; they might bet their ' bottom dollars ' about that. I did not tell them what a fix I had been in, or that I had considered it necessary to collect my fuel and kill my supper.

The most extraordinary instance that has come under my notice of a man being lost for a length of time and surviving, occurred in this very Yellowstone country.

From a detailed account of his adventures, written by himself and published in *Scribner's Magazine*, it appears that in August, 1870, Mr. Evarts, formerly United States assessor for Montana, joined a numerous company about to visit the Geyser region. One day, while the party were with difficulty unravelling their way through thick forests, and the members of it had all scattered out in search of a practicable path, Mr. Evarts strayed so far away that he lost touch of his companions altogether. It was late, and being unable to rejoin them he was compelled to camp out alone on that night. This occurred close to the lake.

The next day Mr. Evarts resumed his search, and seeing, as he thought, some indications of a trail, he dismounted to examine the ground more carefully, and neglected to secure his horse. Something or other happened to scare the animal; and, his attention attracted by a crashing in the brush, Mr. Evarts looked up just in time to catch a glimpse of his horse disappearing through the trees. The loss of his horse was in itself a terrible disaster; but that was not all, for on the saddle were his gun, matches, blanket, fishing-tackle, and all the other appliances which render a man comparatively safe and self-supporting in the midst of the wilderness. He never saw the horse again, and for thirty-five days after that fatal parting this unfortunate gentleman wandered alone, through woods and over mountains, totally unarmed, and with no other instruments or appliances than two knives and a pair of small field-glasses. Strange to say, he allowed himself almost to perish daily, for want of fire, for nearly a fortnight, before he thought of kindling one by means of the lenses of his glasses. One of the fearfully cold storms which suddenly arise in these latitudes came on, and he would have succumbed to cold and exposure had he not managed to reach a group of hot springs. As it was, he was severely frosted on both feet. In that neighbourhood he remained seven days, keeping himself warm by lying on the hot incrustation surrounding a little boiling spring, in which he cooked an insignificant supply of roots.

The day before his rescue he lost his glasses also; an additional misfortune which nearly overthrew the slight remnant of life and reason which still held out against the fatal effects of his prolonged and unparalleled sufferings. At an earlier stage of his adventures he had even lost his knives. In fact, after commencing with his horse, he lost everything of use that he had with him; and the only marvel is that he did not lose his head also, and his life.

As he had become separated from the outfit on a peninsula of the Yellowstone Lake, round which they were making their way, Mr. Evarts took a direction which he thought would cut across this peninsula at right angles, and bring him out on the shores ahead of the party. He did emerge upon the sandy beach of a lake; but it was not the lake he was searching for; it was another sheet of water altogether.

Here he found some edible thistles, and tasted food for the first time in four days; and upon an exceedingly scanty supply of these roots, grass, and leaves, he managed to subsist for thirty-one days more. The only animal food that he contrived to get consisted of one wretched little fowl no bigger than a snow-bunting, which, as it was benumbed with cold, he succeeded in capturing, and the tip of a sea-gull's wing which he picked up. It strikes one as very singular that he could not snare or kill with sticks and stones something to eat in the shape of squirrels, birds, mice, or badgers. But it is easy to talk when one is not in a fix at all, and to think of all the ingenious contrivances one would have invented. When it comes to the point, I dare say the captious critic of his actions would starve as soon as anybody else. I don't want to try it at any rate. I have no doubt an old mountain man would have procured food somehow; but Mr. Evarts must have been entirely unaccustomed to a wild life, else he never would have lost his horse, left his rifle on the saddle when he dismounted, or gone about without a supply of matches in his pocket. This, however, adds much to the interest of his story, and enhances the marvellousness of his escape.

While waiting at the hot springs for fine weather, he manufactured a knife out of the tongue of a buckle, and made a fishing-line and hook out of some red tape and a pin. This is probably the only instance on record of red tape proving of the slightest use to anybody. He subsequently lost all these articles in a forest fire. He tried to make another fish-hook out of the rim of a pair of broken spectacles, but failed. Mr. Evarts was certainly the most unfortunate man that ever was lost. Everything that could happen to him did occur. His feet were badly frozen; he lost all he had originally, and everything that he made; he even got rid of one of his shoes; he slipped into some boiling water and scalded his hip severely; and it was apparently his nightly custom to tumble into the fire and burn himself. He left the group of springs on the eighth day, and returned to the lake. Here he stumbled upon a camping-ground of his party, and found an old baking-powder tin and a fork. He did not attempt to follow the trail, but started in the right direction for Bozeman. He made but little progress and wandered for many days, gradually becoming weaker and weaker, until he was discovered in the last stage of exhaustion, about seventy miles from Fort Ellis, by two men who had been sent out to hunt for him. One of them started immediately for medical assistance from the Fort, while the other remained with Mr. Evarts, who in two days was capable of being moved to a miner's cabin, twenty miles distant. But there he nearly perished, for though the miners most carefully tended and watched him, and did everything in their power to alleviate his sufferings, they had not the medicines necessary for his condition. A thirty-five days' diet on tough fibrous roots had completely arrested all the digestive functions of the body, and he would most undoubtedly have died had not an old hunter and trapper happened to pass by. This man, who had probably been many times starved himself, knew exactly what was the matter, and fortunately he had also the means of overcoming the evil. From the fat of a bear he had recently killed he tried out a pint of clear oil, and administered the draught to Mr. Evarts. This had the desired effect, and rest and good food completed the cure. I envy Mr. Evarts the strength of his brain. How he contrived not to go entirely and irrecoverably mad I cannot imagine. His understanding must be strong indeed. Comparatively early in his wanderings, he experienced, to use his own words, ' one of those strange hallucinations which many of my friends have misnamed insanity, but which was to me Providence.' An old clerical friend seemed to appear to him, and authoritatively ordered him to take a certain direction. Reluctantly, for it was quite contrary to his own convictions, he followed the advice of his ghostly companion, and was saved ; but whether or not, he could have succeeded in carrying out his own intention of crossing the mountains to Virginia City, it is of course impossible to say.

Later on his mind became much affected. The different

members and portions of his body segregated themselves into separate and distinct individualities and identities, who accompanied him as companions, and with whom he, to his great satisfaction, kept up a constant conversation. Yet during this time he was able to reason consistently and sensibly about his condition, the route he ought to take, and his chances of winning out, and to think perfectly naturally of his home ties and affections. Altogether it is a wonderful history, and one worthy of notice, as exemplifying what an incredible amount of hardship, cold, and starvation the human frame is capable of enduring, and showing what apparently insurmountable obstacles and difficulties a man can overcome, if only he can manage to retain even a partial mastery over his mind and reason.

But to return to the subject of Mud Volcanoes. Though disappointed on our first visit, we on another occasion saw two or three eruptions of the principal spring.

The water gradually rises till the inner basin is quite full, becoming more and more agitated as it flows. It then gives one or two convulsive heaves, dashing the waves violently against the sides, recovers itself for a few minutes, and next with still more violent throes it goes off, casting mud and water about twenty or thirty feet high. Then occurs a momentary lull, after which the explosions continue with increased vigour. The whole operation lasts about ten minutes; after which the water gradually subsides and falls to the bottom of the basin.

There is something very comical in the appearance of these great pots of bubbling, splashing, and explosive mud; something almost grotesque in the manner they cast high into the air masses of clay and tons of dirty water.

Round about this central group are a great many mud springs; some large, some small, some intermittent and resembling the specimen described, some constant in their action like the Giant's Cauldron and the Grotto. The former of these two volcanoes is situated on the hill-side, in a little ravine. It has a very large orifice, about forty feet in diameter and thirty feet in depth. This Cauldron is filled with thin mud in a state of most fearfully wild commotion, boiling, spitting, and spluttering like a pot full of stirabout screeching hot. The roar of it can be heard at a considerable distance, and the steam of it ascends in a dense column to heaven. A slight smell only of sulphuretted hydrogen is noticeable here, but with many of these mud springs not only does the steam ascend to heaven but the stench also.

The Grotto is a cavern extending almost laterally, but with a slight downward inclination, into the side of the hill. It is situated close to the river. The mouth is about five feet in diameter, and it is full of clear water, madly boiling, and in a state of most violent gaseous ebullition. The steam from it is so hot that you cannot approach it.

The following extract from Mr. A. C. Peale's field-notes will give a more accurate account of an eruption of the principal mud volcano than can be gathered from my description of it:—

A.M.   August 12th.

6.19.   The Geyser has evidently had an eruption during the night. The basin is full and the centre in ebullition.

6.31.   The eruption commences.

6.35.   There is a lull.

A.M.   August 12th.

6.42.   The eruption ends.   The maximum height was 25 feet, and I noticed
        that the ground shook beneath me while the eruption was
        going on.

10.19. The temperature of the water at the edge of the basin is 148° F., and
        the air is 60° F.   The centre is bubbling, and a black oily sub-
        stance floats on the surface.

10.29. The temperature of the water is from 140° F. to 180° F., and it is
        rapidly filling the basin.

10.49. The eruption commences.

10.55. There is a lull.

10.58. The maximum, 18 feet, is attained.

11.2.   The eruption ends.

11.8.   The temperature at the edge of the basin is 170° F.; air 60° F.   The
        water has fallen a foot already.

11.15. Water 150° F.; air 60° F.   The water has fallen 18 inches.

11.20. The water has fallen 5 inches since the last measurement.

11.24.
 to   The water still has a temperature of 150° F., and has fallen 2 feet
11.29.   10 inches.

11.39. The water has fallen 3 feet 2 inches since the eruption ceased
        (lowest point).

The annexed table gives the results of the observations taken in connection with this spring :—

Data	No. of Eruption	Length of Eruption		Interval between the Eruptions			Interval between commencement and lull	Interval between lull and maximum	Maximum height
		M.	S.	H.	M.	S.	M.	M.	FEET.
August 9	1st	12	30	—	—	—	6	3	25
„ 9	2nd	13	00	4	5	30	6	3	30
„ 11	3rd	13	00	—	—	—	6	4	40
„ 11	4th	13	00	4	18	00	—	—	20
„ 12	5th	11	00	—	—	—	4	—	25
„ 12	6th	13	00	4	7	00	6	3	18
„ 12	7th	12	00	4	13	00	6	4	22
„ 12	8th	12	00	4	12	00	5	4	19

	H.	M.	S.
Average length of eruption	0	12	26.75.
Average intervals between eruptions . . .	4	11	6.
Average interval between commencement and lull .	0	5	34.28.
Average interval between lull and maximum .	0	3	30.

On the opposite page I submit a tabular statement, for which I am indebted to the same writer, of the several springs at Mud Volcanoes.

The water in the river near the springs, and in fact everywhere above the Falls, must be greatly impregnated with various mineral substances, and its temperature considerably raised by the constant streams of hot water and mud that are poured into it.

The trout inhabiting its clear depths are exceedingly large and fine to look at, and will take a fly or any other sort of bait voraciously; but they are almost useless for food, being with few exceptions full of intestinal insects. The ghosts of digested worms seem to have revenged themselves on the living fish here, for instead of being devoured by the trout, the trout afford food for them. Some people eat these fish, and say that they are very good; but I have never been hungry enough to get over the feeling of repugnance caused by the presence of these parasites.

The worms are found, not only in the intestines, but in the solid flesh also; and vary in length and size, the largest being about six inches long. From the scars on the outside of the fish it would seem as if the insects ate their way completely through them. Occasionally you meet with a trout that has escaped the plague, and he is then bright, broad, thick-shouldered, and a very handsome fish; but when the worms are very numerous he becomes a long, lanky, dull-coloured, ugly-looking brute.

The prevalence of these parasites must be due to the warmth of the water, or to the presence of the various

SPRINGS AT MUD VOLCANOES.

General elevation above sea-level, 7,775 feet; boiling-point, 198·5° F.

No.	Size of spring	Temp. of spring	Temp. of air	Time of observation	Remarks
		° F.	° F.		
1	3 feet diameter ·	190	50	. . . .	Very thick mud spring.
2	10 feet diameter	168	50	} 3.35 p.m.	{ These springs are in the same basin with the Mud Geyser, but entirely distinct from it.
3	10 feet diameter	168	50		
4	6 feet diameter	126	48	4.35 p.m.	At head of ravine, 250 yards above the Mud Geyser.
5	15 × 5 feet	156	48	5.00 p.m.	Thirty-five hundred feet from No. 4, in same ravine at the head. There are here some extinct basins and vents for steam.
6	75 feet diameter	134	58	11.20 a.m.	A large green sulphur pool, with many centres of ebullition giving off sulphur hydrogen.
7	3 feet diameter	136	58	11.23 a.m.	Lavender - coloured spring, containing alum.
8	12 × 20 feet	88	58	11.25 a.m.	Yellow sulphur spring, about 14ft. from No. 7.
9	60 × 20 feet	140	58	11.30 a.m.	{ This group is in a ravine near the Giant's Cauldron. No. 9 is on the edge of No. 8, and has clear water, with confervoidæ lining the stream.
10	2 feet diameter	124	58	11.30 a.m.	
11	3 × 1 foot	140	58	11.30 a.m.	
12	Grotto, 3 feet high, 8 feet wide, 20 feet deep	182	58	11.45 a.m.	The grotto is an opening into a sand-stone rock at the head of a small ravine. The top of the entrance resembles a Gothic arch, coated with moss and iron. Steam escapes in pulsations.
13	30 × 15 feet	94	58	11.46 a.m.	A greenish alum pool.
14	2 feet diameter	180	58	11.48 a.m.	A pool a few feet above No. 13.
15	20 feet diameter	163	58	11.50 a.m.	Light grey mud spring, 10 feet deep. There are others too deep to get temperature.
16	Pool 500 × 60 feet	92	58	11.50 a.m.	
17	Small holes, 1 inch diameter	148	58	11.51 a.m.	} Sulphur springs.
18		172	58	11.52 a.m.	
19	. . . .	182	58	11.55 a.m.	Mud spring.

mineral substances in solution; for it is remarkable that, whereas such a thing as a trout entirely free from them is almost unknown above the Falls, I have never heard of a wormy fish being taken below them, or even between the upper and lower cascades.

AN INDIAN AND HIS HORSE.

CHAPTER VII.

NEARING THE END.

MEAT had been growing very scarce for the last few days. We had scraped clean the bones of the antelope we packed with us from Gardiner's River, and afterwards boiled them into soup; and we had killed nothing on the march except wapiti stags, which at this time of year are not fit to eat; so we determined to halt, for a day at any rate, and endeavour to replenish the larder. Accordingly, the next morning before light we all went out—each taking a different direction—to look for game; scanning the ground and peering through the trees, with the eagerness not only of hunters, but of hungry men. But no distant rifle-shot, bearing tidings of dinner, broke the silence of the morning air, or echoed 'supper' through the glades; and about nine o'clock the hunters returned tired and dejected, all with the same story to tell; plenty of old sign, but not a single fresh track, and nothing whatever eatable to be seen. So we hurriedly broke camp and moved about five miles, to a little branch rising among some old beaver dams; and there pitched our tents again, it being the last water to be found on the north side of the divide which separated us from the Fire Hole Basin.

Again we all went out for an evening hunt, buoyed up with emptiness and hope; but our exertions were attended with the same result. I soon made up my mind that there was no game then in the country; and finding a pool in a little stream that was full of small trout, I turned to and caught three or four dozen little fellows only about four to six inches long, but in very good condition and first-rate to eat. None of the others had returned when I got back to camp; and as they straggled in singly I anxiously watched their distant forms to see if any of them bent under the weight of a deer. But, no! They all walked erect, and we had to go to bed again with our guns full and our insides tolerably empty.

A council of war held that night resulted in four of us—Boteler, Wynne, Kingsley, and myself—starting for the Geyser Basin. We took one mule only with us to carry our blankets, small tent, and provisions, such as there were, for a few days. We left the rest of the outfit where they lay, with Texas Jack to take care of them and to hunt during our absence. The mule we took with us, by name Jack, was the best of the lot. He was a most marvellous animal, gifted with an amount of sense, and with a power of judging distances to a mathematical nicety, that were wonderful to see. Moreover, he was patient, strong, wise, willing, and good-humoured:— this last quality is not often to be met with in mules.

Jack could keep up a long swinging trot all day, if not overloaded. He would ascertain, by some means best known to himself, the exact width of his pack, and would measure his distance between the trees to an inch, running through apertures that looked far too narrow for him, but never striking or getting jammed. He had some extraordinary method also of determining the height of his pack, and could tell precisely whether he could pass under an overhanging bough without stooping, and, if not, how much he would have to stoop. If necessary, without pausing for a moment in his trot, he would double-down until his belly almost touched the ground, and wriggle himself through under a fallen tree in the most ludicrous manner. It is no easy task for a man, even though he be accustomed to the mountains and the forests, to make his way through the matted labyrinth of these primeval woods; and Boteler, with all his knowledge and all his instinct—with the acquired ease and natural facility that spring from constant habit—found it impossible to make anything like a straight trail through the tangle, and had not unfrequently to turn back completely arrested by some impenetrable windfall.

But through such places, if they were practicable at all, Jack would run, jump, climb, or crawl, picking his way without pause or comment. His faculty of stooping under branches, though very useful at times, was inconvenient when he was required as a riding animal. He would forget for a moment that he had not a tall pack upon his back, and in passing under some leaning tree, to avoid which the rider would merely stoop his head, not expecting for a moment that the mule would stoop also, down he would go, and with a twist and wriggle of his body writhe himself under the supposed obstacle, much to his rider's surprise and discomfort.

Our path lay for some little distance along the verge of an old lake-bed, now a grass-covered prairie; and then, striking into the timber, it crossed a low divide into the valley system of the Fire Hole, or east fork of the Madison River. Before crossing the divide we passed a few old wigwams, remains of encampments of sheep-eaters. These were the last indications of Indians that we saw, for the natives are afraid of the Geyser Basins, and do not venture into that locality at all.

Beyond the watershed the ground is exceedingly soft, treacherous, and boggy, traversed by streams of hot water, which are by no means easy to cross; and we had much trouble in keeping a direct course. As we advanced, the appearance of the country became more and more strange and interesting. We were near the end of our pilgrimage. We were in the lower Fire Hole Basin.

Presently we rode out into a little grassy plain of perhaps 1,500 or 2,000 acres, a perfectly level bay of the comparatively level plain of some thirty square miles that composes the East Madison Basin; and pulling up our horses we stopped to look round. Close at hand were two untenanted tents, and some very good-looking horses in first-rate condition were picketed hard by. Our stock was very poor, whereas these animals were fat; ours were giving out, and some of them showed strong symptoms of breaking down altogether, while these were strong and capable of doing hard work. There was nobody looking. The epidemic of the country seized us in all its virulence. Horse-stealing is in the air in the West, and if a stranger is not careful he may catch it. But we restrained ourselves; whether from a fear of committing a breach of morality, or from an indistinct idea that somebody might be observing us with a six-shooter handy, I do not pretend to say.

In front of us lay a circular plain, grass-covered at the extremities nearest to us, but bare towards the centre where the surface seemed to be composed of clay. To the west rose a low, massive *mesa*, black as Night and draped with forest; across the eastern sky stretched the high timbered ridge forming the divide we had just crossed; and to the north and south the unbroken forest rolled up to the verge of the prairie. It had been drizzling all the morning; the day was very damp and still; and from the margin of the prairie, and from many places among the pine-trees, rose in the heavy atmosphere dense white vertical columns of steam. The sight was novel and very impressive. The thickly-growing small pine-trees flourished to the very edge of the open space, fringing it with a symmetrical clearly-defined line. It looked as though a giant with a cheese-scoop had taken a sample of the country; as if a great patch of land had suddenly fallen through. It gave one an impression that some horrible catastrophe had happened, —that some modern Cities of the Plain had been overwhelmed, and had so lately sunk amid flames into the bowels of the earth that the smoke of their ruins was still ascending through white heaps of smouldering ashes.

Although the Lower Basin can in no way compete with the Upper in interest, yet there are a great many springs and geysers within its limits presenting an infinite variety of structure, form, appearance, and size; some small, some large, meriting almost to be called little lakes, and containing vast volumes of boiling water; others mere cracks or fissures in the surface, occasionally ejecting air or liquid, like the diminutive puffing-holes one meets with on the seashore.

Occasionally the deposit is composed of almost pure silica; sometimes the principal ingredient is iron; more frequently it consists of iron and silica together, mixed in some cases with sulphur also.

These three substances are found combined in various degrees; and upon their presence or absence, and upon the relative proportion of one to the other, depends the variety of colouring which in most of the springs is extremely beautiful.

The lips, rims, and sides of the orifices and craters,

and the bottoms of the pools and channels through which the water overflows, assume many different colours, and are adorned with a great variety of artistic-like work. The general hue is that of rich cream, and the most usual forms of ornamentation are lace-like fabrics and edgings of bead-work, very delicate and graceful. Frequently, however, the ornamentation takes a larger shape and assumes a spongy appearance, and the sides and bottom of the pool will be seen covered with kidney-shaped or cauliflower-like excrescences. When the temperature of the water is low, it is often filled with a curious gelatinous material, apparently some form of vegetable matter decomposed, and partially filled with mineral deposit. This substance becomes light and friable when dried by exposure to the sun.

In some ponds the water is very blue; in others it has the green tint of a beryl. I cannot account for the difference in colour.

There are six springs in this basin which periodically throw water to a height of about thirty feet, and may therefore be denominated geysers; but there is only one (which is situated at the south end of the plain) that can compare in size and power with the geysers of the Upper Basin. We saw it from a distance spouting. The steam and cloud were voluminous, and rose to a great height; but we were not near enough to judge accurately of the elevation or size of the column of water ejected from it.

A spring which I recognise as the *thud* spring of Professor Hayden is the largest in this group. It has three orifices, all of which are generally very active; and it explodes periodically, making a dull suppressed thud; but it does not throw the water to any considerable distance.

Its basin measures eighteen by sixteen feet, and varies from eight to thirteen feet in depth, not counting of course the orifices, which are of unknown depth.

There is one rather peculiar specimen. It consists of a large basin filled with clear water, with a distinct crater in the centre, just rising above the surface, which also is full of water; it resembles a little coral-reef in the ocean. The water is driven up forty or fifty feet from the inner basin, the aperture of which must be much narrower at the bottom than at the top, for the ascending column slopes outward; and, having attained its maximum height, it droops over very gracefully like the fronds of a palm-tree and falls back into the outer reservoir.

There is also in the neighbourhood a fine example of a mud spring. It contains twenty or thirty puffs, rising continually like great blisters a foot or two above the surface, which, bursting with a smothered thud, scatter the mud around.

These mud springs and cauldrons form the comic part of the entertainment. There is something very ludicrous about them. They fuss and fume and splutter and spit in such a rage about nothing, and with such small results, and are withal so dirty and undignified, that one feels quite inclined to laugh at them.

Very different in appearance to them are the constantly occurring pools, twenty or thirty feet in diameter, very deep, and filled with the most pellucid water. In the centre is generally found a funnel-shaped aperture, descending to goodness knows where, contrasting strongly in its black profundity with the sides which rise from it, richly coloured, and beautifully fretted with lace-like work.

The rim is usually moulded into a series of scallop-shell-like curves, and the edges of the scallops are frequently adorned with rows of pearly flint nodules very pretty to see. Some of these are small, others as large as a walnut. Though these nodules have no more lustre than very dull opaque pearls, which they somewhat resemble, yet they are so regular in size and in order of position that they form a very pretty finish round the circumference of the ponds.

Some springs deposit a very fine-grained black powder; and in the lukewarm streams grows a vigorous, vividly green crop of confervæ.

On the south side of the plain, extending into the mountains, is a fine though not at present very active group, the water from which, overflowing and running down a series of steps, forms numerous little cascades of a few inches in height, separated by brightly-coloured ornamented pools.

The pine-trees in the neighbourhood of the springs look unutterably sad—very pictures of despair. Stripped of every vestige of bark or leaves, encrusted with a coating of white silica, they stand, mutely appealing with outstretched arms against their forlorn condition, like so many vegetable Lot's wives.

That old springs are constantly dying out and new ones bursting forth is evident. The remains of extinct ones are met with at every step; and the pine-trees standing near springs in full activity, coated already with deposit but not yet completely destroyed, show that such springs must be of very recent origin. Numerous bare patches in the forest indicate where craters or springs formerly existed, and in many little lakes and ponds are buried the remains of geysers also deceased.

Professor Hayden enumerates a great number of geysers—flowing or spouting springs—and mud volcanoes in this basin, and says that he has not mentioned more than half of them.

The Fire Hole River is continually receiving contributions of hot water from innumerable little rills, and in this basin it embraces its principal tributary—a small stream heading in a tiny lake in the woods, and having a very pretty miniature cascade 140 feet in height. It has been called Fairy Fall Creek, and the cascade is christened Fairy Falls.

This creek enters the Fire Hole at the lower end of the basin. From its mouth to the mouth of Iron Spring Creek, which enters at the lower margin of the Upper Geyser Basin, the distance is five or six miles as the crow flies. Between the two points lies a large group of springs which cannot well be included in either system, and they have consequently been called the Half-way Springs. There is nothing very peculiar or worthy of notice about them. In fact, the springs, though chemically varying very much one from another, and of course differing widely in size and shape, are yet in their general characteristics so much alike that, unless actual analysis is contemplated, when one good example of each peculiar sort has been seen and studied, the others may well be taken for granted.

From where we entered the Lower Geyser Basin to where we encamped at the Castle Geyser is about ten or twelve miles, and over more extraordinary miles I have never travelled. The journey is suggestive of travelling in, or at any rate towards, and very close to, the infernal regions. The trail runs for the most part along the Fire Hole River, the water of which is warm, and apparently much appreciated in cold weather by flocks of geese and ducks. It is fed by numerous little streams, the beds and sides of which are brightly coloured, and so variegated that they present sometimes an appearance almost of rough mosaic. In some the water is very hot, hot enough to make the mules hop when they tread in it; in others it is comparatively cool, varying in temperature according to the distance the water has run from the boiling source.

The streams and river are lined with very dense green vegetation. The sides of the river, in fact, the whole face of the country, is honeycombed and pitted with springs, ponds, and mud-pots; furrowed with boiling streams, gashed with fissures, and gaping with chasms from which issue hollow rumblings, as if great stones were rolling round and round, or fierce, angry snarls and roars.

The ground sounds hollow under foot. The trail winds in and out among holes that puff sulphur fumes or squirt water at you; by great caverns that reverberate hideously, and yawn to swallow you up, horse and all; crosses boiling streams which flow over beds composed of a hard crust, coloured yellow, green, and red, and skirted by great cisterns of boiling, bubbling, seething water. The crust feels as if it might break through at any moment and drop you into fire and flames beneath, and the animals tread gingerly upon it.

You pass a translucent, lovely pool, and are nearly pitched into its hot azure depths by your mule, which violently shies at a white puff of steam maliciously spitten into its face through a minute fissure in the path. You must needs examine into that ragged-mouthed cavern, and start back with more agility than grace to escape from a sudden flood of hot water, which spitefully and without warning gurgles out and wets you through. The air is full of subdued, strange noises; distant grumblings as of dissatisfied ghosts, faint shrieks, satirical groans, and subterranean laughter; as if the imprisoned devils, though exceedingly uncomfortable, were not beyond being amused at seeing a fresh victim approach. You fancy you can hear the rattle of the loom, the whirl of wheels, the clang and clatter of machinery; and the impression is borne upon the mind that you are in the manufacturing department of Inferno, where the skilled hands and artisans doomed to hard labour are employed. I can compare it only to one's feelings in an iron foundry, where one expects every moment to step on a piece of hot iron, to be run through the stomach by a bar of white glowing metal, to be mistaken for a pig and cast headlong into a furnace, or to be in some other way burned, scalded, and damaged.

It is dangerous ground; I have not heard of any accident up to the present time; no modern Koran, Dathan, and Abiram as yet have been engulfed alive; but the visits to these regions have been, like those of angels, few and far between; and I daresay, when they become more numerous, we shall hear of some premature roastings, and of some poor wretches boiled before their time.

Near the trail, and situated in the woods, is another large mud spring. I call it spring for want of a better word, for there is really no spring about it. It consists of a basin measuring 40 by 30 feet, full of mud, which is constantly rising in puffs and exploding. This mud varies very much in colour at different times.

On the top of a little hill of flinty deposit near the river is one very large spring, nearly circular in shape, and measuring 150 feet in diameter. The water, boiling in the centre and overflowing all round, has produced a series of perfectly-formed concentric steps a few inches in height. The water is perfectly clear, and the ornamentation very pretty. Quite close to the river is another still larger cistern, 250 feet in diameter. The sides are about twenty feet high, and it is full of water in a state of violent ebullition, and throwing off a great quantity of steam.

Late in the afternoon it began to rain heavily, and, amid the usual discomforts attending on a wet camp, we pitched our tents in a small grove of trees close to the 'Castle Geyser.' This geyser is situated on an irregular platform of deposit, measuring 100 feet in length by 70 feet in diameter, and, at the centre, being three feet above the level of the plain. About the middle of this platform rises the active chimney, a cone of 11 feet 11 inches in height, having an aperture three feet in diameter, almost circular in form; and measuring 120 feet in circumference at the base, and 60 feet at the top. It does not taper gradually, nor is the exterior surface smooth; but it is irregular in contour, forming a series of rough steps by which you can climb to the top. The lips and interior of the funnel are lined with large, globular, orange-coloured masses.

Quite close to the crater are two pools simmering and bubbling, which share in the excitement consequent on an eruption, becoming dry when the 'Castle' is in operation.

There is also a third very lovely pool, about 30 feet in diameter and 60 feet deep, with an aperture at the bottom that looks so profound that you might almost fancy it went right through to the other side. The inner lining is of perfectly pure white silica, and the edges are scalloped and ornamented with the usual pearl-like mouldings. But the most noticeable thing about it is the perfect purity and transparency of the water, which is so still, so blue, so clear, that you scarcely know where the surface is, can hardly tell which is air and which is water; indeed, you involuntarily stoop and plunge your hand into it to convince yourself that that translucent element is in reality water. Many of my readers may have seen on the western shores of Scotland or Ireland, on some fine summer's day when the Atlantic dozes in the warm sun, clear, deep pools left by the receding tide. Beautiful they are with the rich golden browns of the sea-rack that streams upwards to the light; the delicate pinks and greens of the seaweed that fringes the rim; the bright or subdued colouring of anemones, sea-urchins, and shells. Somewhat like them, but much more perfect in shape, variety, and intensity of colouring, and above all in purity, are these fresh water-pools.

When we arrived the 'Castle' was placidly smoking. Far down in the depths of the funnel an indistinct rumbling could be heard; but it seemed quite inactive. However, a couple of men, belonging to another party, who had been there some days, told us that they expected it to spout about eleven at night; so we set to work to make ourselves comfortable in camp.

Scarcely had we got things fixed and supper under weigh, when a yell from Boteler, 'He's going to spout!' caused us to drop teapot and pannikin, and tumble out of the tent in half no time.

It was getting dark, but there was quite enough light to see that the fit was upon the imprisoned monster. We ran upon the platform, close to the crater, but were very soon driven from that position and forced to look on humbly from a distance.

Far down in his bowels a fearful commotion was going on; we could hear a great noise—a rumbling as of thousands of tons of stones rolling round and round, piling up in heaps and rattling down again, mingled with the lashing of the water against the sides as it surged up the funnel and fell again in spray. Louder and louder grew the disturbance, till with a sudden qualm he would heave out a few tons of water and obtain momentary relief. After a few premonitory heaves had warned us to remove to a little distance, the symptoms became rapidly worse; the row and the racket increased in intensity; the monster's throes became more and more violent; the earth trembled at his rage; and finally, with a mighty spasm, he hurled into the air a great column of water.

I should say that this column reached at its highest point of elevation an altitude of 250 feet. The spray and steam were *driven* through it up to a much greater elevation, and then *floated* upward as a dense cloud to any distance. The operation was not continuous, but consisted of strong, distinct pulsations, occurring at a maximum rate of seventy per minute; having a general tendency to increase gradually in vigour and rapidity of utterance until the greatest development of strength was attained, and then sinking again by degrees. But the increase and subsidence were not uniform or regular; the jets arose, getting stronger and stronger at every pulsation for ten or twelve strokes, until the effort would culminate in three impulses of unusual power.

The column of water appeared quite perpendicular, and was constantly ascending, for long before one jet had attained its greatest elevation, another had been forced through the aperture; but in the column the different efforts were plainly visible. The volume of water ejected must have been prodigious; the spray descended in heavy rain over a large area, and torrents of hot water six or eight inches deep poured down the sloping platform.

The noise of the eruption was indescribable. I know of but one simile drawn from Nature that conveys the smallest impression of it, and even then the impression is quite inadequate to illustrate the subject. Have you ever sat upon the very verge of a steep sea-cliff in a gale? I don't mean one of your yachtsman's breezes, but a real *bonâ fide* full winter's gale of wind, roaring from the north-west over leagues and leagues of white Atlantic, and striking full against the cliff-face. If you have, you will know that there is at the edge a little space of complete calm, where the sea-pinks are scarcely stirred, and where you can sit and listen to the awful riot around you, untouched by it. If you will sit there, and are unaccustomed to such a scene, you will be half deafened and quite frightened by the strife of wind and rock and sea. Hear with what tremendous blows the gale strikes against the bold front of cliff and flies hoarsely howling with rage just over your head! Listen to its vicious scream, as, baffled, it beats against the crags, and shrieks shrilly round some jutting rock! The ground seems to shake under the shock and thunder of the breakers against its base; and under all you will note the continuous hollow roar of the pebble bank crumbling to the sea with each receding wave. To all these sounds of elemental war add the shrieking of the steam-pipes of many steamers blowing off, and you will have some idea of an eruption of the ' Castle.'

Or, if you don't know much about the sea, you may imagine a gigantic pot boiling madly with a thunder-storm in its stomach, and half full of great stones rolling and knocking about against its reverberating sides. Taken with the above-mentioned steam-pipe accompaniment, which is indispensable, this may convey a faint idea of the noise.

The total display lasted about an hour. Water was ejected for twenty minutes, and was then succeeded by steam, which was driven out with much violence and in great quantities. Like the water, it was expelled in regular beats, increasing in rapidity as the jet decreased in strength until the pulsations merged into one continuous hoarse roar, which gradually but fitfully subsided, and the exhausted geyser sank back into complete repose.

To enjoy such a sight as this, a man should have time to get a little accustomed to it, for the display of such stupendous force exhibited in such an unusual manner is, to say the least of it, startling.

In our case, the grandeur and awfulness of the scene were intensified by the darkness, for before the eruption ceased night had fallen, and obscurity enshrouding the plain rendered even common objects unnatural and strange. From out a neighbouring vent white puffs of steam were forced, which, bending forward in the light breeze, crept slowly past the mound, looking in the dark like sheeted ghosts stooping under the burden of their crimes. The grey plain, and the naked pines stretching out their bared arms menacingly like warning spirits, showed ghastly in the half-light; and with these accompaniments of darkness and novelty, and amid a confused noise and concussion of the atmosphere, and shocks and tremblings of the earth, this great geyser was exhibiting a spectacle entirely new and strange to all of us except one of the party.

We considered ourselves very lucky to have so soon seen one of the principal geysers in action; and damp but happy we went to bed.

The next morning broke very dull. Dense columns of steam rose heavily from innumerable vents into the still morning atmosphere. The air was filled with smothered indistinct noises, emanating from the various springs and smaller geysers.

After breakfast we walked up to the head of the valley and, taking our stand upon the mound of Old Faithful, took a general survey of the basin. Old Faithful is situated at the extreme south end of the valley, and commands a good view of the whole plain.

The morning was still very close and heavy, but occasionally glimpses of sun burst through the thin fog, and lit up the bare ugliness of the plain. The general appearance of the surface is a dingy white, but parts of it are coloured yellowish brown by the jelly-like mud or muddy jelly that I have before mentioned as existing in and around many of the pools. A few grey patches of withered grass are scattered about.

Before us stretched out this plain, broken with a few groves of growing pines, and dotted here and there with dead dilapidated-looking trees, naked or clothed in a white mantle of silica. From this abode of desolation the trees seemed to stand aloof, fearing to share the fate of their companions already caught and turned into stone. Here and there small colonies, pushed forward by the dense population behind them, intruded somewhat on the plain; but, as a rule, the forest appeared reluctant to approach the edge. All around, but a little in the background, rose the thick timber, broken by a few gaps and open spaces which indicate where springs or geysers, active or extinct, are situated. From some half-dozen of these places columns of steam were ascending straight up in the still air.

Far down the valley, ejected by some great geyser in operation, dense clouds were bulging upwards to a height of 1,000, or perhaps 2,000 feet, and were gradually moving southward. Through this plain or valley, flowing in a south-east and north-west direction, runs the Fire Hole River, which drains into the Madison the vast quantities of boiling water thrown to the surface. It is totally unlike any other river that I have ever seen. Its bed and banks, entirely composed of hot spring deposit, are honey-combed, split up and scooped out all over by geysers, springs and pools, simmering, murmuring, gurgling, grumbling, spitting, snarling, steaming, hissing, exploding, boiling, and roaring—in short, making every sort of extraordinary noise. Some grumbled quietly along, as if enjoying themselves pretty well ; breaking out occasionally into a sort of gurgling, explosive laughter. Others, after being quite quiet for a long time, got into a violent rage, spat and snarled, or hissed like angry geese. They were of all sizes and descriptions, varying from minute vents, not bigger than a quill, to great tanks of boiling water. The course of the river is very straight, and it appeared somewhat like a steaming canal cut through a country entirely composed of limekilns, slag-heaps, and the refuse of old smelting works.

Old Faithful is so called because he plays regularly every three-quarters of an hour. The crater is quite low, and contains an orifice, which is in fact only the widening of a crack, which extends across the whole mound, and through which, when the geyser is excited, the steam is driven out and the air sucked in again, as happens in puffing-holes by the sea when a wave entering the cavern below expels the air with violence and noise, which presently rushes in again to fill the vacuum left by the water as it goes out. The mound on which the chimney stands is 11 feet 11 inches high, 215 feet by 145 at the base, and 54 feet by 20 at the top. It is formed of a series of concentric layers or steps of deposit, generally rather thin, raised above each other by little ledges, varying from a foot to an inch or so in height. The summit is covered with the most beautiful little pools, several feet deep, in which wandering trappers and an occasional traveller have dropped fragments of cream-coloured silicate bearing their names in pencil on them—a reprehensible practice and one to be abhorred, but which, in the present case, serves to demonstrate admirably the great clearness of the water.

For about half an hour Old Faithful remains quiet, making a comfortable, soothing, simmering sort of noise in his inside. After a little he gets uneasy, bubbling up occasionally to the mouth and subsiding again. Every spasm becomes more powerful, till with a convulsive and mighty roar up comes the water in a great column. He throws it to a height of from 100 to 150 feet for the space of about five minutes, during which time he keeps the top of the column almost at one level; and from numerous points in the crack which traverses the mound small jets and spurts of water are driven out.

Old Faithful is not to be compared with the 'Castle;' but it is a very fine geyser. When in operation, it displays a great amount of vigour; and it presents unusual facilities for observation, for, if a man does not object to standing up to his ankles in water—and, if he does, he had better remain at home—he can, by keeping to windward on a breezy day, stand within a foot or two of the orifice during the period of eruption.

Every geyser in this group has a different form and appearance, is endowed with different degrees of strength, and throws the water in different ways to various heights; yet the same general description is applicable to them all; and, as it is impossible for me to convey anything but a very feeble impression of the reality, it would be only wearisome were I to try and describe more than one eruption.

Looking down the river from the summit of Old Faithful, that is to say, towards the north-west, the most noticeable craters on the right bank are the Bee Hive and

the Giantess. The name of the former sufficiently indicates its shape. It has a small cone of only 3 feet high
and 5 feet in diameter at the base, the orifice measuring
24 by 36½ inches. I did not see it in active operation.
Professor Hayden describes it as throwing a column of water
of the size of the aperture to a height of 219 feet for
eighteen minutes, and says that the velocity of the water is
such that the column is not deflected more than four or
five degrees out of the perpendicular. No water, he adds,
falls back from this geyser, but the whole mass appears
to be driven up into fine spray or steam, which is carried
away as cloud or diffused imperceptibly into the atmosphere.

A little to the back of the 'Bee Hive' the 'Giantess' is
situated. The crater in this case consists of a very deep
opening of considerable width at the surface, and narrow-
ing below. One of the pipes that convey the water and
steam must be very small, for the strongest jets, those
which are driven to the great height of 250 feet at least,
through a larger mass of water which rises only 50 or 60
feet, are, comparatively speaking, small. The large opening is 32 feet by 23 feet 6 inches across, and 63 feet in
depth, and is filled with water of a deep, clear, green shade.
It is situate on the summit of a gently sloping mound of
geyserite, about 200 yards in diameter at the base.

On the other side of the river, that is to say, on the left
bank, the first geyser you come to is the ' Castle,' already
described. About half a mile below that is the Giant, a
very grand, but rather aged and worn-out geyser. The
crater is a very large rugged chimney about 10 feet in
height, nearly circular, being 25 by 24 feet in diameter
at its base, and 8 feet at the top. The platform on which
it stands is nearly 400 yards in circumference, and the
principal aperture is 5 feet in diameter. The wall of the

chimney is considerably crumbled and decayed, and on one side is completely broken through. The orifice also is broken into from the outside in two places, which must largely spoil the appearance of the jet. There are three pools of boiling water on the mound, close to the crater; and only a few yards away a new and very active geyser, commonly called 'Young Faithful,' has broken out. He has not been many years in existence, and, full of young life and energy, he blows off steam continuously and furiously. I threw him some stones, an attention which he rather seemed to appreciate, for he rolled them about in his throat and did not reject them until he had ground them to powder. He is increasing year by year visibly in strength; and, as it appears that the old Giant is at the same time getting feebler, it is probable that the youthful exuberance of the son is obtained at the expense of the father. At present Young Faithful is in operation all the time. As he gets older he will no doubt find out, with the other geysers, that once in twenty-four hours is quite sufficient.

I was fortunate enough to see the Giant play, but I was not sufficiently near to form anything like an accurate estimate of the quantity of water cast up, or of the height to which it was thrown. The volume of water appeared immense, and huge clouds of steam arose from it. The eruption lasted only a few minutes; which is strange, as Professor Hayden describes it as playing for an hour and twenty minutes, and throwing a column of water to a height of 140 feet. Lieutenant Doane affirms that it threw water from 90 to 200 feet (an estimate which is very liberal in its margin) for three hours and a half; and Mr. Langford says that it threw a jet of five feet in diameter 140 feet high.

About a quarter of a mile west of the Giant are

situated four large basins, the biggest being about thirty feet in circumference. They may be said to be within the same rim, though there is scarcely any appreciable rise above the general level of the plain. The ground all round them is quite soft and spongy, composed of a brownish yellow material, which, when dry, becomes light and brittle, and somewhat resembles a fungus. The surface is covered with little bubbling vents, about the size of a quill. In the largest basin are two apertures, and by one or both of these the water is constantly heaved up in a great rounded mass, like a huge bubble. The different basins are not in connection with each other. I was fortunate enough to see one of them in a state of great activity, but I was at some distance ; and, though I made all possible haste, the eruption, which only lasted a few minutes, had ceased before I arrived at the spot. The volume of water ejected appeared enormous, and I judged the height of the jet to be about 150 feet. I supposed this to be the 'Grand Geyser,' but I see that Professor Hayden locates it at the other side of the river.

Farther back, and near the edge of the forest, are the remains of a great geyser, now deceased, or nearly so. He has buried himself in a steep mound 70 or 80 feet high, and about 200 feet in diameter at the base. From the summit a little smoke was still exhaling, but there were no signs of a recent eruption.

To the south-west are two large geysers quite inactive.

In the rear of the Castle is a very old fellow, the great-grandfather, I should say, of all the geysers in the place. He is now very near his end, but during his active life he has made a deposit covering at least two acres of ground. In the centre of this mound are three apertures, brimming over with perfectly clear water. They are very deep. Two of them are perfectly still, and do not betray the slightest sign of animation, nor is there any appearance in them of an aperture. The third is feebly bubbling in a foolish drivelling sort of way, like an old man in his dotage muttering and dreaming of former and better days, thinking what a grand old geyser he was, and how he had in his time thrown more water higher and further and with more fuss, and made more noise, and been generally livelier than any of the present degenerate age; all of which, to judge by his aspect, may be quite true.

Besides those already enumerated are many other geysers of great interest and importance, well worthy of a visit and meriting description : but the description of one must resemble that of another; and I wish, if possible, to avoid the crime of prolixity. The principal of these are the Grotto, the Fan Geyser, the Riverside Geyser, the Saw Mills, the Turban, and the Grand Geyser.

The borders of the Fire Hole River and its confluent, Iron Spring Creek, and a great portion of the plain enclosed by these two streams, are dotted in all directions by mud ponds, solfataras, fumaroles, warm pools, boiling springs, and the remains of many extinct geysers of considerable size.

To my mind, by far the most beautiful objects are the still, deep, quiet wells. They are perfectly lovely.

Imagine a circular basin of, say, about 15 or 20 feet across, and 50 or 60 feet in depth, the ground surrounding it sloping very gently back from the brink in little concentric steps, varying perhaps a quarter of an inch to three or four inches in height at a time. The edges of these steps are curved into a series of semi-arches, and adorned with mouldings of pearly beads, ranging in colour from a dull white to a coral pink. The rim of the basin is convoluted and gathered in, into a system of irregular curves, scalloped and beaded. The interior is of a most delicately rich cream colour, intensified in places to rose; and over portions of it is spread a fine network of lace-like fabric. Deeper down the ornamentation becomes larger, and the sides are composed of rounded sponge-like masses. The basin is filled to the brim with water, more transparent than anything you can imagine, and deeply blue. As the sun rising or sinking strikes at a greater or smaller angle the surface of the water, its rays, refracted more or less obliquely by the resolving element, give a constantly varying but ever lustrous appearance to the interior ornamentations and colourings of the pool that baffles all attempts at description. One never tires of looking at these fairy lakes, for though language fails to convey the impression of variety, and the character of sameness would appear to be inseparable from them, yet it is not so at all; on the contrary, a constant and beautiful change is going on at every succeeding moment of the day.

In the measurements I have given above, I do not pretend to accuracy. I have merely guessed at them, except in such cases as I have found mentioned in Professor Hayden's reports. There is a great discrepancy of opinion among the several scientific gentlemen who have visited this locality as to the height to which the different geysers throw the water, and also as to the duration of the eruptions. This is attributable, I daresay, chiefly to the great difficulty of distinguishing exactly the point where the water ends and the fine spray or steam commences; also of deciding up to what height the steam is propelled, and where it commences merely to ascend. The geysers, moreover, must vary far more than is generally supposed, both in the amount of force exhibited, in the length of the eruption, and in the interval between the displays. Professor Hayden, for instance, says that the Bee Hive threw 219 feet high for eighteen minutes, while Mr. Peale says over 100; which is vague, but could not mean more than 150 feet. The same authority states that the average of Old Faithful was 121 feet 9 inches; Hayden, on the other hand, gives it as from 100 to 150 feet. The latter adds that the eruption lasted fifteen minutes, while the former says that its duration was only four minutes forty-five seconds. Again, Professor Hayden describes the crater of the Giantess as being 18 feet by 20, and 160 feet deep, and says that she threw a column of water to an altitude of 250 feet; while Mr. Peale, speaking of the same geyser, says the basin is 23 feet 6 inches by 32 feet 6 inches, and 63 feet deep, and the extreme height attained by the water was 39 feet, the average height being only 30 feet. According to Hayden it played for twenty minutes. Of the three eruptions mentioned by Mr. Peale, two lasted about seventeen minutes. Professor Hayden speaks of the Castle as if it had been a great geyser, and represents that it is now inactive, and only keeping up a constant roaring inside; while Mr. Peale mentions that he witnessed three eruptions of it, only, as he did not see the commencement of one, he could not in that instance accurately ascertain the height to which the water was forced; the average height of the other two being 63 feet. I guessed it at 250, and the time to be an hour, and I know that I could not be so very far out. Professor Hayden saw the 'Grand Geyser' throw a column of water 200 feet high, which was held up for twenty minutes. Mr. Peale mentions 173 feet as the extreme height, and gives thirty-two minutes as the duration of the eruption.

In a few instances only have the geysers in eruption been accurately measured by triangulation. They are so far removed from each other, and so little is known of the length of interval occurring between two eruptions of the same geyser (which interval, again, probably varies continually), that it would occupy the attention of a large staff of men for a considerable time to obtain anything like reliable data on the subject of the phenomena exhibited in this wonderful region.

It would be interesting to note the similarity of general character that exists in the various manifestations of extant volcanic force in such widely separated regions of the globe as North America, Iceland, and New Zealand, and to endeavour to compare them one with another, and to judge of their relative value.

Unfortunately it is impossible to arrive at any conclusions so well assured as to permit of one's speaking dogmatically on the subject. The geyser in Iceland has been thoroughly studied for very many years, and, if the other volcanic districts had been submitted to as close and severe a scrutiny, comparison would be easy. But the wonders of the Yellowstone have been laid open to scientific inquiry only during the last four or five years; and, though very much has been accomplished in that short time, yet much remains to be done before any reliable conclusions can be arrived at. Considering that their existence has been known for a comparatively long period, it is very strange how few observations have been obtained of the New Zealand geysers. Whether it be that the intervals occurring between their eruptions are unusually wide, or that the periods of excitement are governed by some obscure effect of climate or weather, and are consequently variable and uncertain to an unusual extent, I do not know; but it is a fact that very few travellers who have visited the neighbourhood of Lake Taupo and the other volcanic districts of the middle island have been favoured with the view of a geyser in actual eruption. We have therefore to content ourselves with unreliable information gathered from native accounts and mere hearsay. Such statements cannot of course be opposed to the observations of scientific men or of the ordinary but accurate traveller. The only mention that I can find of a New Zealand geyser in operation is made by the Honourable Herbert Meade, R.N., who describes the great geyser at Waikite as throwing a vast column of water to a height of forty or fifty feet. He says that on or about the 20th December it rouses itself from a quiescent condition into a state of activity, increasing in vigour till February, when the exhibition culminates and gradually subsides again. This geyser would seem to be governed by totally different laws from those ruling its brethren in any other part of the world, and it affords an exception to the rule of similarity asserted above. Its eruption must constitute a very grand display, not on account of the height attained by the jet, but by reason of its enormous bulk ; but it is not equal to the geyser in Iceland, or to many among the spouting springs of the Yellowstone country. But because this, the only well-authenticated account that I can find, proves that the particular eruption described is inferior to the operations of many geysers in other countries, it would not be fair on that ground alone to prejudge New Zealand.

There is a certain amount of truth doubtless in native stories, and even from their appearance it may be regarded as certain that spouting springs, most remarkable for size and vigour, do exist in New Zealand, although travellers have not been fortunate enough to see them playing. The structure of a true geyser is so peculiar

that it is not easy to be deceived about it. Where you
find a large orifice and deep tube, a great mass of deposit
and plenty of present activity in the neighbouring springs,
it is reasonable to assume that the geyser so constituted,
though probably depending more upon quantity than
quality, upon volume rather than elevation, for its position, must be considered a member of the first class.
Now some of the hot springs and the basins or funnels
of many of the New Zealand geysers are very large
indeed. Te Tarata measures 80 feet by 60 ; the basin
of Otukapuarange is 40 or 50 feet in diameter. The
aperture of Ku-a Kuoi is 16 feet long by 12 wide, and
Pirori at Tokana has a funnel 8 feet broad on the surface, and is said to throw a column of water 6 feet in
diameter to an elevation of 100 feet. The largest cistern
that to my knowledge exists in the Upper Fire Hole
Basin measures 250 feet in diameter ; but Rotomahana
Lake is one mile in length and a quarter of a mile
broad. I think this pond may fairly be considered as
belonging to the class of hot springs, for though it may
not contain any single great central aperture, yet its
waters are throughout raised to a high temperature by
the numerous points of ebullition which break through
the bottom and sides.

Reasoning, therefore, solely from the size of their
orifices, we should be compelled to admit that these
New Zealand fountains excel all others, be they where
they may. But it is probable that the very size of their
craters must in the case of an eruption interfere preju-
dicially with the character of the display. All other
things being equal, it is certain that a fountain having a
long and narrow tube would eject water for a longer
time, and to a much greater altitude, than one provided
with a shallow and very broad orifice ; and consequently

the eruption of the former would far exceed in magnificence and interest that of the latter. A lofty and slender column of water, ejected with such vehemence that for some distance it rises as a solid perpendicular jet, and then gradually losing its momentum sways and rocks in the wind, melting at the summit into white mist and cloud, and drooping over gracefully and falling in long snow-white curves, or in showers of glittering raindrops sparkling like diamonds in the sunshine, streaked and barred with rainbow—such a spectacle is full of grace, and is exquisitely beautiful; but a vast bulky mass of water many yards in diameter, hurled up to a height of 40 or 50 feet in one great effort, though a sight most marvellous as exhibiting a prodigious display of force, is not calculated to fill one with admiration and wonder by its loveliness. The mudpots and solfataras at Waikana Pahapa would appear to be similar to, but larger than, those in America which I have attempted to describe. But, on the other hand, the mud volcanoes on the banks of the Yellowstone are superior to anything of the same sort hitherto discovered in New Zealand. In both countries the areas in which volcanic action at present exists are very large. In New Zealand the district measures in its longer axis about 150 miles. It is impossible to say how extensive it may be in Wyoming and Montana, for the country is not thoroughly explored; but, if the various geyser basins already known to exist be considered as belonging to one system, then it is very large indeed. Probably these centres of volcanic action will be found to connect with other groups of thermal springs which have been observed in states and territories further to the south. In either land, the principal phenomena are grouped near a lake of considerable size, and the country surrounding them is

mountainous.   New Zealand has certainly the advantage in
this respect.   Towering above the plain rise the two great
active volcanoes of Tongariro and Ruapehu, casting out
from their cones of scoria volumes of smoke.   The presence of these burning mountains, standing like sentries
guarding the mysterious region they overlook, proudly
overshadowing the fussing, fuming, insignificant springs
and fumaroles beneath them, and watching the whole
district spread out at their feet, must add great grandeur
and impressiveness to the scene.   Yet, if New Zealand
excels in general beauty of effect, she cannot compete in
excellence of detail, except in the single case of the
terraces of Rotomahana.

Judging therefore by what I have read and heard of
both countries, and by what I have seen of one, I arrive
at the inevitable deduction that the springs, mud volcanoes, and geysers of Wyoming are not only more numerous, but more important than those of New Zealand.

It is a curious fact that, both in Iceland and New Zealand, the geysers are, with few exceptions, described as consisting of a deep, broad pool or spring, existing on a level
platform or in a depression of the surface ; whereas those
situated in the Upper and Lower Fire Hole Basins are
almost invariably provided with a regular chimney, varying from 3 to 12 feet in height, which occupies the centre
of a mound.   Whether this difference in structure would
tend to carry out the theory that the American formation
is older than the others, I do not pretend to say, being no
judge of these matters ; but it seems natural to suppose
that the antiquity of those geysers is greatest where the
tubes are longest, where the orifice is contracted, and
where the deposit has built up a distinct chimney round
the mouth.

The principal spouting fountains in Iceland are the

Geyser and the Strokker, which being translated mean the Roarer and the Churn. None of the others can stand comparison with the ordinary thermal springs and boiling fountains of the Yellowstone country, and it is somewhat doubtful in my mind whether even the Geyser is at present superior or even equal to the Grand, the Giant, the Castle, or any other Transatlantic specimens of the first class. Comparisons are odious; in this case they are impossible also, for though the Iceland geyser is thoroughly understood, the others have not been sufficiently studied; and so much do the eruptive forces vary on different occasions that, unless very many operations were observed and measured, it would be impossible to arrive at a just estimate of the relative value of two geysers.

In former days the Iceland geyser was more active than at present; probably it then exceeded in power and capacity anything we now know of. Mr. C. S. Forbes speaks of it as throwing a column 60 feet high when he saw it play in 1859. No diameter is given on this occasion. In another place the same authority describes an eruption in the following terms :—

'September 10th.—Twice during the night I was aroused by the unearthly complaints of *The* Geyser; but beyond the vast clouds of vapour which invariably follow each detonation, and a gentle overflowing of the basin, they were false alarms. As morning was breaking it sounded an unmistakable " réveille," which would have roused the dead; and I had barely time to take up my position at the brink of the old " Strokker " before full power was turned on. Jet succeeded jet with fearful rapidity, earth trembled, and the very cone itself seemed to stagger under the ordeal. Portions of its sides, rent with the uncontrollable fury it had suddenly generated, were ripped off and flew up in volleys, soaring high above

water and steam, whilst the latter rolled away in fleecy
clouds before the light north wind, and, catching the rays
of the morning sun just glistening over the yökul-tops in
the far east, was lustrous white as the purest snow.

'Discharge succeeded discharge in rapid succession for
upwards of four minutes, when, apparently exhausted
and its basin empty, I scrambled up to the margin, intending to have a good look down the tube, which I
imagined must also be empty ; but the water was still
within a few feet of the brink and boiling furiously.
Hastening back to my former position, the basin filled
rapidly, and I was just in time to witness the most magnificent explosion of all.   Everything seemed to depend
upon this superhuman effort, and a solid unbroken column
of water was hurled upwards of 25 feet in circumference,
attaining an altitude of nearly 100 feet.   Here the column
paused for a moment before reversing its motion, and fell
listless and exhausted through the volumes of vapour
which followed it into its throbbing cup, again to undergo
its fiery ordeal at the threshold of the infernal regions.'

A column of water 25 feet in circumference far exceeds the dimensions of the jet of American geysers ;
but many among the latter throw to a higher elevation,
and keep up the display for a much greater length of
time.   Mr. Symington, who saw the great Geyser in eruption, says :—

'Subterranean noises like thunder were waxing louder
and louder, each earth-shock accompanied by a tremor of
the ground, more or less violent, but quite unmistakable.
Bells of water in quick succession were rising from the
basin and falling again, ever increasing in size, till a large
one burst ; and then jets of water in successive spurts
rushed up in sheafs from the tube ; at first about 10 feet,
then the height was 15, 20, 30, 50 feet, and so on ; each

effort surpassing the preceding, till it attained the height of 200 feet. The fountain did not fall down between each jet, but, nearly holding the elevation once gained, the whole grew up bodily by a series of jerks, each higher than the last. Dense clouds of steam enveloped the whole, and only afforded occasional glimpses of the columns of water from the leeward side. White vapour also spread out above the fountain, rolling away in vast curling volumes, which condensing in the air came down like heavy dew. Tremendous sounds were continuously heard, like the roaring of an angry sea, broken in upon by the near discharge of minute guns. It is at last, what we longed to behold, a grand eruption of the great Geyser.

'The vast body of water from the central pipe continued jetting up, till, as I have said, it attained the height of 200 feet, falling down again into the basin which was brimful to overflowing. The subterranean rumbling sounds and reports, accompanied with vibration of the ground, were fearful. Jets of water rushed up in sheaf with a continuous noise, such as would be produced by 500 rockets discharged into the air at the same instant.

'Even the beautiful clouds of steam which robed the Geyser were regarded by us with an indescribable feeling of mysterious awe and wonder, as if we had actually discovered the fabled magic vapour, from which the Eastern Ufret, or any other vision might arise; while the sharp tinkling plash of the descending water could at times be heard amidst the loud, hissing, roaring, booming, and confused Babel of all unearthly sounds. The eruptive forces having now expended themselves for a time, the fountain gradually subsided in the same manner, though more speedily than it had risen. The whole terrific spectacle lasted about twenty minutes. We were singularly fortunate, as, from what we were told, few eruptions of late have lasted more than four or five minutes, or attained half the height of this which we had just witnessed.'

This account recalls to my recollection what I myself saw in the case of the Castle previously described; but the Castle played about twice as long as the Geyser, and, in my opinion, cast the water to a greater height.

Another authority, Mr. Baring-Gould, in the following quotation describes his experiences :—

' Five strokes underground were the signal, then an overflow, wetting every side of the mound. Presently a dome of water rose in the centre of the basin and fell again, immediately to be followed by a fresh bell, which sprang into the air full 40 feet high, accompanied by a roaring burst of steam. Instantly the fountain began to play with the utmost violence : a column rushed up to the height of 90 or 100 feet against the grey night sky with mighty volumes of white steam-cloud rolling about it, and swept off by the breeze to fall in torrents of hot rain. Jets and lines of water tore their way through the cloud, or leaped high above its domed mass. The earth trembled and throbbed during the explosion; then the column sank, started up again, dropped once more, and seemed to be sucked back into the earth.'

The first accounts we have of the Geyser date about the middle of the eighteenth century. At that time the basin measured, according to Olofsen and Povelsen, 57 feet in diameter, and was 72 feet deep; and a column of water was ejected from it to the enormous height of 300 feet. Shortly afterwards, in 1772, Von Trail estimated its height at 92 feet. Stanley, in 1789, states that the jet of the Geyser attained an altitude of 96 feet. He is the first authority who speaks of the Strokker, which, at the time of his visit, threw a great volume of water

Upper Fire Hole, from "Old Faithful."

130 feet high, thereby surpassing the Geyser; but its supremacy did not last long, for in that same year it was destroyed by an earthquake. In 1804 the Geyser was erupting every six hours, and reaching an elevation of 200 feet; and Strokker, having recovered, was about equal to it in activity. In 1809 and 1810 Hooker and Mackenzie visited Haukadal, and reported that the Geyser operated at intervals of thirty hours, casting its jet 100 feet high in the former year, and 90 in the latter. At the same epoch Strokker was accustomed to play every ten or twelve hours to a height of 60 feet. When Henderson observed it, in 1815, the Geyser had completely changed its manners and customs, for it then spouted every six hours, the average altitude attained being 80 feet, while on one occasion it threw as high as 150 feet. At this time Strokker played during one hour out of the twenty-four. Since 1815 the action of both springs has been very irregular. The two fountains much resemble each other, Geyser being the superior, though on one or two occasions Strokker has surpassed him. The chief difference between them is that Strokker can always be excited by feeding him with turf and stones, while Geyser spouts just when he chooses, and will not suffer himself to be deranged by any insult whatever.

The district of Haukadal is most magnificently situated. Towering peaks pierce through mountains clad in ever-lasting snow, and frown upon great glaciers that creep towards the lava-covered plain. It is a scene awful in its desolation and grandeur, and surpasses in scenic effect the environs of the Mammoth Hot Springs and of the two Geyser Basins.

While it must be conceded, therefore, that the Upper and Lower Fire Hole Basins cannot boast of scenery that can compare in beauty or grandeur with the surroundings that encompass the volcanic regions of Iceland and New Zealand, and while the two latter countries do in some minor respects excel the phenomena exhibited in the former, yet I think there is no doubt whatever that in Wyoming and Montana are to be found not only the most numerous, but also the most noteworthy, remarkable, and beautiful examples yet discovered of the peculiar volcanic phenomena common to all three countries.

In the United States, in Iceland, and in New Zealand, these phenomena may be classed under two heads, acid springs and alkaline springs. The first group contains the quiescent or constantly-boiling pools, called in Iceland 'namur,' in New Zealand 'ngauhas,' and all other springs having no periodical ebullition : in this category must also be ranged the salces, mud-pots, and mud volcanoes. The greater number of the Yellowstone springs and fountains come under this heading.

The alkaline division comprises the New Zealand puias and Icelandic hverjer, to which belong Geyser and Strokker. In this category must be enumerated the geysers—as they have come to be called—of the Upper and Lower Fire Hole Basins, and all the springs or fountains spouting at intervals, regular or irregular, and having intervening periods of complete inaction.

Water filtering through the surface and percolating deep down into the bowels of the earth, mixing with certain mineral substances, acids, and gases, and dissolving others with which it comes in contact, changed into steam by the agency of subterranean heat, and again condensing into water on reapproaching the surface, produces in all countries the causes that have resulted in the construction of these alkaline and acid springs.

The steam, the gases, and the water, holding in solution

various minerals, constantly carry their burdens up from below and deposit them on the surface of the earth. In the first division sulphuric acid is the most active ingredient; and its action on surrounding rocks results in the ferruginous clays of the mud-pots and salces, and in the deposits of alum, sulphur, and sulphate of lime, which are common among the solfataras and other acid springs. When the supply of sulphuric acid becomes exhausted a new system of chemical changes is inaugurated; different minerals and gases are brought into play, and other substances are precipitated. Carbonic acid disintegrates the rocks, and the silica dissolved by the alkaline bicarbonates so produced deposits, in the shape of semi-opal, various kinds of quartz, silicious earth, or pure flint, and forms the geyser-tubes and chimneys, and the beautiful incrustations and ornamentations that I have already attempted to describe. By this theory of chronological succession, which will be found fully explained in Hochstetter's 'New Zealand,' it would appear that the quiet pools and gently-bubbling fountains are first formed. These, changing from acid into alkaline springs, are by degrees converted into spouting geysers, insignificant at the commencement and while the tube is in course of construction, but gradually improving and increasing in vigour as the pipe lengthens and narrows, until their strength culminates at that period of their existence when the tube and funnel have attained that relative depth and breadth, and that proportion of size of bore to length of barrel, which combine to make the most perfect apparatus for their purpose, and enable them to use the force at their disposal in the most advantageous manner possible. They then slowly subside as the orifices become more and more thickly encrusted and choked with deposit, until they revert to their primitive condition of feebly bubbling springs, and finally closing up altogether, give up the ghost, bury themselves in their own crater, and remain monuments of the past, like the Liberty Cap at Gardiner's River.

It has been surmised that the operation of a spouting geyser is caused by the weight of superincumbent and ever-increasing volumes of vapour contained in a subterranean cavern, which, pressing with constantly augmenting force upon the surface of the water beneath, at last acquires sufficient elasticity to overcome the resistance of the water, and drives it violently out through the vent offered by the geyser-tube. Having expelled the water, the vapour frees itself and rushes through the same channel until equilibrium is restored, and the chamber commences again to fill up with steam and water. Equilibrium does not readily assert itself, because, owing to sinuosities and angles in the pipe and cavern, an easy interchange of temperatures is impossible.

But this theory is, I believe, entirely superseded by that evolved by Bunsen in the first place, and adopted subsequently by Professor Forbes. These gentlemen argued that the tube was the only mechanism necessary, and that the whole operation was conducted in it. They proved that water under certain circumstances of position and pressure, and being subjected to peculiar chemical changes, became so cohesive in its particles that it did not boil until an extraordinary temperature was reached ; but that when cohesion was overcome the molecules separated very violently, and steam was instantly generated in vast quantities with terrific force. The superincumbent column of water in the tube, added to the ordinary pressure of the atmosphere, caused this peculiar phenomenon to take place in the lower portion of the pipe ; steam was generated there, and forcing its way upward displaced some of the water, the vacant place below being immediately filled with steam. This process they supposed to continue until the vapour and water were nearly equipoised, when the former, receiving additional impulse from a great volume of steam suddenly generated in the manner before mentioned, would overcome the latter, and cast the entire mass of water violently out of the tube. I can understand how such a mode of procedure might result in a short and vehement explosion, but I do not see how an eruption like that of the Castle witnessed by me, in which water was cast out for twenty minutes, followed by an escape of steam which for forty minutes more rushed through the pipe, can be accounted for in this way. Neither do I comprehend how a tube having the diameter of that of the Castle, and being of any reasonable depth, could contain anything like the quantity of water that I saw ejected from that geyser.

Appended are some tables showing analyses of water and material from New Zealand and Iceland. It may be interesting to compare them with those previously given of deposit and water from various springs in the Yellowstone district :—

CHEMICAL COMPOSITION OF THE WATER AND THE SILICIOUS DEPOSITS OF SOME OF THE HOT SPRINGS.

THE ANALYSES EXECUTED IN THE LABORATORY OF PROFESSOR D. V. FEHLING AT STUTTGART.

I. *Water.*

No. 1. Te Tuia-nui, near Tokanu on Lake Taupo; reaction alkaline; analysed by Dr. Kielmaier.

No. 2. Te Tarata, on the Rotomahana; reaction neutral; analysed by Mr. Melchoir.

No. 3. Ruakiwi, on the Rotomahana; reaction neutral; analysed by Mr. Melchoir.

No. 4. Rotopunamu, on the Rotomahana; reaction neutral; analysed by Dr. Kielmaier.

In 1,000 parts of the water there were contained, of—

	In No. 1	2	3	4
Silica	0·210	0·164	0·168	0·231
Chloride of Sodium .	4·263	2·504	1·992	1·192
Total residuum . .	4·826	2·732	2·462	1·726

Owing to the small quantities of water for analysis (one bottle of each), only silica, chlorine—computed as chloride of sodium—and the total amount of non-volatile ingredients, could be quantitatively ascertained. Qualitatively, however, the presence of magnesia, lime, sulphuric acid, and traces of organic substances has also been proved.

II. *Silicious deposits of Hot Springs on the shores of the Rotomahana analysed by Mr. Mayer.*

No. 1. Te Tarata, two samples: *a*, an earthy powdery mass; *b*, solidified incrustation.

No. 2. Great Ngahapu.

No. 3. Whatapoho.

No. 4. Otukapuarangi.

	1 *a*	1 *b*	2	3	4
Silica	86·03	84·78	79·34	88·02	86·80
Water and organ. sub. .	11·52	12·86	14·50	7·99	11·61
Sesquioxide of Iron } Alumina }	1·21	1·27	1·34 } 3·87 }	2·99 }	slight indication.
Lime	0·45 }		0·27 }	0·64 }	slight indication.
Magnesia . . .	0·40 }	1·09	0·26 }		
Alkalis	0·38 }		0·42	0·40 }	

I. Pattison ('Philos. Magazine,' 1844, p. 495), and

II. Mallet ('Philos. Magazine,' 1853, v., p. 285), give the following analyses of the silicious deposits of the hot springs of Lake Taupo, without, however, specifying the localities.

	I.	II.
Silica	77·35	94·20
Alumina . . .	9·70	1·58
Sesquioxide of Iron .	3·72	0·17
Lime	1·54	Indic.
Chloride of Sodium .	—	0·85
Water	7·66	3·06
	99·97	99·86
Specific gravity	1·968	2·031

From *Srcibner's Magazine* for June, 1871, I submit Dr. Black's analysis of 10,000 grains (about $\frac{1}{6}$th of a gallon) of water from the Great Geyser in Iceland :—

Soda	0·95
Alumina	0·48
Silica	5·40
Muriate of Soda	2·46
Dry Sulphate of Soda	1·46
	10·75

An analysis made by Forchammer of Iceland geyserite gave the appended results :—

Silica	84·43
Water	7·88
Alumina	3·07
Iron	1·91
Lime	0·70
Soda and Potassa	0·92
Magnesia	1·06
	99·97

CHAPTER VIII.

WE left this extraordinary district with great regret : fain would we have tarried longer in it.   An opportunity for exploration such as none of us had ever before enjoyed was most temptingly displayed, and very gladly would we have availed ourselves of it.   Four years ago the white world knew absolutely nothing of the country we were leaving.   The few legends of Indian tribes, and the vague rumours of hunters that occasionally came to the surface and were wafted out from the wilderness to the ears of civilised men, were entirely disbelieved, or were looked upon as fables built on the very smallest foundation of truth ; and its wonders were covered with a mystery as profound as that which broods over the sources of the Nile.   And even now scarcely anything is known about it.   A few parties go in from Virginia City and out at Bozeman, all following the same trail, examining the same objects, halting at the same places. They never stray any distance from the usual route, and there are hundreds of valleys into which no human foot has ever burst, thousands of square miles of forest whose depths have never yet been penetrated by the eye of man.

It is extremely improbable that the area of volcanic activity is confined to the limited space occupied by the two Geyser Basins, and it is very possible that other depressions may be found containing springs and geysers as great as, or even more important than, those I have attempted to describe. The scenery is beautiful, the climate most healthy; game is abundant, and every lake and river teems with trout. It is a district affording infinite scope to the tourist in quest of novelty, the hunter, or the scientific traveller. Compared with other districts equally prolific in big game, it enjoys a wonderful immunity from that great bugbear of the hunter, the hostile Redskin. It is true that on the way into the Upper Yellowstone country, and down anywhere in the valleys that lead out upon the plains, it would be necessary at certain times to keep a good look-out for Indians, for the Sioux come up occasionally out of the boundless wilderness of their prairies, looking after the horses of the settlers, or of the Crows, and lurk for weeks about the passes; but they dare not penetrate far into the mountains; and, terrified at the strange sights and sounds therein, all Indians now carefully avoid the uncanny precincts of ' Wonderland.' A few wretched sheep-eaters are said to linger in the fastnesses of the mountains about Clarke's Fork; but their existence is very doubtful; at any rate, they must be a harmless, timid race. The traveller has to keep a sharper look-out for white horse-thieves than for Redskin robbers, and with ordinary precaution the country can be traversed in perfect safety.

The stock of information concerning it as yet acquired is extremely small, and, with the exception of the compilations of the various Government expeditions, the accounts are untrustworthy and inaccurate. Very anxious were we to add our mite to the general fund in the way of something newly discovered and observed; but winter was drawing nigh, and, as we had no mind to be blocked in to the southward of Mount Washburne, we returned reluctantly to our camp.

It had been our intention to go from the Fire Hole Basin down the Madison to Virginia City, thus making a round trip of it, and obviating the necessity of passing over the same ground twice; but, owing to our stock being so poor and in such bad condition, we were compelled to abandon this idea, and take the back track home; for though the distance from the Geysers to Virginia City is shorter than that to Fort Ellis, we knew that by adopting the latter route we could, if necessary, get fresh animals at Boteler's. We found our camp all right, so far as the bipeds were concerned, except that they were hard up for food, for the country had produced no game; but they had succeeded in losing a mule—an accident that was rather serious, for by it one of the party was dismounted.

The day after our return we packed up and marched to Tower Falls, arriving there many hours after dark. We could not for a long time find any way of getting down to the creek, which rushed foaming beneath, and had much difficulty in selecting a spot suitable for a camp.

Boteler and I had ridden a-head rapidly with the purpose of ascending Mount Washburne in the event of the evening giving promise of a clear view. The day turned out cloudy, and we hesitated about the ascent; but most fortunate was it that we executed our resolution, for we were rewarded with a magnificent sight. We got to the top with about an hour's light by sun. The atmosphere was very transparent, though the day was by no means fine. Heavy masses of vapour were clinging to the higher peaks, streaming out from their summits in long ragged whiffs or encircling their sides; and dense clouds slowly drifting occasionally obscured the sun. Great splinters of light darting through ragged-edged rifts in the clouds struck downward, slanting to the earth, or, spreading out through some larger opening in straight divergent lines of brilliancy, illuminated the landscape. Huge masses of cumulus blazed round their storm-foreboding edges with intense white light; piles of black threatening clouds rolled themselves in fantastic shapes above the horizon. In the distance little fragments of rainbow—wind-dogs, as sailors call them—tipped the verge of the inky blackness of some passing rain storm that swept across the sky. Everything betokened that a tempest was at hand, and the sky, vexed and angry, looked magnificent in its wrath. At one moment the earth was all shadow; then a sun-burst would strike a patch of yellow prairie or belt of trees and gild the earth with golden glory; or it would brush across it a momentary streak of vivid green, and slowly moving would sparkle for an instant like a diamond on some hidden lake, and passing over the landscape fade in the distance and vanish away. The smallest outlines on the horizon were clearly defined, and the whole middle distance was shifting and changing in broad bands of light and shade.

On such a day as this, when the sky is overcast, and the air unnaturally clear foretells a coming storm, far finer effects are enjoyed than can be seen under the cloudless heavens that are so usual in these latitudes.

There is no difficulty in reaching the top of Mount Washburne. We rode to within five or six hundred yards of the crag that forms the summit, from which the view is quite unique. Turn in what direction it may, the eye wanders over a chaotic mass of mountains, and vainly seeks some distinct central object on which to light, until, wearied and bewildered with such infinite disorder, it thankfully rests upon the rolling billows of forest which afford momentary relief, but soon in their turn become irksome from their vast monotony.

Let us examine the panorama somewhat in detail.

Stand by me with your face to the north. Right before us lies the valley of the Yellowstone, golden in the slanting rays of the setting sun, and beyond it are the great up-heaved masses that form its borders. Most noticeable for beauty of outline, cutting clear and sharp against a pale green patch of sky, is Emigrant's Peak, a fine feature in a noble group of mountains. A good deal nearer, but almost in the same line, rises the bold promontory that forms one of the portals of the third cañon, standing out tall and menacing as though warning men not to attempt the gloomy gorges that it guards; and a little to the right of it gapes the grim chasm of Hell Roaring Creek.

To the east is a vague and apparently orderless mass of peaks, tossed about in the wildest confusion, looking as if ranges originally elevated in some sort of decent order had been pressed inwards from the edges with irresistible force, and crumpled up towards the centre; or resembling the waves of a rough sea in a tidal race, when, instead of running in regular billows, the water dashes up pre-cipitously and unexpectedly in all directions. In the fore-ground is a huge flat-topped mountain, bald and scarred, desolate in the extreme; and behind it the notched, jagged horns of Index and Pilot Peaks pierce the clouds; while far in the distance loom the dim outlines of the Big Horn range.

Turning to the right we see the great snow-capped summits cradling the infant streamlets which form Clarke's Fork of the Yellowstone. From their rugged wild barrenness the eye falls abruptly, but gratefully, upon a scene of placid peacefulness rendered all the more striking by contrast. Washing the rough bases of the range with its clear waters lies the lake, shining like a gem in the dark setting of the forest, dotted with islands, pierced by promontories, calm, unruffled, beautiful; a goddess clasped in the mighty arms of the mountain. Still turning, the eye wanders over a vast plateau of undulating woods, broken here and there by open patches of grey or yellow prairie, formerly lake basins, for round the water and the places where water has once been the growth of timber forms an exact fringe. It then gazes in astonishment for a moment on the savage Tétons, looming huge and indistinct of outline in the blue evening mist, and roams over a boundless ocean of forest, extending from the south-west round to west, unbroken, unrelieved by a single peak, till it rests upon the Madison range, which, commencing nearly due west, extends far away into the realms of the mysterious north. A little nearer to us, and trending in the same direction, the Gallatin Mountains surge upwards till their peaks also fade away towards the dim distant north land. Just beneath our feet a heavily timbered valley opens out into a rolling upland prairie, spreading away on all sides towards the river, while to the south and east the Grand Cañon cuts through the bases of two mountains. Although in reality distant, the chasm appears at hand, for from your commanding position you can partly pierce its awful interior, and almost fancy you can catch a glimpse of the white waters of the river foaming below you at a vast and unascertained depth. But no glancing eddy really catches your eye; not even the faintest echo of the roar and tumult of the strife of river and of rock arises from the black profundity of that gulf.

Tired with this excess of mountains, bewildered with peaks, smothered in forest, let the traveller rest awhile, and suffer his mind dreamily to wander in memory or imagination along the banks of those water-courses that rise around him. He will have in thought to travel through many a strange land.

An interest far greater than that produced by mere

scenic effects attaches to the naked crag on which he sits.
That rock is the summit of a mountain which forms the
culminating point of the ridge that rules the water-courses
of the United States. Stretching out its arms between the
streams, it seems to say to one ' Run in this direction,'
and to another ' Flow in that.' It launches into life the
river that forms the valley of the Mississippi, a vast and
fertile region destined in the future to be one of the most
populous places on earth. That rock is the key-stone
of the continent. It is the very crest of ' The Great
Divide.'

From it has been traced out the geography of the
country. The main divisions, the great centres of trade,
together with the natural features that sway the fates of
men and nations, radiate thence ; and by a citizen of the
United States the spot should be regarded as sacred
ground. From it he can overlook the sources of the
Yellowstone, the Wind River, and the Missouri, and
of the Snake and Green Rivers, principal tributaries the
one of the Columbia, the other of the Colorado.

These waters flow through every variety of climate, past
the dwellings of savage hordes and civilised nations, through
thousands of miles of unbroken solitude, and through
the most populous haunts of mercantile mankind ; now
shaded by the great pine-trees of the forest, again shadowed
by tall factory chimneys; there clear and undefiled from the
hand of Nature, then turbid and contaminated by contact
with man ; and from Mount Washburne I believe that the
head waters can be seen of mightier rivers—rivers passing
through more populous cities, through the hunting-grounds
of more wild tribes, through greater deserts, through countries more rankly fertile, through places more uncivilised
and savage, by scenes stranger and more varied—than
can be viewed from any other point on the surface of
this earth.

Impressed by the spectacle, I sat down upon a weather-beaten granite crag, and fell into a reverie.

On the left hand, looking towards the north, spring three streams, the Gallatin, the Madison, and the Jefferson, forks of the largest river on the continent. After short separate courses they unite, and are called the Missouri; and there I in fancy launched my birch canoe. It would be scarcely necessary to paddle. Swiftly by the strong current we should be borne along until, while yet at a distance of many miles, the dim haze of spray and the confused roar of waters would warn us that we were nearing the 'Great Falls of the Missouri.' I wonder how many people know that the river has any great falls at all. Before my visit to Montana all I had of it was an indistinct idea of its length, and a vague notion that the 'mighty Missouri rolled down to the sea.' But there they are, obstructing all further navigation, falls and rapids which in any better known country would be highly appreciated and thought a great deal of. The Missouri, even at the distance of over 3,000 miles from the sea, carries a great volume of water, perhaps three or four times as much as the Thames at Richmond. It varies in breadth considerably, sometimes contracting to 300 yards, and spreading out elsewhere to nearly a quarter of a mile. The Great Falls consist of a series of cataracts and cascades, occupying some fifteen or twenty miles of the river's course. In one place, where the river is very broad, it is traversed by a level, straight-edged, perpendicular ridge of 50 feet in height, over which the water pours in a massive, unbroken sheet. The principal fall is about 80 feet in vertical height. For 400 yards above the brow the stream is compressed, and penned in by two converging sheer cliffs 100 feet in height, which contract the channel to a breadth of not more than 100 yards. The ridge is not, in this case, uniform. For 80 or 100 yards from the left bank it shows an unbroken edge, over which the river plunges in a perpendicular fall; but for the remaining 200 yards it has given way, and forms a steep, broken, jagged slope, down which the current rushes, foaming, leaping, and dashing into clouds of spray. Between these two falls, and for a little distance above and below them, the channel is constantly crossed by dykes more or less broken, forming pitches and rapids of from two to twenty feet in height.

Having made a *portage* of eighteen miles round these obstacles, let us again entrust ourselves to our fragile bark, and the river will carry us for a distance of 120 miles through a wild and savage country, to where, near Fort Benton, it is swelled by a large tributary, the Marias, and turns suddenly to the east, forming the ' Great Bend.' After that it passes through the Judith Basin, a land full of buffalo and other game ; its current navigable, when the waters are high, by steamers, taking stores and Indian merchandise to Benton, and carrying down costly furs from the great north-west. Yet not many men drink of its muddy waters, except the Crows, Grosventres, Black Feet, Assineboins, or Sioux, who hunt or make war along its banks. After a course in an easterly direction of about 250 miles it is joined by the Milk River, which flows from the north-west, having its source in the icy fastnesses of the Rocky Mountains in British territory, and traversing the hunting-grounds of Bloods, Piegans, and Black Feet, Kristeneaux or Crees, and Assineboins or Stonies, as they are sometimes called ; and a little further it is swelled by the current of the Yellowstone, which rises in the lovely lake below me. Here is situated another outpost of civilisation, Fort Buford.

All this time we shall have been gradually changing

for the worse in respect of climate and scenery. If we are journeying in winter, the weather will have been turning colder and more stormy, as we left behind us the warm radiating masses of the mountains and the soft breezes from the Pacific. This deterioration is very remarkable; so great indeed is the climatic change that I have been told that war parties from the neighbourhood of Fort Buford and the Lower Yellowstone, travelling north to strike at their hereditary foes, are frequently compelled to use their snow shoes till they get near the spurs of the hills, where not a vestige of snow is to be seen, and they are enabled to *cache* their raquets, and pursue the journey on unencumbered feet. We shall have been leaving also the rolling prairie, covered with short crisp buffalo grass, and the rich alluvial bottoms, carrying a rank vegetation, in which willows, alders, and wild cherries grow. We shall have passed through the true home and breeding-ground of the bison, through that great plateau over whose vast sad solitudes Sissapapas, Unkpapas, Yauktonaise, Sansarks, and other northern divisions of the Dakotah nation are for ever restlessly wandering, following the herds which supply them with food and with all the necessaries of life, and we shall have gradually entered upon the most dismal, most peculiar region on the continent.

For days and days we dreamily paddle through scenery, heart-breaking in its dull hideous monotony. For hundreds of miles the river washes against its banks of clay, getting yellower and muddier as it flows. If we stop and climb a bluff, we shall see nothing but a brown desert of dried mud, looking as if the waters had left the surface only long enough for it to be cracked and scorched by the sun, and to allow of the growth of a few shrubs of cactus and artemisia. Nothing breaks the dull meaningless stupidity of the round plain ; flat, sad-coloured, grey or olive-green, bounded by blue walls of sky. Not a single bit of bright colour, no object of beauty, not a shade even of pleasant verdure refreshes the tired eye. Everywhere is brown mud, grey clay, or white alkali ; everything is graceless, hideous, and depressing.

As we sweep round the curve of one more link in the endless chain of river reaches, we may perhaps see an Indian, stooping to lap the water from his hands, suddenly leap erect, startled by the paddle-strokes, snatch at his pony, sling himself into the saddle, and vanish over the neighbouring rise. Probably he is one of those fierce warriors of the north, the Black Feet, offshoot of the Dakotah nation, once formidable, now almost exterminated by disease. Or he may be of a kindred but hostile band, and belong to a war party of Minneconjou Sioux, intrepid raiders, who, descending from their northern plains, harry the cattle and lift the stock of settlers on the Platte or the Republican, and penetrate in search of horses away down into Texas, 800 or 1,000 miles from the tents of their tribe. In either case it behoves us to be very careful. No hot coffee for supper, for we dare not make a fire ; the least impression of our feet, the smallest curl of smoke, would betray us. No more landing on the bank, for all such signs as those an Indian can read as a white man reads a book. But all night long we will paddle on, the weather-worn clay banks looking grotesquely ghostly under the dim light of the stars. We are passing through the *mauvais terre* of Dakotahs, one of the most extraordinary districts, geologically speaking, in the world. The high clay, sand, or sandstone cliffs and bluffs that form the shores have been carved by rains, split by heat, and weathered into forms so various and fantastic that only the brush of a

Gustave Doré could do justice to their weird wildness. In places it looks as if the river were running through the ruins of some Cyclopean city; an illusion that is heightened by the fact that on the summits of detached pinnacles and towers the massive forms of mountain sheep may very frequently be seen. It is a desert of clay, alkali, and sage-brush, uninhabited and uninhabitable.

Still through a country of wild tribes the now mighty river pursues its way, gradually bending to the south, bordering the elevated plateau or Coteau-du-Prairie, past villages of Minatarees, Mandans, and Arikarees.

Southward ever roll its waters, shaggy with imbedded pine-trees, yellow with the clays of the 'bad lands,' receiving the currents of the Big Cheyenne, the Niobrara, and many lesser tributaries, slowly, very slowly emerging from utter barbarism into semi-civilisation. Indians still crowd the banks, sit chattering and laughing on the beach, or saunter listlessly about. But many are dressed in European clothes, and are very different men from the free wild savage of the plains. We are passing settlements of the different Téton sub-tribes, and of the Yanckton division of the Sioux.

To the east of us, not very far from the 'grand détour,' lies a district most interesting from the fact that in it is found the great red-pipe stone quarry, where from time immemorial all the Indian tribes have been accustomed to resort in mutual peace, to gather material for the fashioning of their calumets. At these meetings the hatchet was buried, and for the time being hereditary and bitter foes met on terms of friendship. It was a sort of sanctuary, a common property, belonging to no tribe in particular, a place where they could all freely interchange ideas and barter merchandise. And, no doubt, from the facilities of intercommunication thus afforded many good results must have arisen.

Among the sand hills that fringe the western bank, stealing parties and war parties from the two principal bands of the Sioux, the Brulés and Ogallalas, trail and track the hunters of Pawnees, Otoes, Winnebagoes, or Omahas, through whose reservations the river runs. These half-civilised men, who have learned all the vices and few of the virtues of the whites, mix freely with the hunters, trappers, and traders, who pursue their avocations with less risk and smaller profits than their fellows on the upper streams. Steamers ply upon the busy stream, and just before where the Platte—that preposterous river, miles broad in places, and only a few inches in depth—pours in its yellow sands, it sweeps between the rival cities of Omaha and Council Bluffs.

After a brief glimpse of settlements, we should suffer a partial relapse into barbarism.

We should see scattered parties wandering up from the 'Indian territory' of the Cherokee or Chocktaw nations, men who live in houses, cultivate large farms, go to Sunday-school, and tell lies. These tribes are rich and prosperous, and offer almost the only instance of the native race proving strong enough, physically and morally, to withstand the deleterious effect of our superior state of existence. With them we should see members of their affiliated tribes, little remnants of eastern clans, whose very names suggest a history of wrong, bloodshed, and injustice ; of white men tortured, of Indians massacred, of injury unprovoked, of reprisal, revenge, and extermination ; Seminoles, Delawares, Shawnees, Sacks, Foxes, Senecas, Wyandottes, tribes from the borders of the sea, from the misty lakes of the north land, from the red pine-forests of Virginia, the Carolinas and Florida, who till the land of the territory, and look with envy on the few marauding wild men from the plains, Cheyennes and Sioux, Arapahoes, Kiowas, or Comanches, who may chance at rare intervals to water their horses at the brink. But this debateable land is soon passed, and over the broad still bosom of the river, cutting through the rich alluvial soil of Missouri, we slowly urge our boat.

According to geographers, we should soon have to leave, in name at least, the river that we have followed from its birth, for we are approaching the place where the clear-flowing Mississippi pours in its waters from Minnesota, land of lakes. But as the Missouri is altogether the largest stream, has a larger course, drains a far greater extent of country, and carries a heavier body of water, and as, after the junction, it gives its character and colour to the combined rivers, I maintain that below the union of the two the river should be called Missouri, and not Mississippi. After passing the quaint old French settlement of St. Charles, not so *very* long ago a frontier town of importance, we should glide into the shadow of the huge arches of the St. Louis bridge, and haul our canoe up on the levée of the Queen City of the West.

What an awful change has taken place! Can this turbid, sullen flood, reeking with the filth of cities, swirling sulkily through the arches, frothing on its slimy banks, torn and beaten by the paddles of countless steamers, be the same stream that leaped into life in the northern sierras, and sweet with 'the odour of the forest, with the dew and damp of meadows, with the curling smoke of wigwams,' rushed through its 'palisade of pine-trees'? How utterly incongruous and out of place do we appear, and our poor little birch canoe, in this busy hive of men, this great city of 300,000 inhabitants! What do the men who jostle and stare at us know of the free life of the prairie and the woods, though in their warehouses are stored thousands and thousands of buffalo robes and skins? The best thing we can do is to get out of our moccasins, buckskins, and flannels, and, with the help of the barber and the dry-goods store, transform ourselves into civilised beings in white shirts, black store-clothes, and plug hat. How horribly uncomfortable we shall feel! How red and weather-beaten our faces will appear! And as to our hands—well, the less said about them the better.

There is plenty to be seen and done at St. Louis; but, if I linger to describe it, I shall awake out of my reverie before I can reach the sea. We must hurry up, step on board that palatial steamer just about to cast off from the levée, and continue the journey. If we desire to be very luxurious we can have a 'bridal chamber,' all hung with blue satin, 'real elegant.' Very pleasantly pass the days, with the help of good cigars, a few juleps, and a little gambling; the placid monotony of the time disturbed only by the bustle of arrival and departure at the nume-rous landing-stages that line the shores, and at which the steamer takes in or discharges bales of cotton and tobacco, hogsheads of sugar, barrels of pork, and flour for the field hands. Past rich alluvial steamy banks fringed with reeds, where tall canes and palmettoes take the place of the northern pine, we rush along through dreary cedar swamps, where the long funereal Spanish moss hangs dismally forlorn from the rotting boughs, past deserted mansions, abandoned plantations, and ruined homes. It is a country across the face of which 'Ichabod' is plainly written, for the glory has indeed departed from it—a land whereon the stamp, not so much of war as of subsequent injustice, has been indelibly imprinted. Yet we are steaming through the very richest portion of the once-prosperous, happy South. There are large tracts far worse than this, where railways are bankrupt, canals choked, roads impracticable, and the country is fast reverting to its primitive condition. But to no fault on the part of the people is this almost universal ruin to be attributed. Nobly have they struggled against adverse fates and striven to right themselves, and most evilly entreated have they been by their conquerors. With fire and sword the North had to cut out and cauterise the foul sore of Slavery; but the hand that held the knife ought to have been the first to heal the wound. How generously they spoke! What fair promises were lavished upon the beaten foe! The seceded States were to reconstruct themselves; no prolonged military rule was to sully their freed soil! Civil rights and government were to be instituted at once. Arrests were rare, confiscations not frequent—in theory at least; but in practice it makes not much difference whether a man's property in land is sequestered, or whether the taxes on it are so heavy, and so unjustly levied, that he cannot possibly retain the soil. The restoration of civil rights meant too often the enfranchisement of a majority of ignorant men, who, not having had time to educate themselves, or to become accustomed to the novelty of the situation, proved mere foolish tools in the hands of unscrupulous agents. The tax-payers and rate-payers, the employers of capital and labour, had but a feeble voice in their deliberations, and had no control over the reckless system of finance that was frequently inaugurated.

It makes one sad to remember the golden promises that were held out, the flattering prophecies that, now that the stain of Slavery was removed, the South would become more than ever prosperous; to think of the plucky spirit in which the beaten people acknowledged their complete defeat, accepted inevitable consequences, and set to work to build up their shattered fortunes ; and now to see how few of these promises have been fulfilled—how lamentably at variance with prophecies the result has proved to be! There is no doubt that the Northern people wished to deal fairly and kindly by their kindred ; but the exigencies of party strife ran counter to the better feelings of the people. Unfamiliar with politics until the fortune of war raised him to pre-eminence, the Chief Authority in the State could do little in the way of following out his own will, or of controlling and guiding the strong party movement that conducted to his elevation. People wonder and lament that the times are dull and trade is failing ; that immigrants return to Canada or Europe ; that there is no money for legitimate speculation, and no confidence in business matters between man and man ; and every quack has some patent medicine to arrest the progress of the wasting debility with which the State is afflicted. Sorry physicians indeed are they who cannot discern the true nature of the disease when the body politic lies crippled before them, its lower limbs paralysed by the effects of the drugs they have themselves administered. Bitterly will the nation some day repent the short-sighted policy that induced their rulers to harass and despoil the richest provinces of the Union—in the spirit of children, unable to resist the temptation of proving their triumph—' cutting off their noses to spite their faces,' sacrificing the future of the community to the present of their friends.

Still southward rolls the flood; heavier and more stagnant grows the atmosphere ; gloomier and wider spread the lagoons and bayous. Turtles float on the surface ; alligators bask in the sun ; millions of fireflies glance and glitter under the shadows of the trees. The night is too close and oppressive for sound sleep; but towards morning a fresh cool air, smacking of the sea, refreshes one's fevered cheek, and before sun-rise we are landed at the dear, quaint, picturesque, old-fashioned French market at New Orleans.

All hail to the pleasant memories that jostle in my brain, and strive to run down through my pen when I think of you, O crescent city! What a charming place you must have been before the war! Even now—ruined, torn by factions, help-begrudged, government be-Granted, trade-bedevilled and 'busted up' generally, you are a most hospitable and amusing and delightful city. New Orleans is quite different from any other town on the continent, with the single exception perhaps of St. Augustine. Portuguese fishermen wrangle in their harsh jargon on the quay; French creoles—some of them old settlers of Louisiana, some descendants of Acadians expelled from Nova Scotia—gossip in the market-place. Streets are crooked, houses picturesque; the red sashes of fishermen and the gaudy handkerchiefs of the negroes predominate largely over the black cloth or white linen of the clerks. There is a tone of bright colour in the place, and a look of old Europe about it. We ought to stop some time at New Orleans, but we shall be catching cold on our breezy crag; so in spirit let us hurry on still south towards the sea.

Cotton and tobacco are left behind; through swampy, miasmatic savannahs and rice plantations the river dawdles, scarcely moving, old and weary, tired with the long race that it has run, melancholy with the scenes it has passed through, worn out with the strife and struggle of life—all enjoyment in existence gone, the brightness of its youth forgotten, the memory even departed of the days when it leapt flashing and exulting in

the sun, and, brimful of exuberant life, flowed laughing
through the prairies, and brawled and battled noisily
with the obstacles in its way. Very quietly and sadly it
wanders on now through its delta, seeking only for rest
and peace, till at last, after a course of countless miles,
after traversing or bounding numerous states and territories, and draining many thousands of square miles, it
spreads its arms out thankfully, and wearily sinks asleep
on the heaving bosom of the Gulf. And the little grain
of hard sand, the minute fragment of feldspar or quartz,
snatched from its rocky cradle at our feet on Mount
Washburne, finds a tomb at last in the still depths of
Ocean, and sinks to form part of a new continent—a
minute helper in the universal scheme, a humble instrument in the hands of the great Architect of all.

Turning south, and looking towards Henry's Lake,
my eyes rest upon the broken country in which spring
the sources of Green River. Varied are the scenes
and strange the circumstances that attend upon the Missouri in its long course from the mountains to the sea ;
but, apart from mercantile associations, that river cannot
for a moment compare in general interest with the stream
whose course I will attempt briefly to describe. For,
through regions much wilder, more remote, and less
known to white men ; through lands unsurveyed, almost
unexplored ; through valleys, plateaus, and mountains,
equally remarkable with those of the north country, and
having in addition a halo of vague surmise, a mist of
southern romance and Spanish chivalry hanging over
them, flow the waters that I now glance upon.

Green River has a nearly due south course of about
350 miles. At first it runs leaping and laughing through
the hills and fertile valleys or forests like a happy romp-
ing child ; but its youthful season of light-heartedness

does not last long, and it soon enters upon the dry, cold, ungraceful duties of life. For many miles it traverses that portion of the great basin that used to be called the Colorado Desert, a flat miserable country, devoid of beauty, dull and uninteresting in the sad-coloured sameness of its dreary wastes. Plains white with alkali, or shaded green by a partial covering of sage-brush, and deserts supporting only a few artemisia bushes and greasewood shrubs, form the general character of this country.

In the midst of this desolation the traveller would suddenly be recalled to the recollection of arts, sciences, and engineering skill, and to the knowledge that such a thing as civilisation still existed, by passing under the tressel-bridge of the Union Pacific Railway. After leaving behind him this token from the great world of cities and of progress, the scene very much improves. The river strikes upon the bold front of the Wahsatch Mountains, and, forced out of its course, runs along the base of the range, busily seeking an outlet, which it finds at last through a gap between the Wahsatch and the Sierra Escalente. Having passed through the range, it soon bends a little to the westward, to make up for its former easterly digression, and enters upon a country entirely altered in its natural features and principal characteristics, and frequented by different representatives of the human race. It ploughs its way through fertile table-lands, and bursts through mountains; and though Utes, Shoshones, and other Indians kindred to the tribes we have been hitherto accustomed to, still drink of its waters, yet it is hastening rapidly towards the hunting-grounds and villages of very different branches of the native stock. The few white men, too, that might be met with are dissimilar in appearance, clothing, and language to the hunters and trappers of the North.

The barbarous nomenclature of the Anglo-American race is left behind. We are now in a country to which the very names of the mountains, rivers, and passes give a certain amount of melodious interest. There is a remnant of the old chivalry of the Spanish invader clinging to it. We have done with Big Sandies, Little Thomsons, Bitter Creeks, Muddy Creeks, Muggin's Gulches, Smith's Pass, and Brown, Jones, or Robinson's Peaks. Now we pass streams picturesquely named after some saint, or from the anniversary of some particular feast or festival, or from some peculiarity of vegetation or geological appearance, such as the Rio San Rafael, the San Juan River, the Rio de los Dolores; and streams rising in sierras, like the Sierra de los Pinos, Sierra Sangre de Christo, Sierra San Miguel, Sierra de la Plata, Sierra Abajo, or Sierra la Sal, discharge their clear waters into the river. We pass by Ojos and Lagunas, or ride over Mesas, Vegas, and Llanos. Irrigating canals, though still remaining dirty ditches, sound much prettier when called acequias; an arroyo is a pretty paraphrase for a muddy water-course; and villages convey a false but pleasant impression to us when metamorphosed into pueblos. The ordinary circumstances of life and daily travel become interesting and acquire an extrinsic value in our eyes by the mere change of names.

Though still in the United States, we are in a land which could not be more utterly unlike the regions traversed by the Missouri, if it were divided from them by leagues of ocean, or ruled by another government, and owned by another race. The melodiousness of the Spanish names adds, I think, very much to the pleasure of travelling in countries that have been under the domination of that race. What a pity it is that the American people (by American people I mean the citizens of the United States) have not more universally adopted the Indian, Spanish, or French names! It seems impossible for the Anglo-Saxon to invent a picturesque or appropriate nomenclature to describe the principal features of a new country, while the aborigines, and the Spanish or French voyageurs, prospectors, and explorers have generally managed to hit upon some expression which either conveys a just idea of a peculiarity in the place, or is at any rate poetical in meaning and sonorous in sound.

Through mountains, or elevated fertile gently-rolling plains covered with timber and dotted with fresh-water lakes, Green River for 200 miles carves its way, receiving in the first fifty miles of its Alpine course the waters of the Zampah, the Uintah, and the White River ; the Uintah rising among the masses of the Wahsatch, the other two in those great elevated nuclei of mountains which I have already mentioned as existing on the confines of the north and middle parks of Colorado. Clear as crystal run the waters of these two tributaries, which spring among perpetual snows and flow through metamorphic ranges ; the little specks of mica—pilgrims' gold, as it is sometimes called—rolling down among their granite sand, glittering and sparkling in the sun, like flecks of the precious metal. Bright messages they bring from the high islands of Colorado, the Switzerland of America, telling of smiling valleys, warm sheltered parks, of lakes and ever-flowing streams. They linger a moment in the broad glare of sun, and then plunge sullenly into the gloomy depths of the cañon that hides the parent stream.

In the lower portion of its course the river cuts through a region that is better described as an elevated plateau than as a mountain range. Here it is joined by its eastern fork or chief tributary. The wandering hunter or savage, travelling along above the dark depths of the river-bed, would notice on his left as he descended the stream another great rent in the plateau converging from the east ; and, about seventy miles below the crossing of the old Spanish trail from Los Angelos to Abiquie and Santa Fé, he would arrive at the spot where Green River, roaring far down in the depths of its cañon, is joined by the Bunkara, or Grand River, rushing to meet it through a similar gorge. The two streams united form the Rio Colorado Grande.

For 500 miles the united rivers, plunging from cañon to cañon, pursue a tortuous course far down in the bowels of the earth. For 300 miles the stream traverses the Grand Cañon, a chasm of profound depth, which it has worn through various strata of rock, showing the method and order of position, defining their relative thicknesses, and affording the most remarkable geological section in the world. The almost perpendicular cliffs vary in height from 1,000 yards to a mile ; and for many continuous leagues its awful depths have been estimated at over 7,000 feet. It is the greatest cañon or gorge existing, as far as we know, on the face of the globe.

The country traversed by the Grand Cañon consists of a series of plateaus descending in regular steps towards the sea. As the river has no cascades, and not many rapids of any great height, but falls uniformly with a steep but regular gradient, it follows, as a result of the peculiar formation of the country, that at the northern extremity of each cañon the cliffs are comparatively low, and increase gradually in height until the river emerges at the southern end of the chasm from between most stupendous walls. What infinite ages must have been consumed while the current ground out its bed through these elevated plains ! It does not appear that by any convulsion of Nature these chasms were formed, for the stratification is conformable on opposite sides of the cañon ; they must therefore have been slowly sawn out by the friction of water. I know of no exhibition in Nature that could give a man such an adequate idea of the slow but irresistible eroding powers of that element, or that could convey to his mind so accurate a notion of never-ceasing action persisting through an immensity of time, as can be acquired by the contemplation of these and other similarly great gorges, by which a river has levelled its bed through such a gigantic thickness of material as obstinate as most metamorphic rocks and granites.

I suppose the Great Cañon of the Colorado has been formed by a similar process, and in a manner resembling that by which the Niagara River is now creating a small cañon between Lakes Erie and Ontario. If in former ages the Colorado flowed along the surface of the plains, what gigantic cataracts there must have been at the southern edge of each plateau !

All the Indian tribes with which we are acquainted have now been left behind, with the exception perhaps of a few representatives of the Pah Utes, who may occasionally wander down from the mountains. The borders of the Cañon indeed can scarcely be said to be inhabited at all at present, though there are many indications that its safe recesses were at one time tenanted by a tolerably numerous and ingenious people. Who or what they were—these people who have utterly disappeared, but have left behind them, as memorials, their little dwellings and their irrigating ditches—whence they came, and what inducement could have forced them into a country so unsuitable to human life, it is hard to say ; but it has been surmised that they were the inhabitants and the descendants of the inhabitants of villages and pueblos further south, who fled long ago before the mail-clad warriors of Spain.

About sixty miles below the junction of its two forks, the Grand and the Green Rivers, the Colorado receives the turbulent waters of the San Juan, rushing tumultuously from the eastward through a cañon equalling in the immensity of its depths that of the main river. About this point the heights of the chasm walls are said to culminate, and the river is described as rushing madly between vertical cliffs so high that even at midday the light can scarcely penetrate the awful depths. At present there is no very accurate information to be obtained about this district, full reports of Major Powell's exploring expedition, which was undertaken in 1873 for the Smithsonian Institute, not having been published.

On the San Juan, which rises in Southern Colorado, are said to be situated some of the richest silver lodes in the continent; and the upper portions of its valley will probably before many years be settled up. Upon and near its banks are the villages and settlements of Pueblo Indians, apparently a different race to any at present existing on the continent. They dwell in towns, cultivate the land, and have a certain acquaintance with the manufacturing art. Who are they? Is it true that they are the representatives of the Aztecs, and that among them are lineal descendants of the proud, civilised, and luxurious race which succumbed to the valour of Spain? It is hard to say, for they have been so little studied by men capable of solving such problems. It is told of them that from the balconies and flat summits of their houses they wait for the rising of the sun, and worship that luminary, and that they live in daily expectation of the coming of Montezuma. Certain it is, that in their *estufos* they constantly keep burning the sacred fire, and nourish and pay great reverence to a rattlesnake. They are altogether far more civilised in appearance, manners, and customs than the wild tribes who encompass them about, and are evidently sprung from a very different stock.

There is an immense field for ethnological research in the New World. In New and Old Mexico, Arizona and Southern Utah, occur villages of Moquis and other civilised Pueblo Indians; and the remains of a powerful and constructive race are numerous. Very common in Yuchatan and many portions of Central America, frequent in Mexico and all the Gulf States, and occasionally to be found as far north as the neighbourhood of the Great Lakes, are the strange memorials and vestiges of that departed people generally known as 'Mound Builders.' It is a great field, and it lies almost fallow.

Some distance further on, the Colorado Grande receives, also from the south-east, the waters of the Colorado Chiquito, rising in the Zuni Mountains and the great plateau of the Sierra Madre. Could we ascend its rapid current we should find ourselves among pueblos of the Moquis and other similar tribes of Indians, organised communities dwelling in towns and villages, that stand like oases in the wilderness, over which roam wild Apaches and Navajos, savages crafty and warlike— western Ishmaelites, whose hands are against every man, and against whom every man's hand is raised in turn. It is of these Indians and the country infested by them that a 'hardy adventurer' said, in reply to some inquiries, that Arizona was not a bad sort of country, and that it contained a right smart chance for prospecting, but that the Indians were awful mean, especially the Apaches, who troubled him very much, because they filled him so full of bullet-holes he could not hold his victuals. These

Apaches are more dreaded by the whites than perhaps any other tribe on the continent. They have kept up a constant guerilla warfare with the settlers, and up to the present have not only succeeded in holding their own, but have actually turned back the tide of immigration from their country. They have depopulated whole districts in Mexico, and have completely paralysed the energies and stayed the progress of the frontier provinces of New Spain. From their unknown fastnesses in the Mimbres Mountains, and in the many sierras and cordillerras that traverse the desolate plains which constitute the greater part of their country, these marauders sally forth to harry the unhappy settlers of El Paso, Chihuahua, Sonora, and Sinoloa ; or, armed with the guns and clothed in the garments captured and stripped from the bodies of slaughtered Mexican lancers and dragoons, lie in wait for the sturdier but less numerous immigrants and prospectors of the Anglo-American race, who have been induced by tales of the vast riches in gold and silver hidden in these mountains to risk their lives in the pursuit of wealth. What fearful stories are told of these border forays—stories of frontier villages burned and wrecked ; of towns, situated so far in the interior that they were deemed secure, surprised, pillaged, and destroyed ; of quiet peaceful *haciendas*, at eve beautiful in the luxuriant natural foliage of a sub-tropical land and in the rich exuberance of cultivated crops, at morn reduced to a smoking pile of charred rafters and crumbling *adobe* walls ; of wives and daughters torn from husbands' or fathers' arms to grace the lodges of cruel savages ; of expeditions organised in pursuit ; of surprise and recapture ; of the finding of lost ones after years of bitter separation ;— stories varying in detail, but all of them with the same colouring of blood, all of them sounding the same undertone of battle, murder, and sudden death.

Yet these plains, than which no portion of the Great Sahara can now be more inhospitable, plains which support nothing whatever in the shape of vegetation except the huge ungainly cactus, at one time or other were certainly inhabited by a numerous and prosperous race, for you may ride through leagues and leagues of country strewn with the remnants of their pottery, and see evidences of man's work in deserts where now there is not food enough to support a grasshopper.

At last, after a passage of 500 miles deeply trenched in the surface of the earth, the Colorado once more bursts forth into the light of day; and shortly after being joined by the Rio Virgin, a river rising in the Wahsatch range, it issues from its long imprisonment in the mountains and pursues a tolerably even course towards the sea, flowing nearly due south. Near the junction is situated the Mormon settlement of Callville. Below this point it passes through the country of various divisions of the Apache tribes, until sixty miles from its mouth it is joined by a great river, the Rio Gila, flowing from the Cordilleras to the east. Here, in a land scorched and burnt by the fierce untempered rays of a tropical sun which, radiating from the glowing surface of the desert, renders the heat well-nigh insupportable, is situated the most remote post of the United States, Fort Yuma. It is of this post that the story is narrated of a soldier, who, after leaving it for another but apparently not a better world, reappeared at midnight a few days subsequently to one of his comrades, and begged him for goodness sake to give him his blanket and overcoat, because in comparison with Southern Arizona he found his present habitation unbearably cold.

Sixty miles below this the river mingles with the warm salt waters of the Californian Gulf.

The general character of the country drained by the Colorado is that of a great table-land, composed of a series of extensive mesas or plateaus rising from the sea towards the north and east in ascending steps, overtopping each other by a height of several thousand feet. The shape of this table-land is a sort of irregular triangle, the apex lying about the intersection of the 38th parallel and the 110th meridian, and the base being upon the sea, or rather upon the sea-coast range. The eastern side forms the divide between the Rio Grande del Norte and the Colorado. This watershed follows in places the crests of the Sierra Madre, and of the many other sierra offshoots and spurs of the main range, but during the major portion of its length pursues a devious course along an imperceptible ridge in the Sierra Madre plateau. Its principal tributaries, the Gila, Bill William's Fork, and the San Juan, flow from the east. The Rio Virgin, though entering it from the right hand, yet flows from the north, and it receives no confluent of any size from the west except the Mohave. From its south-western angle extends a very peculiar feature in American geography. A long depression sunk about 70 feet below sea-level, comprising some 30,000 square miles, stretches from the San Bernardino Mountains to the 38th parallel, a distance of about 250 miles in length. This oblong basin is a perfect desert, and is commonly and not inaptly called the 'Valley of Death.'

Very little indeed is known of Arizona and parts of New Mexico, Colorado and Utah. Constant hostility on the part of the Indians has frustrated all efforts at successful colonisation. Though the greater portion of Arizona, as far as our knowledge of it extends, is parched and barren in the extreme, yet it undoubtedly must contain fertile land, and that on a large scale. No human beings, not even Apaches and Navajos—those Western Bedouins—could exist in it if the usual surface of their country was of a character similar to that portion of it with which the whites are acquainted. Far in the recesses of the mountains are the homes of these wild horsemen ; and in those secluded valleys must be hidden parks and pasture lands in plenty. There, too, in the imagination of many a hardy prospector, are valleys strewn with balls and lumps of native silver, and hill-sides where the precious metal crops out of the surface. Legends of stately cities where Incas still reign, where the sacred fire has never been extinguished, where the ordinary utensils of the people are of solid gold and silver, float out from this land of misty rumour and vague tradition, and fire the brains of reckless men. Many a poor fellow has met a cruel and violent death from the hands of savages, or has perished in slow, solitary misery, of thirst and starvation, wandering through these trackless wastes in search of the fulfilment of his dreams. It is a country a great portion of which can never be settled up, for by constant irrigation only could it be cultivated ; and who is going to expend labour and money there, when to the south, in the highlands of Mexico, is a fertile land, a garden country situated within the influence of tropical rains, and while to the north and east are the valleys, parks, and plains of New Mexico and Colorado freely watered by perennial streams ?

The best description that I am acquainted with of this part of the United States is to be found in ' New Tracks in North America,' by Dr. Bell ; in the pages of which interesting work will be found a most graphic account of the passage of the Grand Cañon of the Colorado by a man of the name of White, who, most miraculously escaping all dangers and overcoming almost incredible difficulties, succeeded in navigating the river on a raft from above the two forks to Callville.

Let us turn to streams that will lead us through very different scenes and climates.

Numerous little creeks and rills combine to form Snake River, and it is difficult to say where its head-waters should really be placed; but in any case we shall not have to look far from the sources of the river that occupied our attention last. In some maps the sources of Snake River are indicated as existing about twenty miles south of the south end of Yellowstone Lake; but I fancy that those streams are joined by other branches having their springs further from the mouth of the main river, and contributing to it a stronger body of water. Old trappers and hunters used to talk of 'Two-water Lake,' a sheet of water so called because from that mutual spring two rivers ran —the one to the Atlantic, and the other to the Pacific Ocean; and, though not literally true, yet their statement turns out to be very nearly correct. The Yellowstone River, after a course of 1,300 miles, falls into the Missouri, and through that channel finds the Gulf. It flows from out the lake of the same name; and though it cannot be said actually to rise there, for there is a river flowing into the lake also that heads some distance to the south, yet the Yellowstone Lake may not inaptly be described as the source of a river running into the eastern seas. On the south-western side of the Yellowstone Lake, about five or six miles from its shore, lies a little sheet of water called Hearts Lake; from which flows a strong stream, which is certainly one of the most important branches of Snake River, and is probably its principal source. Hearts Lake is fed by a small creek, which rises in a promontory jutting out some distance into the waters of Yellowstone Lake. Thus within the encircling arms of that lovely sheet of water is contained the fountain whence bursts into life the southern fork of the mighty Columbia River. The sources of the Snake and the Yellowstone overlap and interlock, and the old uncredited legend of Two-water Lake turns out after all to be almost literally true.

The stream to which I ask my readers now to turn their attention is called indiscriminately Snake River, Shoshone River, and the southern branch or Lewis Fork of the Columbia. I respect it for having so many names. Every river ought to be voluminously baptised for the convenience of those who wish to write about it. It obviates such a lot of painful repetition. The Snake, however, is a river of uncertain temperament and undecided mind. It is incapable apparently of striking out and maintaining an independent course of its own, but goes wandering aimlessly about, feebly trying to find a way out of the deserts that encompass it during the early part of its career.

First it flows south, receiving many accessions from the neighbourhood of the Yellowstone Lake and the north-western slopes of Wind River Mountains; then, at the earnest solicitation of several tributaries rising in or about Lewis and Shoshone Lakes, it turns suddenly to the north and, having met and received their currents, bends again to the southward, making a bold curve round from south to west for about 180 miles. Then it flows nearly due north for 200 miles or so, its course being almost conterminous with the boundary of Idaho and Oregon, until it receives its principal confluent, the Salmon River; and after a western course of 80 miles it discharges into the Columbia. Soon after leaving Wyoming, the land of its birth—a land sparkling with streams and shining lakes, swathed in solemn folds of forest, or bedecked and rendered gladsome with flowery vales and grassy prairies—it enters upon a district of clay, sand, and alkali, prickly pear, artemisia, and sage-brush, such as I have many times previously attempted to describe. The valley of its drainage has an average width of 70 or 80 miles, and the desert lies principally on its northern or right bank. It rises in Wyoming, and traverses the entire breadth and almost the whole length of Idaho, and, together with the Columbia, forms the boundary of Washington and Oregon territories.

About the centre of its great southern curve is Fort Hall, a small military establishment situated in the reservation of the Shoshone and Bannack Indians, and some 60 miles west of that post is the principal feature of the river, the great Shoshone Falls.

Lewis Fork is a river that depends very materially upon snow melting for its supplies, and consequently it varies very much in volume, being in spring and early summer nearly equal to the Columbia, but in winter dwindling to a comparatively small stream. But this epithet of small is comparative only, and is not really applicable, for it is at all seasons a large river, being over 200 yards broad just above the principal fall. Like all other rivers on the continent that flow over a series of mesas or table-lands, it has worn its way gradually back from each precipice, and formed a tolerably level bed by sawing out for itself a deep gorge. Above the fall the cañon is between 600 and 700 feet in depth, the upper portion of the sides being composed of steep clay bluffs and buttress-like intrusions of basalt, while the lower half is of grey porphyritic trachyte. Above the brow of the fall the course of the river is broken by several small islands and large fragments of volcanic rock, among which its waters rush and rend their way in numerous shoots and rapids. The transverse trachyte dyke that forms the cascade curves up stream, like the great Horseshoe Fall at Niagara. Over this ledge the river plunges in one vast solid mass, striking full upon the surface of the water about 190 feet below. There are no rocks beneath to break and dash to pieces the descending column, which drops vertically into a mist-enshrouded cauldron of seething, surging foam; and though the face of the ridge is broken into rough jutting ledges and shelves, yet their presence is indicated only by occasional lateral jets of foam, the mass of water being so heavy that it falls in an almost solid, shining, uninterrupted wall. About four miles above the chief fall is another cascade. Here the river just before its leap expands considerably, and is divided into two channels by a low island that reaches to the very brow of the fall. On the north side of the island the current springs boldly over a projecting cliff, and falls a distance of 150 feet, striking the green surface of the pool beneath. On the other side the ledge has given way; and the current plunges madly, foaming down a steep and broken slope covered with fractured fragments of the dyke.

The formations being in many respects very similar in both instances, these falls must somewhat resemble those situated on the Yellowstone and in Tower Creek. Both are to a great extent indebted for the strange wildness of their scenery and for the savage desolation that so gloomily envelopes them and that impresses the visitor so very powerfully, to the peculiar structural effects produced by the rounded water-wrought masses of trachyte, the long lines and square buttresses of columnar basalt, the angular fragments of other volcanic material, and the weather-worn eroded masses of indurated clay, of which their surroundings are chiefly composed. The Shoshone cañon is wanting entirely in the gorgeous colouring which

distinguishes that of the Yellowstone, and the falls and
the scenery surrounding them are endowed with no particular form of loveliness or grace. But this lack of
beauty may perhaps be partially made up for by the
peculiar quality of desolation that pervades them, and
which they possess in a preëminent degree. Very few
men have visited these falls, but all who have done so
agree in thinking that the perfectly level, utterly monotonous plain, the dingy, neutral-coloured grey greens of
sage-brush, and the browns of sunburnt clay—tints
so sad that not even the fierce light of Midsummer's sun
blazing in a sky of cloudless blue can strike out the
smallest particle of bright cheerful colour—combined
with the long gloomy endless sides of the cañon, and the
forbidding blackness of the volcanic rocks that encircle
the falls, make altogether a scene most savage and strange
in the extreme. After passing the falls the Snake River
flows towards the North, and traverses the country of the
Peu d'Oreilles and Cœur d'Alênes.

At their junction the two forks of the Columbia are
in early summer nearly equal to each other in volume,
but the northern branch (or Columbia proper), taken from
year's end to year's end, is by far the more important river
of the two. Its current maintains a more consistent level,
being fed by the numerous reservoirs through which it
passes, such as the upper and lower Columbia Lakes and
Lakes Peu d'Oreille and Cœur d'Alène. With it we
have nothing to do. It is noteworthy principally as forming part of a natural highway to the extreme north. Its
course is very tortuous. For a long distance it flows
nearly north, striking the eastern flanks of the Selkirk
Mountains; and then, bursting through that chain and
turning sharp round, it pursues a direction nearly parallel
with its former channel, running between the Selkirk and

the main or snowy range of the Rocky Mountains. Not far from where it turns suddenly to the south, but on the other side of the chain, are clustered the sources of the Athabaska River. The pass is not a difficult one, I believe, though it is overshadowed by one of the loftiest peaks on the continent, Mount Brown, which attains an altitude of 16,000 feet. The distance between the Columbia and Athabaska is not great, and the waters of the latter river, after joining the Mackenzie, flow mingled with that mighty current into the Arctic Ocean. It is a long path though, that leads by this route from sea to sea; and a weary way it is to travel; for from its mouth to where it breaks through the Selkirk Mountains close to Athabaska pass, the Columbia has a course of 1,500 miles; and from the head of the Athabaska to the mouth of the Mackenzie, descending Slave River and traversing Athabaska and Slave Lakes, is over 2,000 miles more.

Shortly below the junction the Columbia is a magnificent river of from one to two and a half miles broad. For several hundreds of miles it flows through upland sparsely-timbered plains; but, as it nears the sea, the shores of its fine estuary are densely clothed with all manner of valuable hard-wood trees, such as various species of oak and ash. Alders, poplars, and beech also are mingled with them, and help to relieve the sombre monotony inseparable from forests of unmixed coniferous trees, while some of the pines attain gigantic proportions, being second only to the 'Big Trees' of California. The navigation of the river by vessels of any burden is interrupted 170 miles from the sea by the 'Dalles,' or narrows, a series of low rapids over which the river tumbles, falling seventy feet in ten miles. These rapids are, I believe, passable by boats at high water. The banks of the lower river are inhabited by Chinnoocks and other tribes, who live entirely on fish, and hunt but little, though they pay some attention to trapping and collecting the furs which the country produces in tolerable abundance.

Oregon is naturally one of the richest portions of the United States. Its climate is good, being superior to that of California. It is admirably adapted for tillage, farming, and stock and sheep-raising; it is covered with valuable timber; and it is traversed by fine rivers, which are stocked with salmon and other fish. Settlements were established in it, and the trade with the natives secured by the Hudson's Bay Company, or (as I am not sure that the establishment of trading-posts did not take place prior to the amalgamation) I should perhaps be more correct in saying, by the adventurous pioneers of the North-West Fur Company. There are but four or five harbours on the Pacific coast, and Oregon possesses two of them. And yet, with all these advantages to be considered, Great Britain did not think this fine territory worth the trouble and difficulty of keeping; but gave it up almost without disputing her claim, and suffered herself to be nearly crowded out of the Pacific coast altogether. There is a legend current, which I do not exactly remember, but it is to the effect that the cession of Oregon was not strongly opposed at home because some plenipotentiary sent out to examine into the matter reported that it was a useless and disgusting country, for the salmon in the Columbia would not take a fly. I am afraid that this myth is too good to be true, and that the Colonial Office has no such valid excuse to offer for its conduct. Certain it is that, actuated by whatever causes, we abandoned Oregon very easily, not to say supinely. And the worst of it all is, that under the fostering care of the United States the salmon have become so educated that they will now take a fly.

Very slow to look after the advantage of herself and of her children has Great Britain been. We will not now discuss such grave questions as those affecting Maine and British Columbia, or springing from the consideration that the only road to Red River and the West runs of necessity along the boundary line for a long distance. But look at the nice little hitch up North which the line makes in Lake Superior, thereby sweeping in Isle Royal and all its copper. Observe, too, the absurd way in which—to suit the letter of a badly worded stipulation—the boundary goes up into the North-west angle of the Lake of the Woods. Perhaps it may be thought that a few acres in the North-west angle of the Lake of the Woods are not worth troubling about, and that the Yankees might as well have them as not; but does any one imagine that they would go there for nothing? Not a bit of it. That corner contains one of the best *cranberry marshes* in North America.

And so for a full hour I sat upon the rocky summit of Mount Washburne, and, without moving, surveyed with my outward eyes the springs of these great rivers, and with my inward vision followed them in their long journeyings from their sources to the sea.

It is pleasant thus to gaze out upon the world from some lofty standpoint; to hold as it were in the hollow of one's hand the lives and destinies of great rivers; to stretch out and to grasp threads which, unwinding their interminable length, lead one through so many countries and peoples and climates. It seems to expand the mind; it conducts one by easy pathways down long lanes of thought penetrating far into the future of nations, and opens out broad vistas of contemplation through which glimpses of what may be can dimly be discerned. The outlook from such a commanding point elevates the mind, and the soul is elated by the immensity of Nature. An appreciation of man's superiority over all other works of the Creator asserts itself, and the world seems to lie subject at one's feet. A feeling of wonder seizes one that man can be so weakly foolish as to suffer himself to be moved and vexed by the trivial crosses, the disappointments, the thwarted ambitions, and vain bickerings of life. Calm, soothing philosophy is taught, is forced upon one by everything that the eye sees and the ear hears, or that can be otherwise apprehended by the senses; and peace permeates one's whole being.

Those strange thoughts and problems over which men uselessly shatter their brains intrude themselves unbidden upon the mind, and a man asks himself involuntarily how it is that in a scene like this, and surrounded by circumstances differing as much as can be from the outcome of all those products and results of civilisation that in our estimation constitute the best part of life, he feels infinitely superior to his civilised self. Have we turned our back upon the light? Is our progress a retrogression, and not an advance? Are we in the darkness pursuing a shadow? Or is the present conflict between Nature and man only a passing incident, a fleeting phase in the ample roll of the history of the world?

Long could I have pondered and wondered, but day was fast declining; and from my musings I was roughly roused by Boteler, who reckoned that, unless I had concluded to take root there, I had better get up and look for camp.

I jumped to my feet. It was indeed high time to be moving. The sun was getting very low, and the valleys were already steeped in shade. To the east all was dark, but in the western heavens long flaming streaks of yellow were flashing across a lowering sky. The masses of black cloud were glowing red with an angry flush. The clear white light of a watery sun had changed into broad streaks of flaunting saffron. Across all the hemisphere opposed to it, the setting orb was shaking out the red and yellow folds of its banners, challenging the forces of the storm which was marshalling on the horizon its cloudy warriors resplendent in burnished gold. As I looked the sun sank into a mass of cumulus, and all was grey.

So we turned to descend the mountain; but, as we went, the sun, invisible to us, broke through some hidden rift in the cloud strata, and shone out bright and strong, splashing its horizontal rays full against the opposite slope, and deluging the lower portions of the valley with a flood of intense cherry-coloured lurid light. The hills reddened as if beat upon by the full glare of a great furnace. It was a sight most glorious to see. The beauty of it held us and forced us to stop. The glow did not gradually ripen into fullness, but suddenly and in all its intensity struck upon a prominent ridge, lighting up the crags and cliffs, and even the rocks and stones, in all their details; and then by degrees it extended and spread on either side over the foot-hills, bringing out the projecting slopes and shoulders from deep gloom into clear light, and throwing back the valleys into blackest shade. Every rock and precipice seemed close at hand, and shone and glowed with such radiance that you could trace the very rents and crevices in the cliff-faces, and mark the pine-trees clinging to the sides; while in comparison the deep recesses of the chasms and cañons seemed to extend for miles back into dark shadow.

As the sun sank so rose the light, rushing upwards, surging over the hills in a wave of crimson most rarely beautiful to behold, and illuminating the great bulk of the range, while the peaks were still darkly rearing their sullen heads above the tide, and the valleys were all filled with grey vapour. At last the glare caught the mist, and in an instant transformed it from grey cloud into a gauzy half-transparent veil, light, airy, delicate exceedingly, in colour like the inner petals of the rose. Then, as the sun dropped, suddenly the light flashed upon the summits ; the peaks leaped into life for a moment, and sank back into their clay-blue shrouds.

In silence we descended the mountain, picking our way through the gathering darkness, and leading our horses until we regained the trail, when we mounted and pushed on as rapidly as the jaded condition of the animals would permit.

The first thing we saw in the gloom was an unusual-looking object, apparently nearly all head, standing erect upon its hind-legs, swaying about and making a strange grumbling noise. Bear, thought I ; but, on closer inspection, it turned out to be Maxwell, stumbling along with his saddle on his head, very tired, almost drunk with fatigue, and in a very bad humour. His horse had given out in crossing the pass, and after bestowing a parting kick on the unfortunate cook, which vastly accelerated the progress of that worthy down the mountain and very nearly broke his leg, had utterly refused to proceed any further. The rider had consequently been compelled to abandon the horse to its fate, and to take up his saddle and walk home ignominiously, like a man coming in amid the jeers of the populace from a disastrous steeple-chase. We tried consolation, but in vain ; Maxwell was weeping for his horse, and would not be comforted. A little further, and we came upon another member of the party driving his jaded animal before him, propelling the beast with a constant stream of rapidly-uttered swear-words, delivered in a steady and sustained jet with much strength and precision. It was not strange that something stirred at an appeal so moving; the only wonder was that the man, being the lighter of the two, was not knocked backward by the force of his own language. Further on we overtook other individuals, some riding, some walking, all in bad humour and tired out. My horse lay down twice under me, and I also had to take it on foot. The ground was very rough, the night pitch dark, and altogether it was ' a hard road to travel.' We were all scattered about the country, out of sight and hearing of each other; but at last the leading men got down by the river and lit a fire, and, attracted by the blaze and by whoops and whistles, we straggled in somehow, and made camp and supper.

CHAPTER IX.

TRACKING BACK.

THE next day we rode to the Mammoth Hot Springs
Our outfit was getting exceedingly demoralised, and on
this occasion also it was long after dark before we got into
camp. We had counted upon getting plenty of game,
deer or elk, all through the trip, and had arranged the
commissariat accordingly. But we had grievously miscalculated either our own skill or the resources of the country,
for not an atom of fresh meat had we tasted for days.
This sort of perpetual fast began to tell upon us. We
were a hungry crowd. Trout I had devoured till I was
ashamed to look a fish in the face. When I saw them,
their heads just sticking out of the weeds and their broad
tails fanning the water, take a look at my grasshopper,
and sidle across the stream, I fancied that I could discern
a wink in their expressive eyes, a drawing down of the
corner of their eloquent mouths; and imagined I could
hear them say: 'No, no, my boy: you have had your
share; things are getting pretty fishy; you will be developing fins yourself, if you go on in this sort of way.'
A trout diet is all very well in warm weather, and taken
with moderate exercise ; but when the mercury gets
below freezing, and you have to work hard all day, com-
mend me to venison and fat pork. So not only were the
horses and mules tired and sulky, but the ' humans ' also
were beginning to show signs of dissatisfaction.

Mammoth Hot Springs, on Gardener's River.

Before leaving the Mammoth Hot Springs we had provisioned the party with five prong-horns killed on the trail we were to take to-day. Why not, said we, do the same again, or at any rate part of the same? So Wynne, Boteler, and I formed ourselves into a committee of supply and started off ahead of the column, determined to get something to eat.

We rode for some two or three hours over the rolling upland, and then espied some antelopes. Wary and wild as hawks, the villains saw us at the same moment, and soon put themselves out of our reach. A little further on we saw three more feeding on a hill-side about a mile off. I dismounted, stamped the geography of the country as well as I could on to my brain and, while the others sat down and waited, ran 'along under cover of a ridge to circumvent and get to leeward of the game. The ground was good for stalking, and I expected to get a nice shot; but when I had got round under the brow on the other side of which I fancied the antelopes were feeding, and, after breathing a mild imprecation, had dragged myself to the top and craned my head over the ridge, the deuce a living thing was to be seen except Wynne and Boteler, on a mound ever so far off, making antics like a couple of mountebanks, indicating that the prong-horns had ' *vamoosed.*'

I felt much inclined to take a pot-shot at my gesticulating friends, but did not indulge my fancy, consoling myself with reflecting that perhaps the antelopes were bucks and not in good condition, and that there were plenty more of them about. Of course they said when I rejoined them that it was all my fault, and that I had made noise enough brushing through the dried rustling sunflowers to scare a dead antelope into blue fits. I did not believe a word of it. After that we rode all the morning without seeing a single solitary creature fit to eat, until in the afternoon we crossed the trail and got up on some bluffs almost overlooking the cascade on Gardiner's River. Here was a nice country, little open parks and glades, with pools of water in them occurring frequently in the pine-woods; and we had not gone far before Boteler, who was leading, jerked his pony on to his haunches and motioned me to get down. Over the ridge he had just caught a glimpse of an antelope. At the same moment a storm that had threatened all day burst, and choked and pelted us with such a driving deluge of hail, sleet, and rain as is only to be met with in these youthfully violent and unfinished countries. Wynne, who had lagged behind, got under a rock somewhere; Boteler and I, who were on the open, put out for the nearest pine-tree and backed up against it.

I have seen storms on the plains, when the hailstones were so large and descended from such a distance that a man exposed to them would be glad to whip his saddle off and protect his head with it. This storm was not quite so bad as all that, but it was severe enough; and the hailstones cut cruelly. We waited until the worst was over, and then, as we could not afford to waste time, started out to look for the antelope. We found him right enough; an old buck he was, and lying—the cautious, crafty old sinner—on the top of a little knoll in the very centre of a small circular plain, of perhaps 1,000 yards in diameter. On one side, and about 200 or 300 yards from him, was a little outcropping fragment of slate, a few inches high and some five or six yards long. To crawl up behind that ledge and take a shot from it, appeared to be the only chance. So I told Boteler to make a long round and ensconce himself behind a clump of trees on the opposite side, so as to secure the off-chance of a running shot in case the antelope went that way, and I, with a woeful glance at the cold soaking grass, proceeded to wriggle myself up to the stones. I don't like wriggling like an eel in the wet grass, particularly when you 'have to go a long way prone upon the streaming face of mother earth, dragging yourself through shallow pools of standing water, and through tufts of tall, drenching weeds that flick the spray down your neck. Rain water is cold, *beastly* cold ; and, favoured by your peculiar attitude, it insinuates itself through interstices in your garments which would not otherwise be accessible, percolating into all sorts of queer places, and making you quake and shiver.

When I got up to the last shelter, there was the prong-buck ever so much further off than I expected, lying down, but by no means in a quiet frame of mind, for he was looking about him in all directions, evidently inspired with a notion that something was the matter. There was not so much as a stalk of sage-brush or a tuft of long grass between me and him ; so I had to take my shot from where I was. Of course I could not discover a crack or cranny through which I could catch sight of him without giving him a chance of seeing me ; and of course I could not, to save my scalp, find a nice, convenient place to lie. When I had slowly, by hair-breadths at a time, dragged myself to the top and had at last settled myself comfortably, and gently pushed my rifle forward, and was taking a long breath preparatory to firing, a great raindrop must needs splash right on top of the foresight, causing me to wink violently. So I came down and, levelling my gun the second time, hardened my heart, and was just feeling a strong pressure on the trigger and wondering nervously why the thing did not go off, when flick ! a hailstone, under the especial patronage of Satan, strikes me on the nose. I felt that

I should miss him, and I began to hate that buck. However, I came down again, wriggled an inch or two further up the hill, crossed my feet, filled my lungs, set my teeth, and got a nice sight upon him. How ridiculously small he seemed, and how absurdly the foresight would keep wobbling about! At last I got it pretty steady, and pulled. As I did so he caught sight of my expressive countenance, and jumped as only an antelope can jump, and my bullet splashed up the mud a foot or two behind and under him. Do you suppose he ran towards Boteler? Not a bit of it, but just the other way; and in half a dozen jumps was out of sight.

It was blowing so hard, and there was such a noise of storm, that there was no danger of the shot having disturbed anything, and so, as the country looked very gamey, we walked on on foot, leading the horses, and presently came upon a little band containing six antelopes. We were by this time near the summit of a long sloping mountain. The ground fell away rapidly on either side, and in a long but narrow glade the antelopes were lying. While we were peering at them, two does—nasty inquisitive females—got up, walked forward a few steps and stared too. We remained still as statues, and after a while they appeared satisfied and began to crop the grass. We then left our ponies, and signing to Wynne, who just then hove in sight, that there was something ahead, and that he was to catch them, hastened up under cover of some brush. By the time we reached the tree nearest to them we found the does had all got up and fled to some distance, but a splendid buck with a very large pair of horns was still lying down. At him I fired, and nailed him. He gave one spring straight into the air from his bed, fell back into the same spot, kicked once or twice convulsively, and lay still. I fired the second barrel at a doe and struck her, for she 'pecked' almost on to her head, but she recovered and went on. Out we rushed : ' Never mind the dead one,' shouts Boteler, his face all aglow ; ' let's get the other ; she's twice as good, and can't go far. You take one side of that clump and I will take the other.' So off we set, best pace, bursting up the hill after the wounded doe. We followed her for half an hour, running our level best, and got each a long shot, but missed ; and, as she was evidently quite strong, we gave up the chase and walked back.

We found Wynne driving up the ponies ; and as he appeared to have some little trouble with the poor beasts, rendered sulky and ill-tempered by the wet and cold, I said to Boteler, ' You go down and help him, and I will butcher the buck.' I had scarcely got the words ' butcher the buck' out of my mouth, when the darned thing, apparently not appreciating my intentions, came to life, bounded to his feet, sprang into the air, coming down all four feet together, and, with his legs widely extended, gave a *phwit*,—a sort of half whistle, half snort of surprise, I suppose at his own resurrection, — stared a second, and made off. ' Shoot, Boteler,' I cried, ' shoot. In Heaven's name, man, can't you see the buck ? ' and I threw up my own rifle and missed him, of course. ' By George,' says Boteler, wheeling round, ' look at the ——— ; ' and he let go at him with the same result. Wynne yelled and dropped the lariats ; Boteler ejaculated terrible things ; and I also, I fear, made use of very cursory remarks. But neither for swearing, shouting, nor shooting would he stop. He ran about fifty yards, fell on his head and rolled over and over, jumped up again, ran one hundred yards, pitched head over heels the second time, got up, and went down the hill as if he had never felt better in his life.

We followed of course, and wasted an hour in searching for him in vain. Never again will I pass a beast, however dead he may appear to be, without cutting his throat by way of making sure.

We were all thoroughly disgusted; and as it was getting very late, and Wynne and I did not know anything of the country, we two took a direction that would cut the trail, while Boteler persevered and went over the other side of the mountain to try one more shot.

By the time we had got down the hill-side and skirted round the margin of a little reedy lake, it was nearly dark, and we had just barely light enough to find the trail. We crossed it on the other side of the pond, and followed it as fast as we could; but we had some difficulty in finding our way, and did not get in until about ten o'clock that night. The expedition was in a very sad plight. Another of the horses had given up, and Campbell and Maxwell had been obliged to walk all day. One or two of the mules had sore backs, and could carry only very light loads; the others consequently were too heavily laden, and the column had made but very slow progress. We overtook them just before they made camp, and went on ahead. Maxwell was quite beat and exhausted, poor fellow. He was so done up that, in crossing the west fork of Gardiner's River, he came mighty near being drowned. The water there is not deep, but it rushes violently over a bed strewn with round, smooth boulders. Maxwell, instead of waiting for a horse to be led back to him, thought he could ford it on foot. He tried, lost his balance, fell, and was swept some distance down the stream before he could get his footing again. Eventually he was fished out, half choked, by Campbell. Wynne and I found both men and beasts dismal and in bad humour; but we kept up our spirits, and instilled imaginary warmth into our wet and clammy limbs by thinking and talking of the great luxury we should presently enjoy in the shape of a hot bath at the Springs. How delicious it would be, we mutually speculated, to lie up to our chins for an hour in the warm, soft, invigorating water, calmly smoking the calumet of peace. Thoughts of supper too at the hotel reconciled us a little to our present discomforts.

We knocked at the door of the hotel, but no answer was returned. An ominous darkness enveloped the house; the door was fastened; we burst it in, but beat a hasty retreat from two or three skunks who appeared inclined to resent our intrusion. There was not a human being in the place; and, when the inhabitants had left, they had taken with them every available article in the shape of food, drink, and utensils. We tried the other shanties, but with a similar result; there was not a man, woman, or child left in the settlement. They had all gone 'up the cañon or down the valley.' Our disappointment was acute, for we were in want of food, and the only thing in the shape of provision to be found was the fag end of a knuckle of ham. This we were afraid to touch, thinking it might have been used for poisoning rats. The river of course was full of trout, but at that time of night it was too late to go to it for supper. Wynne looked unutterable things. Slowly drawing from his pocket a newspaper cutting, and unfolding it, he exclaimed, 'Just read this and look around you. Is this abomination of desolation the luxurious summer resort mentioned by those unprincipled prophets in Helena? Can such a gigantic fraud have been perpetrated in Virginia? Exists there an advertising medium in Bozeman so base as to prostitute its columns to such a vile purpose as the deception of the traveller? Are these things really so? Or is it only a horrid nightmare? Can there be a newspaper so mean as to talk of coaches, horses, hotels, stores, and baths that exist not, and delude the unwary wayfarer with a piled-up heap of specious crammers? According to this document I hold in my hand, the weary visitor will find a first-class hotel, a luxurious club-house, and several quiet, retired boarding-houses. The elegant bathing establishments are under the supervision of one of the most eminent physicians of the West. All the luxuries, in and out of season, are to be had in abundance, at moderate prices. In fact, the innocent individual who trusted to this document would have expected to find a sort of Saratoga in the wilds of Montana. Only contrast this ideal with the stern reality!'

It certainly was rather a gloomy look-out. The Springs presented a very different appearance from the highly-coloured accounts in the advertisements. On our former visit there were two or three people in the place, and it was possible to get something to eat, for the hunters had brought in some elk; but now there was not a solitary human being in the whole establishment. Where were the luxurious bath-houses, the commodious club-house, the restaurant, the lodging-houses, the eminent physician, and the civil and obliging guides, who were willing to convey travellers to the geysers and back again for a modest remuneration, or to show them herds of wapiti and bands of sheep, and do anything and everything to add to their comfort?

An owl, who might have been the ghost of the learned doctor, hooted dismally round the solitary shanty—I mean the elegant restaurant; a skunk walked disdainfully and slowly, trusting to the prowess of his tail, out of the saloons of the hotel; squirrels were the only visitors at the club-house. We had to camp as best we could upon the bare, dirty floors, and go well nigh supperless to bed. We should have fasted altogether, but for a solitary individual who appeared, very late at night, with a string of trout. He was 'the last rose of summer,' and had come back after something or other that had been left behind by one of the late dwellers at the Springs.

However, Wynne and I got a candle-end and proceeded to the bath-house, determined that we should not be done out of that luxury at any rate, and that if we were hungry we would at least be clean. We carefully stuck up our little light, and stripped ourselves; and Wynne, who was the more expeditious of the two, stepped into the water. With a yell of agony he instantly drew out his foot, red and scalded. The water was nearly boiling hot. There we sat for about half an hour, two shivering wretches, waiting in vain expectation that the water would cool, for we had plugged up the conduit that conducted it to the baths. But it did not cool a bit. It is the most provoking, obstinate, and peculiar water, so far as its powers of developing and maintaining caloric are concerned. It does not appear so intensely warm when you first insinuate your feet into it, but it seems to get hot all at once, and then it becomes hotter and hotter. You may cautiously immerse yourself up to the knees without suffering much pain; but scarcely are both feet down before your legs begin to tingle, and before you can get out again you are about parboiled, and expect to see the skin peel off your shins. So after waiting a long time in vain, we were obliged to get into our clothes again; and, rather colder and dirtier than before, we walked back to the shanty to try and forget our disappointment in sleep.

I did not get much of that, for about three in the morning I went up the mountain with Boteler to see if we could not get a deer. There is a regular *bealoch*

there through which the black-tail pass in great numbers
at certain times in the year, when moving to and from
their winter pasturage, and we expected to be lucky
enough to come across some, as it was the right time of
year, and the weather had been stormy for the last few
days; but, though we walked hard and fast for about four
or five hours, we did not see anything, not even fresh
tracks. It was evident that the herds had not yet come
down.

We found some fresh trout, and consumed the last of
our tea and flour for breakfast; and after a somewhat
scanty meal Wynne and I left, intending to ride into
Boteler's the same day. Kingsley had started some two
or three hours before, as his horse was very jaded, and he
wished to have plenty of time before him.

We got along very pleasantly, leading our ponies up
and down the steep places and saving them all in our
power. We had not gone many miles, however, before we
spied Kingsley's horse standing with his head down and his
legs very far apart, propping himself up as if he was afraid
of falling, a miserable and dejected-looking object. Close
at hand, his rider was peacefully reclining in a sage-
brush, philosophically smoking. His horse, he said, could
not go a step further, and he would wait where he was
until the outfit came up. In order to lighten his load he
had left his gun behind, and he said that in consequence
scores of antelope had suffered him to approach quite
close to them. Reflecting that his fate was not unlikely
to overtake us also, we gave him some tobacco and our
blessings, and proceeded on our way. We saw a great
many antelope that day; but as we were now close to
the end of our journey, and our horses moreover
were so beat that it would have been unwise to give
them any extra work to do, and as the day was scarcely

long enough for the journey we had to make, we did not take the trouble to try and kill anything.

We therefore made the best of our way along our old trail, galloping cheerily over the level, and walking and driving our horses before us over all the steep places; keeping a look-out for Indians, but not troubling our heads about game. Just about sunset we passed the corral, and saw that most marvellous old dame, Mrs. Boteler—marvellous for the sprightliness with which she bears the burden of her many years—busily engaged milking her cows; a sight that was highly refreshing and suggestive of luxurious feeding. A few minutes afterwards we pulled up at the ranche and were heartily greeted by Phil Boteler, who warmly bidding us to get right off, and sit right down, and not trouble ourselves about the stock, for he would manage all that, put chairs for us, called in his mother, and went out to drive our tired horses down to pasture. What a refreshing wash we had! And how we did enjoy our supper of fresh eggs, chicken, cream, butter and cheese, and plenty of Japan tea! Honestly tired we were, and heartily glad to have got to the end of our troubles.

We had brought to a safe termination a most enjoyable expedition, the pleasant recollections of which will never fade from my memory; but we had also experienced a somewhat rough time. Our horses and mules were scarcely up to the work; we had been greatly hurried; we were unfortunate as regards weather, and still more unlucky in not getting half enough game to keep us properly supplied. So the pleasures of the trip were mixed up with just enough hardship to make the return to civilisation exceedingly pleasant.

We lay at Boteler's for three days, full up to our eyes of hominy, milk, and other products of the dairy and the farm. We also managed to get hold of some whisky, and not very bad whisky either. The evening of our arrival Wynne and I noticed a keg, but, fearing that our honesty might not prove equal to the temptation which a conversation on the subject would have held out, we avoided the cask and the topic, and asked no questions about it. We thought that if we resisted the Devil he would 'flee from us.' We did resist that keg manfully, but it did not budge an inch. The next day Jack came in and hovered round it like a hungry fish about a hook, getting bolder all the time. Finally he tapped it to see if it was full, and found it was. It gurgled pleasantly when he shook it, and that gurgle finished Jack. He asked Boteler 'what it was anyhow?' and Boteler replied it was some of the best whisky that could be got in Bozeman. Upon which Jack looked unutterable things and walked away, speedily returning to renew the interesting conversation. It turned out that the keg was on its way to the man who used to live at the Hot Springs. 'But,' we all cried in a breath, 'there is nobody at the Springs at all.' 'Well,' said Boteler, 'I don't know anything about that. It was left here for me to send on by the first chance. I don't suppose there will be any chance now till next spring ; and, if you fellows feel like taking some and leaving ten dollars a gallon for it, I don't know that there will be any great harm done; but you must take it on your own responsibility.' Jack was quite willing to take it on his own responsibility ; and it was not long before there was an auger-hole in the head of that cask.

Although we had made a decidedly successful trip, having accomplished all that we had resolved upon, and having seen all or nearly all we had intended to see, yet in the hunting line we had done very little. It is true that we had devoted but little time to the noble pastime, but we were rather disappointed at the results. With the exception of one grizzly and three wapiti, we had nothing to show as evidence of our adventures. I felt that we ought to have a good mountain-sheep head to take down with us; and I determined, as the weather was still open, to move up into the mountain to a locality where 'Ovis montana' was reported to be tolerably numerous.

Accordingly, when we had sufficiently recruited ourselves and our horses, I moved the whole party up a creek running from the westward into the Yellowstone.

The trail was easy at first, and we got along very pleasantly, winding our devious way along the foot-hills; but presently the creek cañoned, and we were compelled to keep down close to the water's edge. The rich soil bordering the stream was thickly bristling with a dense growth of cotton-wood and aspen, their branches matted and interwoven with various vines. The signs of many a winter's storm were apparent in the leaning trees arrested in their fall by their stronger brethren, and the ground was strewn and littered with prostrate trunks. Through this mass, more like a gigantic cobweb than anything else, we had to thrust ourselves; and such a falling of beasts, swearing of men, upsetting of packs, and smashing of branches, I have seldom seen.

Hot and breathless, our eyes full of dust and our shirts of bits of dry stick which had showered themselves down our backs, we at last burst through the gorge, and emerging into the fresh air pursued a course along the hills, until, a little before dark, we came to a beautiful camping-ground, nicely sheltered and affording plenty of wood and grass. But, alas! no water was to be found, except that which was descending most bountifully and disagreeably from heaven; and we were compelled to descend to the creek bottom.

The next day four of us started early to explore the

tops. The ascent was very steep and fatiguing, but by no
means difficult, though there were of course a few bad
places. In one of these Campbell and I got stuck. We
could get up, using hands, feet, and eyelids, but could not
carry our guns with us. Fortunately the bad step was not
very long, and by utilising all available compass-cords,
whistle-strings, belts, and handkerchiefs, we were enabled
to make a rope long enough to reach from top to bottom.
So I climbed up first, and having reached a secure place,
much to my own satisfaction, let down our improvised
rope and hauled up the two rifles one by one, after which
Campbell clambered up. Careful climbing thenceforth
enabled us to overcome all difficulties ; and, the crowning
ridge once reached, all trouble was at an end.

The mountains here do not consist of isolated peaks, but
are for the most part connected by a narrow ridge composed
of slate very much tilted, the strata being occasionally
quite perpendicular, sometimes inclined to one side and
sometimes to the other. Along this connecting crest of a
foot or two feet in breadth you can walk for miles, bending and turning in all directions, for the range does not
seem to possess any method or order, but to consist of
just a jumbled up mass of mountains. In this range the
principal valleys run east and west, towards the Madison
in the first case, and the Yellowstone in the other. The
summits rise now and then to elevations perhaps 200 or
300 feet above the average level of the ridge, but they can
generally be surmounted without much difficulty. Occasionally you meet with a peak of rugged, massive rock,
which bars the passage and necessitates a détour. Having once ascended the chain, you can thus, without much
further climbing, get a fine view of the valleys and slopes.
In this way two men, one taking one side and his companion watching the other, can with good glasses survey a

great deal of ground, and well rewarded for their trouble they probably will be both in game and scenery.

The general configuration of the country is, as before stated, a great jumble of mountains, bounded by the Madison on the one side, and by the Yellowstone on the other.

Flowing into these rivers are numerous creeks and streams, which in their turn are fed by smaller creeks and branches, entering them generally at right angles to their course, and draining through most picturesque valleys and gorges the snows which never melt entirely from the summits.

Ascending from the foot-hills along the boundary ridge of one of these valleys, we wound our way, first through dense woods, and, after climbing over or skirting round steep cliffs, along more level ground,— the ridge becoming narrower and more knife-like, and the vegetation more stunted and scanty as we proceeded, until we emerged from the region of trees altogether, and, after traversing in single file a tract of bare slate, stood upon what was evidently one of the highest points of the range. By a slight difficulty in getting sufficient breath, by the deliciously cool, clear, exhilarating air, we rightly judged we had climbed to a considerable elevation above the sea, and we gladly sat down to rest and look about us.

All around peaks and crags, bare, savage, and storm-tormented, surged up in constantly recurring waves. The scene was utterly desolate and wild, yet man had trodden these riven rocks before ; for at my feet lay a chipped obsidian spear-head or scraper, dropped perhaps ages ago by some wandering savage hunting the goats and sheep scarcely wilder than himself. The ground immediately about us was covered with slate débris curiously encrusted with a substance resembling a coating of dirty frozen snow.

The head of the valley may be described as a *fell.* Large patches of snow lie upon it, hard and frozen on the north side, but melting fast and distributing quantities of mud and small stones where exposed to the powerful sun. A little further down, the whole of one slope of the valley is covered with loose stones, constantly falling, making a very nasty and dangerous ground to walk upon, for if you with incautious steps set a portion of it in motion, the whole hill-side starts and moves in a mass. A little below timber line, which in these latitudes is about 11,000 feet above sea-level, the upper part of the valley forms a sort of basin; and in the bottom of this depression nestle three calm unruffled little lakes, sheltered by stunted pine-trees, and surrounded with a carpeting of short sweet pasture. They communicate with one another, and finally lip over in a tiny rill, which, first trickling through grass and Alpine flowers, and gathering strength and courage on its course, goes foaming and leaping down precipices, rushing noisily through the cool shadows of the forest, until it mingles its icy waters with the creek on which we are encamped below.

As the valley spreads out, the mountains on either side throw back their great shoulders and rear their hoary heads towards the sky, depelling the cloudy tresses from their summits capped with snow. Then an interval of fell occurs, and then comes the timber struggling to ascend. And so the valley expands and the mountain masses break up, throwing out great naked promontories, wooded spurs and huge castellated cliffs, till they merge into the blue undulations of the foot-hills, which look in the shimmering autumn haze like a great, heaving, restless sea of pines.

Turn right round; walk a few steps, and you will see another valley and lake beneath you, and a stream flowing in the opposite direction. We are on the 'divide' between the Yellowstone and the Missouri, and the panorama unrolled on either side cannot easily be surpassed on the continent of North America. I wish I could convey to my readers a just impression of a scene of such excellent beauty that I never can forget it. It is only necessary for me to close my eyes to see it in all its graceful details of wood, water, valley, field, and cliff. But so exceedingly lovely is the view that I should consider it scandalous to pollute so fair a memory by clumsy and unavailing efforts at description.

But as I sat soaking myself in sunshine, inhaling the joyous air, and revelling in the scenery, with a sudden start I become aware of something moving on the opposite face.

Out with the glass! Yes! there are one, two, three, by George! sixteen sheep, quietly feeding. 'Any big ones among them?' says Boteler. I screw the glass in a trifle, and steady my elbows well on the ground, for I am lying at full length *ventre à terre*, and drawing a deep breath reply, 'Ne'er a big horn; all young rams or ewes. See how they are all skylarking, butting at one another, and jumping about.' 'No use going after them anyhow,' drawls Jack; 'but I can see two other bands;' and so in truth they were, a small party of three sheep crossing the stream far below, and twelve more moving slowly along close to the lake beneath us. But there did not appear to be a good head among them all.

As we looked at the herd by the lake, suddenly they all spread out like a lot of minnows when you drop a pebble in the midst of the shoal, and darted up the mountain falling into single file, stopping occasionally to look back, and then bounding up with inconceivable rapidity. Why, in a few minutes they were up the mountain and over the ridge ;—a good day's work for a miserable man who would follow them. What on earth could have scared them? There was nothing in view and nothing came in sight.

'Well, boys,' says Jack, 'there's no use in fooling around here all day. Let's go ahead and try and strike something.' So, shaking ourselves together, we started again, Jack and Boteler on one slope, Campbell and I on the other, carefully examining the ground on either side for sign.

We had not gone far before I threw up my head, like a hound, sniffed violently, and swore I could smell sheep quite plain. Campbell smiled incredulously. Because *he* could not *feel* the smell, he would not believe that I could be endowed with a keener nose. But I was right, for a few yards further on we came upon the beds the sheep had slept in the night past, found where they had been feeding a short time before, and discovered the quite fresh track of four big rams.

Fatigue was forgotten ; every sense seemed quickened ; and I became aware that I had a heart beating rather violently, as Campbell whispered, 'Tread light ; they must be close by somewhere, lying down likely.' So we cautiously crossed the ridge, stooping very low to inform our companions that they were close to game. While we were running along as fast as our bent position would admit, crack! went a rifle ever so far in front of us, followed by a rattling of stones ; and presently appears Jack, trying to look as if nothing had happened. He had walked right into the herd and fired, killing nothing, but wounding one. Campbell and I were silent, but our thoughts were powerful.

We had not proceeded more than half a mile when, looking back, I saw Boteler apparently stark, staring mad. He was gingerly, but with much gesticulation of his legs, running over the rocks as if they were red-hot, his eyes staring, his face working with excitement, his mouth open as if he were yelling, but no sound coming therefrom, and his hands going like the arms of an old semaphore. When he got close he shouted in a whisper, 'Bighorns! bighorns! twelve or fourteen of them! quite close! this way! come on!' Grabbing him by the shirt-sleeve, I said, 'For Heaven's sake don't excite yourself; let me stalk this lot myself; you and Jack keep back well behind us, and don't on any account show until I have fired.' So Campbell and I started. How well I remember my sensations! How my heart beat! One's circulation is rather queer at those high altitudes; and Boteler had said there were very large rams in the herd; and good specimens of mountain sheep are rare. What infernal walking it was to be sure, all loose slates and stones, over which a cat could not have passed without displacing some and making a noise.

Cautiously but swiftly, as if treading on eggs, we stepped, well covered by the ridge, till we thought we must be nearly opposite the band; and then, crawling to the top, I motioned Campbell to look over.

With eyes contracted, nostrils dilated, and lip quivering, inch by inch he raised his head. Down it dropped again; and, without a word, he slid back feet first. I followed his example; and, when well under cover again he whispered, 'Two hundred yards further on, feeding up; we must be quick and catch them before they cross the ridge; go ahead you now.' So away I went, till with a pull at my coat-tail Campbell signed to me to crawl up.

Mercy! How sharp the stones were just there! How they did cut one's knees and elbows; and what a nice thing a round, compact young prickly-pear—something like

a pincushion stuck full of barbed needles, points out—
is to place the palm of one's hand on with the whole
weight of one's body resting on it!

As I got near the top I began to think, 'Goodness!
what a noise my heart is making; enough to scare all the
sheep in the country! How hot I am, and there's a great
drop of perspiration run into my eye! I wonder whether
the sheep are to the right or left of me. Had I better
crawl up and try and get a lying shot, or rise up suddenly at the top and pitch both barrels into them? What
an infernal steep place this is to get up! There, now,
you great fool, you've clicked your gun-barrel against that
stone, and it's all over. Hark at that idiot behind. If
he hasn't sent a stone clattering down the face! Con-
found these slate flakes, how they do cut!' At last I
could level my eyes over the ridge. Cautiously I took
off my hat and peered all round. Not a single solitary
beast was there in sight, but I could *hear* them grazing
and coughing, so close were they. I did not know what
to do. I looked back. Campbell was lying flat, occasionally
squinting at me with an agonised expression of countenance, and then dropping his face between his hands as
though muttering an incantation to some private Highland
family devil. A little further back were Jack and Boteler
squatting, guns ready, eyes staring, both looking as if
saying, 'Why the blazes don't you shoot, or do something?'

The eyes of Europe and America were upon me, and
I felt aghast and uncertain how to act. If I stayed
where I was I should of course get a shot at the leading
sheep; but probably it would be a ewe, and she would be
bound to see me. Could I only get to that dwarf juniper-
bush some thirty yards down the slope before they came
in view, I should be all right.

Stalking the Ram.

I determined to chance it, and, Campbell being beckoned to, we rapidly wriggled, after the manner of serpents, towards the bush. Scarcely had we crept into the friendly cover when a ewe stepped into full view, and, feeding quietly, passed so close I could have almost touched her with my gun. Fortunately the wind blew strong, and she did not notice us. Another and another followed, till eight or nine sheep were in sight, and not a good head among them. How slowly they did pass! Sometimes one would look right at us. I could see straight into its eyes, and it appeared impossible but that the beast would distinguish us also. How motionless we lay! A photographer would have been charmed with us. We scarcely dared to breathe or wink. The suspense was awful. I felt hot and cold alternately all over, and began to get the buck-ague to such an unbearable extent that I felt as if I must let go at something and before long, when at last out stepped a great ragged-skinned old ram. I need scarcely say that, whereas all the others had presented fair broadside shots, this one most unceremoniously offered me his tail, and would *not* turn round.

At last I caught sight of his shoulder through a little opening in the branches, and let him have it. With one bound he disappeared. 'Missed, by Jove!' I heard from behind me; and then such a row as there was! I jumped up and fired the second barrel at something, I don't know what; but I noticed a sheep stumble on to his head, get up again and plunge down the hill. Campbell let drive into the brown of them; Jack and Boteler too ran up and fired a volley; and then the latter rushed down the slope after the wounded ram, which by this time was going very short. I also pursued, and should have had a fair shot at him, for on entering a belt of timber he stopped and stood looking at us for some seconds; but unfortunately Boteler was in an exact line with the beast; and, though I swore that if he did not lie down I would shoot through him, he did not pay the slightest attention to me, but continued running till he had got his gun loaded, when he fired and missed the ram.

Poor Boteler came back very disconsolate, for he supposed we had got nothing; but I knew better, and reassured him; for I felt certain that I could not have missed, and sure enough we found the sheep as dead as Julius Cæsar, lying doubled up in a bush within twenty yards of the cover from which I had fired.

When they got to the bottom of the gulch four of the rams bunched up together, and stood five or six hundred yards off gazing at us. We all sat down and had some very pretty practice, for they let us fire in all five or six shots before they made off. When the bullets struck the ground they would all jump straight up into the air, run a few yards, and gather up together again. It is hard to judge distance across a valley; and as they moved at each shot we could not get the range, and killed nothing; and they, after satisfying themselves that it was about time to quit, broke into a steady run, crossed the valley and plain, and went away up another mountain and over it without ever stopping to look back.

Thereupon Jack volunteered to fetch one of the ponies up as near the scene of action as possible, and said he would afterwards look for the sheep he had wounded in the morning. Campbell and Boteler took a diverging ridge and followed it in hopes of finding another herd, and I continued along the crest on which we had found our game; but, seeing no fresh sign, I soon came back, and, like a dissatisfied idiot, must needs go down the gulch to look for the wounded sheep.

It was the steepest place I ever climbed without going

on all-fours. I went *down* in about ten minutes, jumping
in the loose gravel and then sliding; but it took me a
good hour and a half to get up again. I had no chance
to trail my sheep, for the ground was completely covered
with tracks, and I could not hit off the right one; but
with a dog I might have got him, and he was a big one.
I was so thirsty when I got back to the top that I was
obliged to make a little fire, melt some snow, and have
a small tot of cold grog; after which refreshment Boteler and Campbell, who had joined me, and myself turned
to, skinned the sheep, cut off his head, and carried the
hide and skull till we found the pony; when we
packed them on his unwilling back and, tired but contented, made the best of our way to camp.

After much consultation round the camp-fire that
night and the consumption of a great deal of tobacco, for
opinions were different on the subject, we decided to move
camp; and the next day, having retraced our steps some
five or six miles, we struck up a long heavily-timbered
spur of the range, and, having ascended as far as was
practicable for the animals, camped in a most picturesque
spot and drove the beasts down to pasture below. The
country looked a very hunter's paradise, and is reported
to swarm with black-tail deer when they are moving to
or from their winter quarters in the spring or fall. We
ought to have found them. I cannot say I expected to
find them, for I have invariably observed on these occasions that there is something wrong with the weather or
the year. It is a very early season, or the latest that
ever was known; there never was so much snow on the
range, or who ever supposed that the mountains would
not be white by this time? The oldest inhabitant will be
dog-goned if he ever remembered such weather. Bill will
turn to Hank, and he with many oaths will corroborate

his statements that this time last year every bush held a buck. Jim will, with profuse expectoration, give it as his opinion that the present is the very worst time in the year, and that if you were only there in the spring, when the deer begin to move westward, you would be tired of shooting at them. 'Elk did you say?' he will answer to your inquiries as to wapiti; 'you bet your life there's elk. Did not Joe What's-his-name and I sit right down on that bad-worded peak there and shoot seven big bulls without ever moving? Bears is it? Lord! you should be here in the spring when they first come out hungry! Why, you couldn't walk three steps then without meeting one. Now you may look till h—ll freezes over and never see a bear.' And so on; it is the same story everywhere, in all quarters of the globe, and among all people. What says the Eme-rald Islander in reply to the indignant query of some dis-appointed Saxon who has hired a shooting in the wilds of Ballybog, and who, weary and disgusted, has just emerged out of fifty acres of morass through which he has been plunging up to the chin, and which have not afforded him a single shot? 'Well, my good man,' says he to Paddy leaning complacently on his spade, ' can you tell me if there are *ever* any snipe in this infernal bog?' ' Is it snipe? Sure your honour's joking. It does be full up with snipe; the sun do be darkened with them; but it is a little early yet in the season.' 'Oh, indeed, too early is it? Any ducks here?' 'Ducks! Is it ducks? Begorra, the place do be crawling with them if there was the least taste in life of frost; maybe it's ducks you see; 'tis wishing them out of it you'd be for the noise of them.' ' Dear me! And do you get any barometers here?' 'Faix, then, we do get an odd one at all times; but, if your honour would come quietly—very quietly—in the dark of the moon, the place would be alive with them.'

And have we ever gone barbel-fishing, or roach-fishing, or any other kind of fishing, without hearing that in that very pitch only last Tuesday two gentlemen caught so many tons of fish; our stock, however, consisting at the end of the day of some flat beer, a great many crawling gentles and other abominable beasts, and a few, a very few, small fishes? And so it was in this case. The deer had not come down. In vain we wandered over the foot-hills; softly with moccasined feet trod the mazes of the forest, or rode over the swelling surface of the rolling prairie. But what a pleasant wandering it was! Some times through parks dotted with giant hemlocks, rearing their ruddy, rugged stems to heaven, and filling the air with fragrance and with the low cadence of their song as the wind murmured melodies to the branches, and the boughs whispered back to the breeze. I could sit for hours under one of those splendid trees, gazing up into its sturdy branches, wondering at the colony of life among them—the insects, the birds, and squirrels, and watching the chitmunks hard at work throwing down fir-cones and burying the seeds. I love a squirrel, he is such a jolly little beast, and so active withal. Always busy, always happy, and full of larks, he manages to instil into the every-day routine of his life any amount of fun and good-humour. If men would only follow his example, and go through their business with his cheerfulness, and take the same comical, humorous view of life that he does, the world would move with about half the moral friction that now stops its progress and wears out our lives.

Sometimes we passed through glades of aspen shivering in the autumn breeze; across little sparkling streams, on whose white sandy beaches merrily danced the sha-dows of the broad flickering poplar-leaves, and through whose glancing waters darted numerous red-spotted trout;

through dark aisles of the forest, chill, mysterious, solemn, filled with a silence which seems to awe and subdue every living thing save and except the irrepressible squirrel, who, impudently chattering with rage at your intrusion, waves defiance with erected tail; then out into a prairie, under the full blaze of the sun, cheerful and bright, instinct with insect life, full of chirpings, hummings, hoppings, and sometimes, if truth be told, of bitings also.

In vain we climbed the mountains, scaled giddy precipices, penetrated the range to the head waters of Trail Creek, and other streams flowing to the Madison River. Not a thing did we see except a few small sheep, two of which Jack shot, two or three antelopes as wild as hawks, and the dead carcass of a bear.

So one afternoon, coming in tired and disgusted, we suddenly determined to go back to Boteler's, and, hastily packing up, started for the ranch. Jack was the only one of the party absent, but leaving a *square* drink of whisky suspended in a flask from a tree with an intimation of where we had gone, we abandoned him to his fate. It was a pitch dark night; but Jack, guided by the instinct of an old prairie man, had no difficulty in finding his way, and joined us long before we reached Boteler's, bearing on his saddle a quarter of lamb.

We remained a day at the ranch in order to clean up, and arrange for the transport of our trophies; of which we were reasonably proud, for all the natives agreed that the heads of two out of the three wapiti, and the ram's head, were the finest specimens that they had seen for a long time. The taye, bighorn, or mountain sheep (*Caprovis canadensis*) is a splendid beast. There is nothing whatever sheeplike about him, except in the shape and appearance of the horns and face. His form resembles that of a large black-tail buck, but is much thicker, sturdier, and more majestic. The hair is like that of a deer, only longer and thicker in texture; it has, when the coat is in good condition, a slightly bluish tint, and the fibres are very closely set together. The connection between the wild sheep and our domestic varieties is chiefly shown in the appearance and quality of the flesh, which looks and tastes like most excellent mutton. Without exception it is the best meat that the mountains afford. The bighorn is very white behind, and seems as if he had been sitting in the snow. Sometimes the whole skin is white; and this does not depend upon the time of year, for I once killed an almost white ewe in Colorado in the month of June. The slot is squarer than that of a deer of equal size, and not nearly so pointed at the toes. Both sexes have horns, those of a full-grown ewe being about the same size as those of a two year-old ram. Sheep generally run in bands of from five or six to twenty or thirty, with the exception of very old rams, who are solitary in their habits, and usually betake themselves entirely alone to some secluded ridge backed by the highest peaks of the range, to which they can retreat in case of danger. The rutting season varies, of course, somewhat according to the locality and climate; it occurs about the same time as that of the deer. They drop their young about April. In Colorado, where I have chiefly observed their habits, the ewes separate from the rams in the winter or early spring, and go down among the lower foot-hills almost to the plains; while the males at that time betake themselves to the high mountains, where they remain in spite of wind, frost and snow. Very severe weather will, however, sometimes drive them down; and I have met with a large band of rams in thick timber in Estes Park during a mid-winter's storm. About June and July you will meet with the ewes returning to their mountain homes, accompanied by their lambs. Very pretty little creatures the young ones are. I once caught one, about two months old, in Estes Park after a severe chase, and succeeded in carrying it to the ranch, where I had hoped to rear and tame it; but the poor little thing died in spite of all my care. They are not difficult to domesticate, I believe. A ram of about seven years old carries a fine head. To see such an one bounding hundreds of feet above you, along the verge of a precipitous cliff, or standing on some jutting crag, with his head thrown back a little, as gracefully and easily poised upon his massive shoulders as though those huge horns weighed no more than a feather, and with his feet gathered up ready for a spring, is a sight worth going a long journey to see. He is a noble animal, worthy of the grand scenery of the mountain ranges among whose peaks and precipices he loves to dwell.

The bighorn is closely allied to the argali or Asiatic wild sheep (*Caprovis argali*). In fact, as far as general appearance goes, they are indistinguishable one from the other; but I suppose minute differences, sufficient to constitute a variety, do exist. The moufflon, or European variety, is a much smaller animal than the American or Asiatic sheep. The only noticeable difference between the argali and taye lies in point of size. I do not think that the latter ever attains to as large proportions as the former. The British Museum possesses a gigantic specimen of the argali; the horns of which are beautifully shaped, and measure 48 inches in length, following the curve, and are 19 inches in circumference of the burr. I do not believe there exists a specimen of the bighorn equal to that. The best American head that I have seen belonged to the ram whose death I have attempted to describe. I took the dimensions at Boteler's ranch, and found them to be as follows :—Weight of the head thoroughly cleaned, cut off at the first joint of the neck, but with the skin of the neck left on as far almost as the shoulder, 40 lbs.; circumference of horns, measuring just above the hair and following the hair round, 21 inches. I did not at that time note the length of the horns.

But either the measuring tape at Boteler's must have been very much in fault, or, what is more probable, the horns have shrunk a good deal; for, on taking the dimensions now, I find that, following the curve, the right horn measures 38 inches long, and the left horn 36 ; and they are $17\frac{1}{2}$ and 17 inches respectively in circumference, following the hair and measuring just above it. The weight cannot now be obtained, as the head is affixed to a wooden shield. The finest specimen in the British Museum is almost identical with the last-named in size; the horns measuring 17 inches round the burr, and 36 inches in length along the curve.

The largest example mentioned in Lord Southesk's book, 'Saskatchewan,' measured 42 inches in length.

It will be seen that none of these American sheep are nearly equal, in point of size, to the Asiatic specimen first mentioned.

Unlike those of deer, the horns of mountain sheep are not shed annually ; but they certainly are occasionally cast, whether as the result of accident or disease I know not ; for I have picked them up lying quite alone, and have searched in vain for any skull to which they could have belonged. They appear to be in their prime when the animal is from six to eight years old. I doubt if they increase in girth much after that ; but, even if they do grow larger, their symmetry is sure to be spoiled, for the horns of very old rams become scaly, and invariably are much damaged and broken about the points by fighting and falling among rocks.

There are legends to the effect that the bighorn does cast himself incontinently down precipices of vast height, and, falling on his horns, bounds up again into the air like an India-rubber ball, alighting unhurt upon his feet, much to the surprise of the baffled hunter; who, however, if he believes in such tales, might confidently cast himself down after the sheep, imitating its manœuvres and alighting also on his head, for wood is hard and elastic, and he would likewise bound up and down to the detriment, perhaps, of the rocks, but not of his own skull.

It is marvellous what stories are told and created about game. I have frequently heard it gravely asserted by people who, I am sure, were incapable of telling a deliberate falsehood, and who believed in the fact themselves, that it was not uncommon to find a wapiti head of such dimensions that, when the antlers were placed upright, their tips just resting on the ground, a full-sized man could walk between them without stooping his head or touching the skull. This has been told me scores and scores of times, as a sort of rough general way of estimating the size of a wapiti stag; and I might have ended by believing and repeating the tale myself, if I had not actual measurements to oppose its adoption. There are no very good specimens of wapiti heads in the British Museum; nothing so large as some that I have in my own possession; I therefore took the measurement of one of my Montana stags having very *long* horns, though in other respects it is not particularly large. The dimensions are as follows :—Circumference of horn at the burr, 12 inches; circumference of beam above brow-antler, 7¼; length of tip to beam along the curve, 56 inches; distance between the outer tips, 45 inches; ditto middle tips, 34 inches; ditto inner tips, 29 inches; length of brow-antler nearest the skull, 12 inches; ditto furthest from the skull, 15 inches; distance between tips of brow-antlers nearest the skull, 3 inches; ditto furthest from skull, 24 inches; number of points, 14.

From Mr. Ward, of Wigmore Street,[1] I obtained the following measurements of the largest wapiti head in his establishment :—Circumference of horn at the burr, 11 inches; circumference of beam above brow-antler, 8 inches; length from tip to beam along the curve, 54 inches; distance between the outer tips, $49\frac{1}{2}$ inches; ditto middle tips, $41\frac{1}{2}$ inches; ditto inner tips, $31\frac{1}{2}$ inches; length of brow-antler nearest the skull, $16\frac{1}{2}$ inches; ditto furthest from skull, 17 inches; distance between tips of brow-antlers nearest the skull, 16 inches; ditto furthest from skull, 26 inches; points, 14.

These heads are, as will be seen by comparing their measurements, almost identical in size; and either ot them may be safely taken as a fair specimen of a large wapiti stag. I selected my stag for trying the experiment with, because his horns were somewhat the longer of the two, and I found that, when placed upright, the tips just resting on the ground, a line dropped from the skull at the centre of the burr to the ground measured 42 inches in length. Now, three feet six inches would be the stature of a very short man; and thirty inches, added to the length of the perpendicular line, would necessitate a prodigious increase in the size and weight of the antlers, out of proportion to the endowments of any species of deer now existing.

The next day saw us started,—this time, thank good-

---

[1] I learned that a much larger head had passed through his hands, of which no record was kept.

ness, with our plunder in a waggon—to Trail Creek, bound on a wild moose chase.

Now the moose is ' the most subtle of all the beasts of the field' (the serpent has no right to claim that proud distinction); and to hunt him, save under most favourable circumstances, is labour lost. Circumstances were adverse to us. We had plenty of snow when we did not want it. Now we would have given a good deal for the fall of a few inches, and there appeared no chance whatever of it. The nights were getting very cold, but every day the sun rose bright and warm in a cloudless sky. Still as it appeared certain that there were some moose in the country, we thought it a pity not to give Fortune an opportunity of doing us a good turn. The result of the expedition was that Campbell and I covered ourselves with ridicule as with a blanket.

It fell out in this wise. Be it known, in the first place, that the hunting-ground was a very large depression extending in numerous valleys far back into the mountains, drained by Trail Creek, Bozeman Creek, and other smaller tributary rills. On these streams the beavers had been for ages busy, damming the waters back and forming swamps, in which willows, the favourite food of the moose, luxuriantly grow. The general surface is covered with an almost impenetrable crop of dry, brittle, diminutive pines.

On the very first day, Boteler, Campbell and I went out together and found plenty of old sign, and the tracks of two bulls, not more than a week old (I refer to the age of the tracks, not of the bulls). The second day, Boteler being anxious to ' play a lone hand,' Campbell and I went out together and very soon struck the fresh trail of a young bull descending the creek towards Bozeman, right down wind. We followed it some distance, and then taking different sides of the valley searched carefully to see if he had passed up again. We crossed no return trail, but discovered a pretty little lake or pond called Surprise Lake. I had been told that it was unfathomable! In one sense it is so, for nowhere could you get a fathom deep; the greatest depth being, I should say, two feet, and the average twelve inches. The water is perfectly clear, and the bottom is soft mud. It is inhabited by many trout, who swim about like young sharks with their back fins out, there being scarcely water enough to cover them. I caught a couple of dozen for supper. The mode of capture is somewhat peculiar.

To secure these unsophisticated fish, it is not at all necessary to be especially prepared for that species of sport. A string, a hook, and a knife constitute a complete fishing outfit. You cut a long pole, attach a cord to the end, tie a hook on to the cord, and on the hook fix a fragment of your luncheon if—fat pork so much the better. This bait you then hurl out into the still water with a great and unavoidable splash, thereby causing much commotion among the fish, who fly for refuge under the fallen trees and stumps that fringe the pond. Presently they emerge, and all those that espy the bait swim at it like atoms attracted to a magnet, at first slowly, and then with ever-increasing swiftness. The smartest trout gets the pork, and you heave him out of water. If you are lucky, he falls on the ground; if you are not, he lodges and immediately tangles himself up in the top of a pine-tree, which you must climb or cut down (the latter process is easiest) to get your trout. Having then mercifully killed your fish, you extract his eyes, which prove a tempting morsel to his fellow-creatures.

We caught as many trout as we wanted, and, knowing it was useless following the moose down wind, climbed a ridge overlooking Bozeman's Cañon, lay down in an open space, and went to sleep. A little before sundown we awoke to the consciousness that some beast was making a strange and diabolical noise far down the cañon. ' What like beast is that?' drawls Campbell. ' Don't know,' said I; ' must be moose, I suppose, but I never heard one.'

At intervals of ten minutes the strange cry—a sort of cross between a roar, shriek, and whistle, as if a wild beast, an owl, a bull, and a locomotive were singing quartet—would swell up against the wind, gradually approaching.

We waited as long as we dared, but saw nothing; and not relishing the idea of camping out on a cold night without blankets, and with nothing but trout without salt for supper, we started for camp, where, having detailed our experiences, we were told by the authorities that certainly we had heard a bull moose calling.

Thus the next morning found us two, full of hope and porridge, making the best of our way to Surprise Lake, where we separated, taking opposite sides of the valley.

For three or four hours I diligently quartered the ground, but not a fresh track did I see. The day was very still, hot for the time of year, and dull, with a sensation of coming thunder in the air; and I began to feel quite drowsy, and oppressed with an uncomfortable feeling of solitude, when I was startled into full wakefulness by the same unearthly noise proceeding as before from the lower end of the cañon. Toned down and softened by distance, the cry came wailing up the valley, making my flesh creep—it sounded so mournful and yet so savage. Three times in perhaps half an hour I heard the cry, still at a long distance, but evidently approaching me; and this time down wind, for the breeze had changed.   ' Bound to get a shot this time,' thought I to myself; and, selecting a nice convenient spot, I lay down and waited.

Not a sound for a long time broke the oppressive stillness of the air, but the dropping of an occasional fir-cone or the fluttering fall of a dead leaf; and then a distant cry. Another long interval of silence ensued, broken by a crushing and tearing of something bulky through the brush; and instead of a moose out bursts Campbell. Scared and breathless, he exclaims, 'What is it?' 'What's what?' inquired I. 'Why,' he gasped, 'I heard a most extraordinary yell; it sounded like a man in distress calling for help.' 'You great idiot,' said I, 'there is a moose coming up the gulch calling, if you haven't frightened him out of the country by running through the woods in that fashion. Listen!' And, as I spoke, our ears were assailed by the same unearthly yell, a good deal nearer to us. It *did* sound partially human, but still it certainly was not that of a man. Legends of forest devils and Jibbonainosays flitted through my brain; and Indians, for a moment, I thought of, for they can and do make noises unutterably hideous; but there were no Indians in the country, and no sign of them. I glanced at Campbell, whose face looked quite white and anxious; and Campbell looked at me, and I daresay I presented the same bewildered appearance. Be that as it may, I am sure we each felt glad that the other was present, for there was something very uncanny, devilish, and altogether uncomfortable in this unknown yell ringing through the forest. 'There it is again!' we simultaneously exclaimed, as the same quavering cry echoed through the woods, swelling into a roar and dying away in a shrill whistle or scream. This time it was answered a little above us. 'There can be no doubt,' said I; 'I know it is not a wapiti, neither is it a mountain lion. It is not exactly like what I imagined the call of a bull moose to be, but there is no other beast in the woods that *could* make such a noise. Let us wait for another call.' Again came up the noise from the cañon, answered as before. 'You are right; it can be nothing else but moose,' whispers Campbell; 'two bulls; and the upper one is close to Surprise Lake. Come on; let us get up to him. They will be thinking of each other, and if we have luck we may get a shot at both.' Accordingly, after taking off our coats, moccasins, and socks, we advanced, walking like Agag delicately, pointing our naked toes like ballet-dancers, worming our way noiselessly through the trees without cracking a stick, rustling a leaf, or snapping a twig.

Goodness! How anxious I was! I had killed all the principal beasts of the continent, except moose and carriboo. The latter I anticipated no great difficulty in getting in Lower Canada; but the moose is nearly extinct, save in the far-away swamps of the Peace River Valley; and was I now to be so favoured by the gods as to witness a fight between two bulls, and kill one, perhaps even both, of them? With stooped bodies, heads craned forward, scarcely venturing to draw breath through our dry parched lips, inch by inch we noiselessly advanced, treading softly on our bare feet, carefully putting aside every twig and branch, and using extra caution as we neared the lake; presently we caught the glint of water through the trees. A pull at my shirt arrested me; and Campbell, putting his mouth to my ear, whispered, 'I see the reflection of his antlers moving in the water.' Motionless as statues we stood for a few seconds, then gently dropped on our knees, when I too saw the reflection of something pass across the surface, followed by a slight splash in the water and cracking in the bushes. 'Feeding on the water-lilies,' gurgles Campbell, shaking with suppressed excitement. I too felt quite ill, but bottled-up my feelings and said nothing, my attention being too much taken up by the peculiar colour I saw reflected in the lake. Craning my neck a little further forward, I perceived it distinctly. 'Why, Campbell,' I said, 'it's blue! Who ever heard of a blue moose?' Another inch or two forward, and I turned my expressive eyes on Campbell, whose responsive orbs spoke volumes of unutterable words. 'Durn the trout, they ain't biting worth a cent,' we heard; and there, placidly unconscious, stood a free and independent citizen in a pair of blue military pants, fishing for trout with a young pine-tree! He had come up from the saw-mill below to get a dish of fish. 'I think,' said I, 'we had better go back and put on our shoes and stockings; this gentleman might wonder what we were doing without them.' As we turned, the same unearthly yell rolled up from the cañon, answered by a horrid howl from our friend in blue, and followed by a muttered inquiry as to what the bad-worded fool meant by losing himself, and making such a bad-worded row in the bad-worded woods for.

We did not hunt moose any more that day.

We remained about a week on Trail Creek, and explored the country thoroughly. Every day two of us took the valleys, and scratched our way through the matted pine-woods, or floundered about among the swamps; and the other two went up the ridges and hunted the tops for sheep. But as none of us got a shot, or ever saw anything, we got tired of it. The weather too was turning very stormy; winter was evidently close at hand, and we therefore determined to give it up. A slight fall of snow we had been praying for, but it appeared likely now that we might get too much. Day by day the sun sank in heavier and wilder-looking banks. The weather was exceedingly hot and oppressive, a condition of atmosphere that surely indicates the approach of a decided change; and, as we had no mind to undertake a stage journey in deep snow, we bade adieu to hunting, broke camp, and went into Fort Ellis.

There we were received with the greatest kindness by General Sweitzer and the officers of the garrison, whose hospitality we enjoyed for three days, while we were occupied in disposing of our stock and settling up matters in general.

It was a stormy day on which, with great regret, we left Fort Ellis and the pretty little town of Bozeman; and it was snowing heavily and bitterly cold when we drove into Virginia City, where we remained two days, and then took the stage for Corinne.

Oh that drive! Can I ever forget it? It occurs to my mind like the memory of some horrid dream—some dreadful nightmare. Four days and four nights in the interior of that vehicle; worse a great deal than Jonah's three in the whale's belly;—four mortal days and nights going 340 miles, or thereabouts. We got on pretty well for the first two days, thanks to the unfailing cheerfulness and indomitable good-humour of Jack; but the third night was very severe, and on the fourth our miseries culminated, and we collapsed.

The road was over a level plain of soft clayey soil, recently flooded with torrents of rain. It was cut into, not ruts merely, but trenches, by the heavy ox-teams carrying northern freights. There were great holes in it feet deep. Over or through this we were somehow dragged by four horses, at a rate of about two and a half miles per hour during the whole night. The coach, as I think I have before stated, was an old-fashioned, leathern inconveniency slung on straps; and the way that engine of torture jerked, kicked, plunged, and pitched us about is past all telling. Wynne, being a man of fine proportions, and moreover dressed in Ulsters and other voluminous garments, jammed himself between the back and middle seats, and got a little sleep; while Kingsley sat in the opposite back corner, half asleep from sheer fatigue, his head wobbling and chucking from side to side in a manner that must have severely tried the toughness of his neck. His face wore an expression of stolidly calm indifference; but an evidence of internal suffering was occasionally jerked from between his chattering teeth in the shape of an explosive d——n. There was a moral force, emphasis, and energy about that monosyllable that signified more than a whole column of strong language.

Jack sat beside me on the front seat, his six feet of lissom frame tied and knotted up into inextricable confusion, his head appearing in strange and unexpected places, hands and feet turning up promiscuously, and without the slightest regard to the anatomical positions which they are usually supposed to occupy. He would fall over asleep on my shoulder, and the next moment I would awake to the consciousness that his toe was intruding into my mouth; or, if he lay in the other direction, with his feet in my lap, I would be astonished to find him grabbing wildly at my hair to prevent himself falling into the bottom of the coach. Jack, best and cheeriest of companions, was for once out of humour. Fervent and frequent were his prayers, having reference to the future condition of driver, horses, coach, road, those that made it, the teams that had cut it up, and everything and everybody that had to do with the line. But swearing did not last long. Things soon got too bad for that. Language, even the most violent language, is quite inadequate to express one's feelings on certain occasions. No one knows what mean, weak, and sickly things are mere words until he has stubbed his toe against the leg of a chair in the dark, or has become utterly fretful and demoralised by such a stage journey as we had to undergo. Hindostanee might possibly be of service if thoroughly understood and judiciously employed; but English is of no use whatever; and we soon gave up the attempt to express our sentiments, and relapsed into and maintained a gloomy silence.

As for me, I endeavoured to sit still in my corner; but, being of a light frame and spare body, I found that, not being provided with any suction apparatus in those parts, my efforts were unavailing, and I spent most of the night bounding about the coach like a pea on a drum, causing much dissatisfaction to myself and my fellow-travellers. If I did lie down across the front and middle seat, not being stout enough to stick between them like Wynne, I speedily doubled up, feet and head together, and fell through after the manner of a clown in a pantomime, who, lying on his back across a barrel, and being smitten violently on the stomach, folds up and collapses therein. I soon got beyond the consolations of swearing, and confess that I felt more inclined to cry than to do anything else.

But all things come to an end; and at length, tired, sulky, and giddy, we arrived at Corinne eighteen hours late, and just in time to step on board a train bound east.

How luxurious appeared the Pullman car, how smooth the motion, how soft the cushions, how snug the beds! With what awe did our unaccustomed eyes regard the ladies! How gorgeous they appeared, how graceful they were, how marvellous their costumes, and how stupendous their back hair! How extraordinary seemed the harmonium, and the singing thereto! How full of pictures were the periodicals, how full of lies the newspapers! How clean one felt in a ' boiled rag' and fresh suit of clothes, and how sound we all slept that night!

Having now fairly returned to civilisation, I must say good-bye, reluctant to banish from memory the souvenirs of an extremely pleasant tour. At this distance of time, the recollections of annoyances and discomforts have faded and grown dim, and scarcely cast a shadow across the bright and happy memories that crowd my brain. Could I but transcribe and paint the scenes and pictures that pass before me when I shut my eyes and think, I should, I am sure, induce some of my readers to spend a holiday in those far-away Western wilds, and to make a pilgrimage to the ' Great Divide.'

HEAD OF MOUNTAIN SHEEP.